The Backcountry Towns of Colonial Virginia

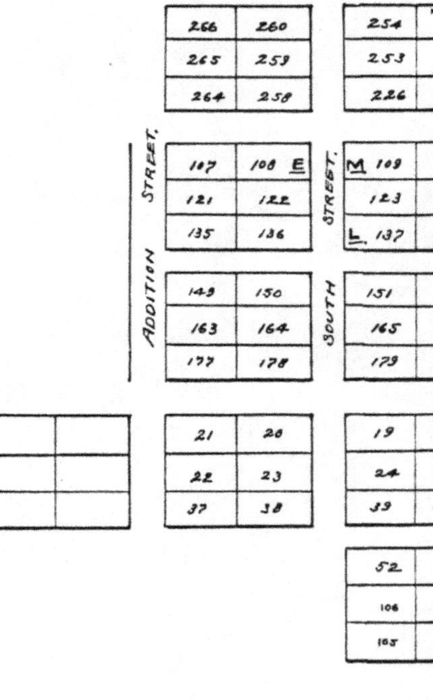

ADDITION STREET.
SOUTH STREET.
STEPHEN STREET.
269 263 257 225
268 262 256 215
267 261 255 226
266 260 254 194
265 259 253 187
264 258 226 186
107 108 E M 109 110
121 122 123 124
135 136 L 137 138
149 150 151 152
163 164 165 166
177 178 179 180
21 20 19 18
22 23 24 25
37 38 39 40
52 53
106 65
105 104
H
102 101
103

The Backcountry Towns of Colonial Virginia

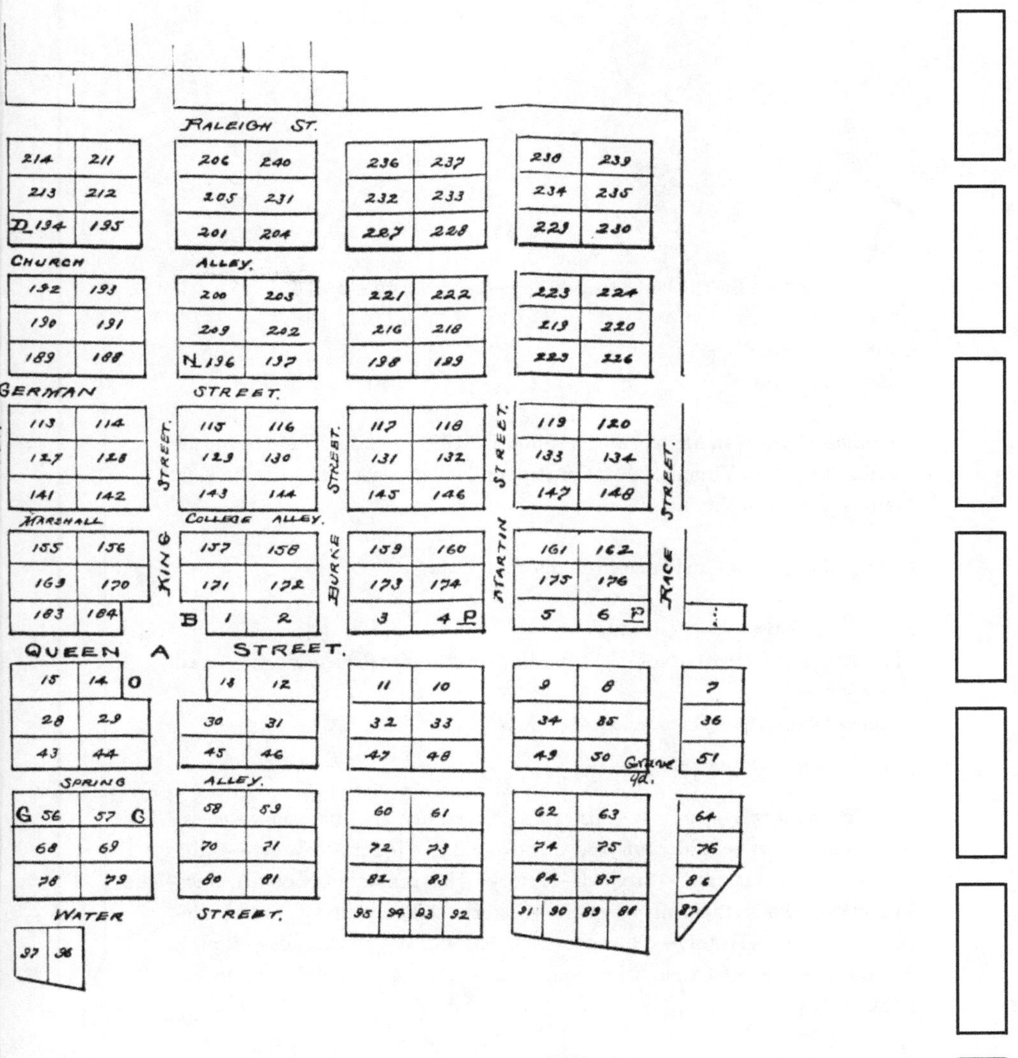

Christopher E. Hendricks

The University of Tennessee Press / Knoxville

Cloth: 1st printing, 2006.
Paper: 1st printing, 2017.

Frontispiece: Geo. Van Metre, "Martinsburg, Va. 1779." Berkley County Courthouse, Martinsburg, West Virginia, 1904. Courtesy of the Berkeley County Clerk's Office, Martinsburg, West Virginia.

Library of Congress Cataloging-in-Publication Data

Hendricks, Christopher E., 1963–
The backcountry towns of colonial Virginia / Christopher E. Hendricks.—1st ed.
p. cm.
Includes bibliographical references and index.

ISBN-13: 978-1-62190-309-3

1. Cities and towns—Virginia—History—17th century. 2. Cities and towns—Virginia—History—18th century. 3. City planning—Virginia—History—17th century. 4. City planning—Virginia—History—18th century. 5. Colonial cities—Virginia. 6. Land settlement—Virginia—History—17th century. 7. Land settlement—Virginia—History—18th century. 8. Frontier and pioneer life—Virginia. 9. Virginia—History—Colonial period, ca. 1600-1775. 10. Virginia—History, Local. I. Title.

HT167.5.V8H46 2006
307.7609755'09032—dc22 2006007749

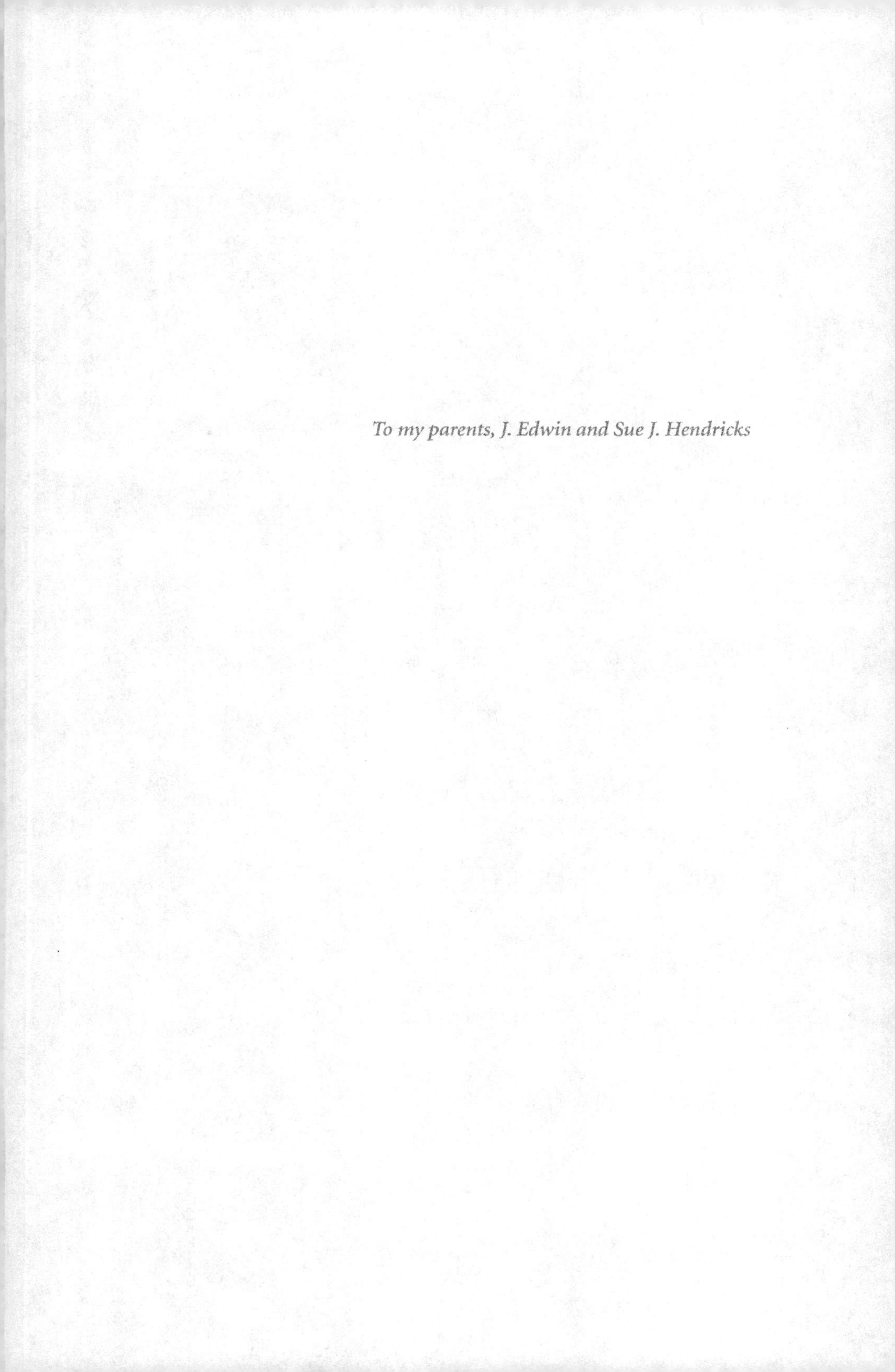

To my parents, J. Edwin and Sue J. Hendricks

Contents

Illustrations

Acknowledgments

Town plans have always fascinated me. As a kid, I spent a lot of time in the hallways of my father's office scrutinizing the framed plans of historic cities that were hanging there. The idea of studying towns and town design in the Virginia backcountry developed during a lunch conversation I had with James P. Whittenburg at the Short Stop Café in Williamsburg several years ago. While, as often happens, other research interests and responsibilities kept me from finishing the work as soon as I would have liked, this project has never strayed far from my mind. Then, in 2001, my colleagues at Armstrong Atlantic State University made it possible for me to return to Williamsburg to teach at William and Mary for the academic year and complete my research. I took the next couple of summers to write and revise, and what follows is the result.

I long ago lost track of all of the individuals who helped me complete this project, but there are several people who deserve special recognition. First, I would like to thank Brian J. Martine, Kathy Graydon Lisiewicz, Sue Hendricks, Ed Hendricks, Barbara Fertig, and June Hopkins, who read early drafts of the manuscript and whose editorial comments and suggestions have made this a much better work. I thank John Dickinson for his invaluable assistance preparing the maps and illustrations. Turk McCleskey at the Virginia Military Institute provided me with several insights into the development of Staunton. Melinda Byrd Frierson of the Albemarle/Charlottesville Historical Society helped me track down maps of Charlottesville. And Jennifer Davis McDaid at the Library of Virginia assisted me in unraveling a couple of different map mysteries. Scot Danforth at the University of Tennessee Press has made publication a remarkably gentle and enjoyable process. The members of my family (Brian, Ed, Sue, Jim, Lisa, Lee, Dennis, Grayson, and William) have been extremely supportive throughout—thank you. I'd also like to thank my friends in the Department of History at Armstrong Atlantic for helping to create a unique and special atmosphere in which to teach and work.

Just as I am unable to thank personally each individual who assisted me, I am also unable to thank the staffs of all of the libraries, archives, courthouses, museums, and other repositories I have utilized over the years for their invaluable contributions. However, there are five institutions where I did the bulk of my work, whose staffs I need to thank profusely. I spent most of my time researching this project at the Earl Gregg Swem Library at the College of William and Mary and the John D. Rockefeller Jr. Library at the Colonial Williamsburg Foundation. I also took great advantage of the resources of the Library of Virginia and the Z. Smith Reynolds Library at Wake Forest University. And I need to recognize the staff of the Huntsville/Madison County Public Library in Huntsville, Alabama, where I did much of my writing. The remarkably complete historical collection housed there puts many college libraries to shame and more than once saved me a trip to Virginia.

Finally, I'd like to end where this project began. I'd like to thank Jim Whittenburg for being a wonderful teacher, mentor, and friend. I owe you lunch.

Introduction

Planned urban settlements account for the rapid expansion of colonial Virginia into its backcountry. The key factor in town development was the individual or group who actively engaged in a town project, functioning in an entrepreneurial spirit. Almost all of the successful towns of the region were the consequence of such initiative; they were the result of careful planning and thoughtful design, not chance. The people who put these plans and designs into action were motivated by a variety of economic, social, or philanthropic factors and sometimes purely by circumstance and opportunity. These individuals did not act in concert, nor did they follow any systematic economic or urban theory in their approach, but each was convinced that backcountry development was dependent upon the creation of a town as both attraction and catalyst for further expansion. Their actions resulted in the rapid occupation, settlement, and development of the Virginia backcountry by the conscious creation of economic and social forces.

Various individuals attempted to establish at least twenty-five towns in the Virginia backcountry during the colonial period. Not all twenty-five grew into large urban centers. Indeed, some of them did not make it off the page onto the ground. Others flourished for a time only to fade into obscurity. And while most continued to exist, they remained small, so small in fact that until the last thirty years or so, historians and geographers overlooked them and their important roles, choosing instead to cast the development of the colonial South as an exclusively rural phenomenon in contrast to the urban Middle and New England colonies.[1] For the most part, these historical studies tried to develop or apply economic models to explain how town and country functioned in the colonial South, typically using just a few towns (or in some cases only one) to demonstrate the particular model. While this is an interesting exercise in the abstract, it only describes at most one aspect of town development—the economic interplay among a small sample of towns that succeeded. However, many factors shaped the success or failure of towns that simply cannot be explained by economic systems. Missing from the studies are elements such as the human motivation and the individual events that went into a town's founding and the story of its development. Through an examination of the narrative history of every town attempted in the Virginia backcountry, this study reveals a fuller picture of backcountry urban development by exploring a wider array of factors that shaped the success or failure of these communities.

Virginians constantly tried to develop ways to make the vast and rich lands of their colony pay, and one means they utilized to accomplish that was to lay out a town.[2] Landowners knew they could take a large tract of land and break it up into smaller pieces to sell, creating town lots that were much more valuable than the unbroken whole. However, the simple act of surveying lots was not enough, for the process was much more complicated than that. There was an art to founding a successful town, and a potential founder had to take into account a host of environmental, geographical, political, and economic factors. And, as with all speculative ventures, no matter how well towns were planned or researched, a great deal was left to chance. The end result of the process for the Virginia backcountry, whether or not a town succeeded, was that the land was opened up and made more accessible, attracting people to move into new areas or take part in new business opportunities. Backcountry towns furthered settlement by offering new opportunities to own land, influencing immigration, creating family and social networks, and developing trade and systems of credit.

Because of the importance of towns in the expansion and settlement of new territory, from almost the very beginning of Virginia's history, people expressed concern that a dearth of towns was hampering the colony's development. Searching for an explanation, many looked to Virginia's geography.

1. (Previous page) Scholarship first began recognizing southern urban development in the 1970s and includes John W. Reps, *Tidewater Towns: City Planning in Colonial Virginia and Maryland* (Williamsburg, VA: Colonial Williamsburg Foundation, 1972); Joseph A. Ernst and H. Roy Merrens, "'Camden's turrets pierce the skies!': The Urban Process in the Southern Colonies during the Eighteenth Century," *William and Mary Quarterly*, 3rd series, vol. 30 (Oct. 1973): 549–74; Lois Green Carr, "The Metropolis of Maryland: A Comment on Town Development along the Tobacco Coast," *Maryland Historical Magazine* 69 (Summer 1974): 123–45; Hermann Wellenreuther, "Urbanization in the Colonial South: A Critique," *William and Mary Quarterly*, 3rd series, vol. 31 (Oct. 1974): 653–68; Carville Earle and Ronald Hoffman, "Staple Crops and Urban Development in the Eighteenth-Century South," *Perspectives in American History* 10 (1972): 7–80; and Carville Earle and Ronald Hoffman, "The Urban South: The First Two Centuries," in Blaine A. Brownell and David R. Goldfield, eds., *The City in Southern History: The Growth of Urban Civilization in the South* (Port Washington, NY: Kennikut, 1977), 23–51. For scholarship on ports and town legislation, see footnote 9 below. For a discussion of the historiography of the urban colonial South, including the early theme of the lack of urban development, see Christopher E. Hendricks, "Town Development in the Colonial Backcountry—Virginia and North Carolina" (Ph.D. diss., College of William and Mary in Virginia, 1991), 2–16; and James O'Mara, "Urbanization in Tidewater Virginia during the Eighteenth Century: A Study in Historical Geography" (Ph.D. diss., York Univ., 1979), 6–56.

2. Town founding was only one of the ways Virginians tried to profit from their land. A good case study of another type of investment scheme is Charles Royster, *The Fabulous History of the Dismal Swamp Company: A Story of George Washington's Times* (New York: Borzoi Books, 1999).

Writing in the middle of the seventeenth century, Anthony Langston, a military officer whom the General Assembly commissioned to explore and report on ways to develop the colony, explained that a lack of cities in Virginia was due to the "manner of seating the Country," particularly blaming the "conveniency of the River for the Transportation of . . . Commodities" throughout the Tidewater.[3] John Clayton, a Yorkshire minister who traveled through Virginia in the 1680s, agreed, saying, "This, (i.e.) the Numbers of Rivers, is one of the chief Reasons why they have no Towns: for every one being more sollicitous for a private Interest and Conveniency, than for a publick, they will either be for making forty Towns at once, that is two in every Country, or none at all, which is the Country's Ruin."[4] In 1724 Anglican rector and William and Mary mathematics professor Hugh Jones wrote that towns were not developing because every plantation afforded "the owner the provision of a little market."[5] And three years later, the authors of *The Present State of Virginia and the College* observed that "if Towns and Ports can be brought to bear, the Chief Obstruction to the Improvement of that Country will be removed," but they did not think the task would be easy. Indeed, they held "that the bringing of the People of that Country to the Improvements of Cohabitation, must be against their Will, by Virtue of the King's Prerogative and not by expecting the Concurrence of their General Assemblies, the major Part of the Members whereof having never seen a Town, nor a well improv'd Country in their Lives, cannot therefore imagine the Benefit of it, and are afraid of every Innovation that will put them to a present Charge whatever may be the future Benefit."[6]

Their comments were a bit harsh toward the General Assembly, which, after all, had made several attempts to further urban growth in the colony and had chartered several towns, though these were not entirely successful. English clergyman Andrew Burnaby, traveling through the colony in 1760, noted that "by act of assembly there ought to be forty-four towns; but one half of these have not more than five houses; and the other half are little better than inconsiderable villages." Like Langston and Jones, he blamed the availability of land and the ease of navigation rather than government inactivity and predicted that only when the colony was more heavily populated and land more expensive would people turn away from farming and establish "towns and large cities;

3. Anthony Langston, "On Towns, Corporations; And on the Manufacturing of Iron," *William and Mary Quarterly Historical Magazine*, 2nd series, vol. 1 (Jan. 1921): 101.

4. John Clayton, "A Letter from Mr. John Clayton Rector of Crofton at Wakefield in Yorkshire, to the Royal Society, May 12, 1688," in Peter Force, ed., *Tracts and Other Papers, Relating Principally to the Origin, Settlement, and Progress of the Colonies in North America, From the Discovery of the Country to the Year 1776*, vol. 3 (Washington, DC: Peter Force and Wm. Q. Force, 1836–46), tract 13, p. 11.

5. Hugh Jones, *The Present State of Virginia: From Whence is Inferred a Short View of Maryland and North Carolina*, ed. Richard L. Morton (1724; Chapel Hill: Univ. of North Carolina Press, 1956), 73.

6. Henry Hartwell, James Blair, and Edward Chilton, *The Present State of Virginia and the College*, ed. Hunter Dickinson Farish (1727; Williamsburg, VA: Colonial Williamsburg, 1940), 5, 13. Hartwell was a member of the Governor's Council, Blair was the founder of the College of William and Mary, and Chilton was Virginia's attorney general.

but this seems remote, and not likely to happen for some centuries."[7] Even Thomas Jefferson in his *Notes on the State of Virginia* repeated the early themes, writing almost apologetically that Virginia's river network allowed trade to come "directly to our doors, instead of our being obliged to go in quest of it," to the detriment of towns.[8]

Much of the confusion in the discussion of southern urbanization, regardless of the period, is the result of definition. By the seventeenth century, Europeans had developed conceptions of cities, towns, and villages, creating a hierarchy of size and importance. It is significant that much study of southern colonial urbanization focused largely on the ports and the failure of legislative efforts to create new urban centers, revealing a tendency dating back to the colonial period to equate population with urbanization.[9] Historians' suggestion before the 1970s that urban development in the South was insignificant was attributable in part to period travelers' and observers' care in noting the small populations of the towns through which they passed.[10]

In eighteenth-century accounts, when the basis of comparison to European cities was population, towns in the colonial South did not fare well. When listing urban centers at the turn of the nineteenth century, even Jefferson wrote about Virginia's "Towns, but more properly our villages or hamlets."[11] Earlier accounts, especially those of European travelers, were often highly subjective and impressionistic, usually lacking an examination of the communities' functions. Those writers who were careful enough to observe the functional side of a community did so only for the larger towns and still tended to make function secondary to size. Furthermore, descriptions of town functions tended to stress trade and commercial activities and often neglected industry and governmental services.[12]

Do these tendencies imply that period accounts are not useful in the study of urban development? To the contrary, the eighteenth-century author was an

7. Andrew Burnaby, *Travels through the Middle Settlement in North America, in the Years 1759 and 1760; with Observations Upon the State of the Colonies*, 3rd ed. (London: T Payne, 1798), 16.

8. Thomas Jefferson, *Jefferson's Notes on the State of Virginia* (Baltimore, MD: W. Pechin, 1800), 111.

9. Examples of historical studies of the failed town acts include Edward M. Riley, "The Town Acts of Colonial Virginia," *Journal of Southern History* 16 (Aug. 1950): 306–23; James C. Rainbolt, "The Absence of Towns in Seventeenth-Century Virginia," in Kenneth T. Jackson and Stanley Schultz, eds., *Cities in American History* (New York: Knopf, 1972), 50–65; and Beth-Anne Chernichowski, "Legislated Towns in Virginia 1680–1705: Growth and Function: 1680–1780," M.A. thesis, College of William and Mary in Virginia, 1974. Studies primarily focusing on southern ports include Thomas Jefferson Wertenbaker, *Norfolk: Historic Southern Port* (Durham, NC: Duke Univ. Press, 1931); Leila Sellars, *Charleston Business on the Eve of the American Revolution* (Chapel Hill: Univ. of North Carolina Press, 1934); Carl Bridenbaugh, *Cities in the Wilderness: The First Century of Urban Life in America, 1625–1742* (Oxford: Oxford Univ. Press, 1938); Carl Bridenbaugh, *Cities in Revolt: Urban Life in Colonial America, 1743–1776* (New York: Knopf, 1955); Thomas H. Preisser, "Eighteenth-Century Alexandria, Virginia before the Revolution, 1749–1776" (Ph.D. diss., College of William and Mary in Virginia, 1977); and Mary Catherine Ferrari, "Artisans of the South: A Comparative Study of Norfolk, Charleston, and Alexandria, 1763–1800" (Ph.D. diss., College of William and Mary in Virginia, 1992).

10. Ernst and Merrens, "'Camden's turrets,'" 552–53.

11. Jefferson, *Jefferson's Notes*, 111.

12. Ernst and Merrens, "'Camden's turrets,'" 554.

observer, writing to an audience that in all likelihood shared views common to his society. The purpose of writing was to describe, to recount the unusual. If a traveler simply named a community and then described it concisely as a "county town," for example, he was not making a judgment. Rather, he simply felt he had provided an adequate description of something his reader would immediately understand in terms of function as well as approximate size.

In modern studies, the chain of city, town, and village persists as a viable way to describe the spectrum of urban places, from large heterogeneous communities with labor and class divisions and diverse economies to small largely classless agricultural settlements. But a problem lies in the fact that the terms themselves remain highly subjective. At what point does a village become a town or a town become a city? Furthermore, are the standards used for one region or culture valid for others?[13] Certainly, the eighteenth-century observers underestimated the important roles of Virginia's backcountry towns, based on their notions of European rules and patterns.

Population is one of the most typical determinants in defining an urban community. Even today it is quite common to use population figures as guides to define a community's status as well as its eligibility for incorporation.[14] But the idea of using arbitrary population divisions, saying, for example, that a community consisting of one to forty-nine people is a "hamlet," fifty to ninety-nine a "village," etc., is not helpful in a historical study.[15] Governments at all levels have used such definitions to provide consistency in evaluation, but the definitions differ from place to place and frequently change over the years within the same government body.[16] And when such categories exist, governments do not always follow their own policies. In colonial Virginia, for example, it took around one hundred people or twenty to twenty-five families to be granted the legal status of a town, but as Andrew Burnaby noted, the Assembly did not always follow its own standards. On the other hand, settlements of sizeable populations that otherwise might legally have been defined as cities or towns frequently remained unchartered either by choice or through neglect.[17]

13. Stephanie Grauman Wolf, *Urban Village: Populations, Community, and Family Structure in Germantown, Pennsylvania, 1683–1800* (Princeton, NJ: Princeton Univ. Press, 1976), 17–21.

14. Emrys Jones, *Towns and Cities* (New York: Oxford Univ. Press, 1966), 3–5. There was also confusion later caused by the use of census data and inaccuracies in the data itself. See Lisa C. Tolbert, *Constructing Townscapes: Space and Society in Antebellum Tennessee* (Chapel Hill: Univ. of North Carolina Press, 1999), 5; and Thomas Field Armstrong, "Urban Vision in Virginia: A Comparative Study of Ante-Bellum Fredericksburg, Lynchburg, and Staunton," M.A. thesis, Univ. of Virginia, 1974, 8–10.

15. For a list of scholars' attempts to classify places by population breakdown, see Charles J. Farmer, *In the Absence of Towns: Settlement and County Trade in Southside Virginia, 1730–1800* (Lanham, MD: Rowman & Littlefield, 1993), 21.

16. David J. Russo, *American Towns: An Interpretive History* (Chicago: Dee, 2001), xi.

17. Burnaby, *Travels*, 16; Robert D. Mitchell, *Commercialism and Frontier: Perspectives on the Early Shenandoah Valley* (Charlottesville: Univ. Press of Virginia, 1977), 196; and Robert D. Mitchell, "The Settlement Fabric of the Shenandoah Valley, 1790–1860: Pattern, Process, and Structure," in Kenneth E. Koons and Warren R. Hofstra, eds., *After the Backcountry: Rural Life in the Great Valley of Virginia, 1800–1900* (Knoxville: Univ. of Tennessee Press, 2000), 35.

Another criterion for defining a town is function. A generally accepted characteristic of an urban center is that its population is not engaged primarily in agricultural production.[18] In this light, towns become centers of collection, exchange, trade, manufacture, government, and other services, and size need not be considered. However, in the colonial South, these kinds of activities often took place in the smallest forms. For example, isolated stores (many begun in the mid-eighteenth century by Scottish mercantile firms) often opened and closed depending on market forces, providing rural areas access to imported goods, markets, and elaborate systems of credit—services usually associated with urban centers.[19] Likewise, inns, ferries, and mills provided manufacturing and service functions in sparsely populated regions—functions important enough for them to appear on maps of the period.[20] Similarly, during certain days of the year, county courthouses transformed from isolated structures standing alone in the midst of the countryside into government, market, and entertainment centers.[21] Yet while Scottish stores, inns, mills, or courthouses may have provided loci for urban activities, they were not towns.[22]

The models scholars have proposed provide interesting insights into how towns may have functioned as parts of larger economic systems, though certainly no one in the colonial period would have been thinking in such terms when they were busy pioneering their communities. Economic models are descriptive, not explanatory, and as such leave out much of the story of how the systems they describe came into being. And, as is often the case with theories, their proponents frequently hold that only one model truly works. The Virginia backcountry was vast, consisting of different geographical regions, and many models could apply, no one of them individually providing an adequate account of the creation of all the backcountry towns. Even collectively, they provide at most a descriptive account. In order to move toward an explanation, it is much more useful to consider not only these theories in combination, but also what lies behind them. The deliberate plans and circumstances of individual players enter into this, and that is what is often missing from such systematic approaches. Nonetheless, such models may be helpful in understanding backcountry town formation.

18. Jones, *Towns and Cities*, 4, 25; and Mitchell, "Settlement," 34–35.

19. Ernst and Merrens, "'Camden's turrets,'" 555.

20. See, for example, "Ashbys Ferry" and "Watts Ordinary" in Joshua Fry and Peter Jefferson, "A Map of the most Inhabited part of Virginia containing the Whole Province of Maryland with Part of Pensilvania, New Jersey and North Carolina. Drawn by Joshua Fry and Peter Jefferson in 1751," in Richard W. Stephenson and Marianne M. McKee, eds., *Virginia in Maps: Four Centuries of Settlement Growth and Development* (Richmond: Library of Virginia, 2000), Map II-21 B.

21. Rhys Isaac, *The Transformation of Virginia, 1740–1790* (Chapel Hill: Published for the Institute of Early American History and Culture at Williamsburg, VA, by Univ. of North Carolina Press, 1982), 88–90; A. G. Roeber, *Faithful Magistrates and Republican Lawyers: Creators of Virginia Legal Culture, 1680–1810* (Chapel Hill: Univ. of North Carolina Press, 1981), 73–80; and E. Lee Shepard, "'This Being Court Day': Courthouses and Community Life in Rural Virginia," *Virginia Magazine of History and Biography* 103 (Oct. 1995): 459–70.

22. Wellenreuther, "Urbanization," 660.

Central place theory is a model that suggests that trade patterns are more important than geography in explaining the size and locations of towns. The basic premise is that people will travel greater distances for increasingly specialized or unusual types of products. For example, many communities had blacksmiths, because a large number of people in a small area required their services. On the other hand, only a larger place could support a more specialized craftsman such as a watchmaker. This resulted in a hierarchy of population centers including hamlets, villages, towns, and cities. These urban places would be arranged in such a way that they could feed into one another, each providing certain services for its own citizens, and increasingly specialized services being provided in the larger population centers. On a flat plain where there are no distinctive geographical features (such as rivers) and the population is evenly distributed, the theory suggests that a perfect web of urban places would develop. A hamlet would form, providing the most basic services for its inhabitants. Six hamlets of the same size would grow up to surround a village where the citizenry could obtain more goods and services. Six villages would in turn surround a town, six towns would surround a city, and this development would continue until the plain was filled and the area combined into a unified whole. The sizes of the towns, the distances between them, and their locations would be perfectly predictable. The development would be natural from within the community, coming as the needs of the agricultural region matured. Of course, no such perfect plain exists, so in actual practice, many factors influence the size and locations of towns including geography, climate, culture, transportation, and even chance.[23]

Mercantile or *wholesaling theory* proposes a scheme of thinking about regional development as being influenced more significantly by forces external to the region itself. It posits that entrepôts or contact points would develop between areas of different strengths or development. These entrepôts would develop on the borders of the frontier region and would function as the chief points of trade into the area. Manufactured goods and finished products would flow into the region from the entrepôt, which would also serve as a collection point for raw materials and agricultural goods coming out of the area. These would then be shipped from the entrepôt to distant markets. Eventually, places in the frontier region would develop to serve as collection and distribution points that would receive goods from the entrepôts and exchange them in for agricultural products. The connections between the entrepôts and collection points would be linear until the region's population grew to a point at which a network of towns would develop.[24]

23. Walter Christaller, *Central Places in Southern Germany*, trans. C. W. Baskin (Englewood Cliffs, NJ: Prentice-Hall, 1966); Edward Ullman, "A Theory of Location for Cities," *American Journal of Sociology* 46 (May 1941): 854–61; Farmer, *In the Absence*, 8–9; and Paul M. Hohenburg and Lynn Hollen Lees, *The Making of Urban Europe, 1000–1950* (Cambridge, MA: Harvard Univ. Press, 1985), 19, 50.

24. Farmer, *In the Absence*, 15–16; and James E. Vance, *The Merchant's World: The Geography of Wholesaling* (Englewood Cliffs, NJ: Prentice-Hall, 1970), 80–96.

A third proposition, *staple theory*, argues that the type of agricultural products produced in a region is the principle factor in shaping its town development. Primary staple goods such as rice or tobacco, which require little or no processing, are exported directly from the farm to a port, negating any need for a town. According to this theory, the towns that did develop would be small and completely dependent on trade, lacking craft industries and institutions such as churches and schools. However, areas that produce secondary staples such as grains, which need processing and contain greater bulk, use towns as collection and processing centers before the products take their final form and are either distributed in the region for local consumption or sent along to port towns for export. A variety of industries necessary for processing or shipping would develop, further necessitating the creation of towns filled with a wide range of skilled workers and a diverse economy.[25]

A final theory often helpful in the understanding the role of backcountry towns is known as *functionalism*. It focuses on the purpose each urban place serves. The size and shape of the town is not important in this system; indeed typical urban functions including collection, storage, distribution, and exchange could occur at isolated places that operate as urban places only at certain times of the year. According to this view, what is important is not the place itself, but the economic function it serves. That is what makes it urban.[26] All four of these theories offer useful ways of interpreting how towns developed in the different backcountry regions and how they may have operated as a system. But at least in the case of backcountry Virginia, no single theory is adequate.

Population, function, and trading patterns certainly are elements of cities and towns, but they do not provide a complete picture of an urban center. Towns and cities are not stagnant collections of people any more than they are isolated retail outlets. A town grows or fails. Its population increases or decreases according to any number of shaping forces. Urbanization involves external growth as a town physically expands in a region, its form influenced by factors such as geography, population, trade, manufacturing, ethnicity, tradition, and culture. There is internal growth as well, as a town struggles to meet its population's social needs of governance, education, and religion.[27] An aggregate population is not urban until it develops a diverse economy and its members begin to identify with the community. Nor is an inn, mill, ferry, or courthouse urban until people begin to congregate nearby, adding different economic activities to the society and laying out streets and constructing houses, helping it take shape physically. In the colonial South there was also an integral relationship between the town and the surrounding countryside which so camouflaged the southern urban experience that it confounded attempts of contemporary and (occasionally) modern observers to recognize

25. Earle and Hoffman, "Staple Crops," 7, 11, 22, 39, 64–66; and Farmer, *In the Absence*, 13–14.
26. Ernst and Merrens, "'Camden's turrets,'" 574, 555, 557; and O'Mara, "Urbanization," 9.
27. Russo, *American Towns*, xi; and Armstrong, "Urban Vision," 14–16.

it.[28] Finally, at the root of it all, one last factor was essential to the development of towns in the backcountry of colonial Virginia: the *idea* of the town—the deeply held view that towns were essential to civilization and the desire of individuals to try to establish urban places. So deeply ingrained was individuals' desire to create towns, that they often seemed to be working from a moral imperative.

What follows is an exploration of town development in the backcountry of colonial Virginia. The definition of the backcountry changed as time passed, so that it could be argued that a town founded near the falls of a river on the eve of the revolution was no longer in the backcountry, while it would have been during the seventeenth century. For the purposes of this study, the backcountry will include the area extending from the fall zone along the rivers demarcating the Piedmont from the Tidewater and stretching into the Appalachian mountains. Although the study is meant to be inclusive, modern Wheeling, West Virginia, and at least four places beyond the mountains in what is now central Kentucky were founded during the colonial period (Harrodsburg in 1774, Leetown in 1775, Boonesborogh in 1775, and St. Asapath in 1775) in what were then the extreme reaches of Virginia. They are excluded because they were located hundreds of miles from the other backcountry communities and were settled along different migration routes from the rest of the colony. Wheeling was populated largely by people moving in from western Pennsylvania, and the Kentucky sites were populated by people moving north through gaps in the North Carolina mountains. For consistency, the geographical boundaries of the backcountry described above are used for the whole of the colonial period in this study.

Another consideration is the type of place discussed as a town. The study is meant to be inclusive, examining all twenty-five backcountry towns, but the five places mentioned above would not be included even if they were in the geographical region because all five were forts during the colonial period and were not laid out as regular towns until the early national period. Although they existed, so did places further east such as Harper's Ferry, Lynch's Ferry (modern Lynchburg), and Scott's Ferry (Scottsville), which were also later laid out as towns, but have also been excluded.

The story of the colonial Virginia backcountry towns that follows explores the circumstances of each town's establishment, intended purpose, design, and actual development—in other words, its form as well as its function. The goal is not only to provide a regional town survey, analyzing and interpreting a significant urban movement, but also to identify commonalities in town development, including methods of establishment, economic activities on local and regional levels, the roles of public institutions, and what factors may have led to success or failure of each town. Furthermore, while not the whole

28. Darrett B. Rutman with Anita H. Rutman, *Small Worlds, Large Questions: Explorations in Early American Social History, 1600–1800* (Charlottesville: Univ. Press of Virginia, 1994), 233.

story, the connections between different towns and between towns and their surrounding countryside are important, with each backcountry region operating as an economic unit uniquely suited to its development and interacting with the other areas through trade and communication links, network systems, and areas of urban influence.

Towns made land attractive, drawing people into the Virginia backcountry. Their promise, the types of opportunities and economic services that they offered, helped to expand and accelerate the settlement of the region, offering an ever-increasing range of economic activity, security, government, society, family, and a variety of other benefits. Towns prospered as long as land, trade, and people remained abundant. Some succeeded, some failed, but they were all part of a larger story. The backcountry towns of colonial Virginia led to the faster expansion of settlement, serving as "spearheads of the frontier."[29]

29. Richard C. Wade, *The Urban Frontier: The Rise of Western Cities, 1790–1830* (Cambridge, MA: Harvard Univ. Press, 1959), 1. Wade is referring to the Trans-Appalachian West, but the same was true for earlier frontiers.

Chapter 1

The Promised Fruits of Well-ordered Towns

In the eighteenth century, the notion that *civilization* could exist without *cities* was inconceivable. Indeed, the words share the same Latin root. Throughout history, the city has represented the flowering of a society's achievements. It was a physical manifestation of culture, the site of technical advancement, artistic endeavor, and education. But more than a location for intellectual pursuit, the city was also the measure of a nation's power, offering its populace safety, order, and a means of control.[1] When nations spread out beyond their own borders, they carried their culture, their ideas of civilization with them. The city proved an excellent tool of colonization as pioneers built settlements in conscious imitation of the forms and styles of their homelands. Once established, these towns became islands of alien culture and power, providing stepping stones into conquered territories and previously unoccupied lands. Towns hastened settlement.

The seemingly inherent link between city and civilization was a natural and unquestioned reality of human existence for many nations, and England was no exception. From the beginning of their colonial efforts in America in the sixteenth century, English administrators of settlements in Massachusetts, New York, New Jersey, Pennsylvania, Maryland, Virginia, and Carolina all provided their colonists with directives for the construction of towns. These centers served as market areas for the collection and distribution of agricultural

1. Russo, *American Towns*, 47, 242–43; Jones, *Towns and Cities*, 1; and Lewis Mumford, *The City in History: Its Origins, Its Transformations, and Its Prospects* (London: Secker & Warburg, 1961), 3.

products and trade goods, bases for further exploration, safe havens for religious and ethnic refugees, and protection against foreign threats posed by the Spanish, the French, and Native Americans. But British officials simply assumed that cities would rise in the New World, and so these instructions tended to be secondary to other matters. However, by the middle of the seventeenth century, when a decentralized economy developed in the southern colonies, matters took on a more serious tone. Colonial leaders began to press urgently for town development.[2] The Lords Proprietors of Carolina explained to their colonists "that it is your and our Concerne very much to have some very good Towns in your Plantations for other wise you will not longe continue civillized or ever bee considerable or secure, there being no place in the world wither of these without them."[3]

Some writers believed that even more than culture was at stake; so were people's immortal souls. In a pamphlet addressed to the bishop of London in 1661, one author suggested that "the Heathen who lived in the Cities and Towns with the Christians" of Virginia would be won over to Christianity by "beholding the comely order of the Christians Government, the amiablenesse of their Conversations, their Meeknesse, Humility, Charity, their Righteousnesse shining as the Noon-day." While the author concerned himself primarily with the religious lives of Virginians, he also explained that the Christian community in towns offered even more:

> To contemplate the poor Church (whose plants now grow wilde in that Wildernesse) become like a garden enclosed, like a Vineyard fenced, and watch'd like a flock of Sheep with their Lambes safely folded by night, and fed by day; all which are the promised fruits of well ordered Towns, under Religious Pastours and Magistrates, with what joy, and delight may you likewise think upon their comely and most ingenious Children, like hopefull plants growing up in Nurseries of learning and piety, and when their time of fruit is come, Transplanted into the enclosed gardens of God, and becoming fruitfull and usefull trees of righteousnesse; which is the promised happinesse and benefit of well ordered Schooles, in well governed Towns.[4]

The quest for urban development in the southern colonies came from many quarters, as British policymakers struggled to reconcile the conflicting philosophies of cultural and economic thought. The rural nature of the southern

2. Earle and Hoffman, "Urban South," 24; and David R. Goldfield, "Pearls on the Coast and Lights in the Forest: The Colonial South," in Raymond A. Mohl, ed., *The Making of Urban America* (Wilmington, DE: Scholarly Resources, 1984), 13.

3. "[Lords Proprietors] To the Present Government and Assembly of the County of Albemarle," [Oct. 26, 1676], in William L. Saunders, ed., *The Colonial Records of North Carolina*, 16 vols. (Winston, NC: M. I. & J. C. Stewart, Printers to the State, 1895–96; Goldsboro, NC: Nash Brothers, Book and Job Printers, 1896–1906), 1:229.

4. R. G., "Virginia's Cure: Or an Advisive Narrative Concerning Virginia: Discovering the True Ground of that Churches Unhappiness, and the Only True Remedy," in Force, *Tracts*, vol. 3, tract 15, pp. 13, 17.

plantation system suited mercantilist theories of restricted trade, limited manufacture, and production of raw materials, yet it ran counter to the demands of civilization. Similarly, officials realized that the mercantile system needed towns as administrative and trading centers in order to control the economy, yet they also discouraged town development because of their fear of creating manufacturing centers that might compete with English towns.[5] As a result of these contradictions, English directives often left colonial governments frustrated.

One solution colonists offered to alleviate this schizophrenic impasse was for England to relax its mercantile policies and allow some manufacture and limited trade in the colonies. In 1657 Anthony Langston, blaming the lack of industry in Virginia for the absence of towns, outlined a plan to the General Assembly that he believed would spawn urbanization through the importation of skilled craftsmen. He proposed that mass immigration take place in two waves, with "Brickmakers, Bricklayers, Sawyers, Joiners, Plaisterers, Coopers, Glasiers, and Smiths, Tanners . . . Shoemakers, Millwrights . . . and Boatwrights" arriving the first year, followed by "Hemp and Flax Dressers, roape makers, Soape Boilers, Potash men, Felt makers, Beaver makers, & divers other Trades" in the second.[6] Langston suggested the resulting advantages of the rise in land values, increased population, employment, and education were obvious. But such a plan was unrealistic, if well meant, and decentralized settlement continued unabated.

Early in the next century, Presbyterian minister Francis Makemie also sought to promote towns in Virginia, writing "I have been justly amazed to see the unaccountable Humour and singularity" of the colonists "who have so patiently, and for so long a time, sat down with a kind if stupid satisfaction under those pressing and Innumerable Disadvantages both they and their Posterity must still endure" without towns. Makemie could see numerous advantages. Towns added "worth and value upon our whole Country," "fill our Country with people of all sorts, and so add to our strength," "render Trade universally more easie," "prevent and soon regulate a great many Frauds, Irregularities, Abuses, and Imposition on Trade," as well as foster religion and "Learning and School-Education." The benefits seemed obvious, and Makemie categorized those who were

> averse to Towns, to be three sorts of Persons: First, Fools, who cannot, neither will see their own Interest and Advantage in having Towns. Secondly, Knaves, who would still carry on Fraudulent Designs, and cheating Tricks, in a corner or secret Trade, afraid and ashamed of being exposed at a Publick Market. Thirdly, Sluggards, who rather than be at labour, and at any charge in transporting their Goods to Market, tho idle at home, and lose double thereby rather than do it: To which I may add a fourth, which are Sots, who may be best Cured of their Disease by a pair of Stocks in Town.[7]

5. Reps, *Tidewater*, 60.
6. Langston, "On Towns, and Corporations," 101–2.

A category that Makemie failed to mention was that of colonial administrators, who were simply unwilling to sacrifice any mercantile principles, even to foster the creation of towns. Instead, Virginia officials attempted to maintain a strict economic system while simultaneously embarking on a campaign to legislate towns into existence.

Aside from trying to inspire town growth by giving counties names such as James City and Charles City, the early attempts in Virginia to influence urban development focused on the first capital, Jamestown. English officials repeatedly instructed governors or their lieutenants to direct their attentions to rebuilding the town despite its unfortunate location and poor track record.[8] However, matters took a different course after the arrival of Governor Thomas, Lord Culpeper, who informed the Assembly that King Charles II considered towns a necessity, "without which noe other nation ever begunne a plantacon, or any yet thrived (as it ought,) and observed that all other means have bin unsuccesfull, hath in order thereunto Resolved as soon as storehouses & conveniencyes can be provided to prohibit Shipps tradeing here to loade or unloade but at certain fixed places."[9] This speech marked a shift of focus away from Jamestown, and provided an outline for a period of town legislation that extended from the middle of the seventeenth century into the first decade of the eighteenth.[10]

The Virginia General Assembly made several attempts to fulfill the king's wishes. In 1680 an "act for cohabitation and encouragement of trade and manufacture" went into effect, establishing twenty ports on the major rivers.[11] This act required that imports and exports pass only through these ports, bypassing privately owned docks and warehouse facilities. To further encourage settlement, the act exempted goods in the towns from attachment for debt and granted artisans who settled in them a five-year tax exemption. But despite the inducements, for the most part the ports failed to attract populations, and ship captains, who found the wharves and storage facilities at the new towns to be poor, if they existed at all, continued to trade at private wharves along Virginia's rivers as they had in the past. Finally, the English government disallowed the

7. (Previous page) Francis Makemie, "A Plain & Friendly Perswasive to the Inhabitants of Virginia and Maryland For Promoting Towns & Cohabitation. By a Well-Wisher to Both Governments," *Virginia Magazine of History and Biography* 4 (1897): 259, 261–65, 271.

8. Jamestown remained the capital of the colony until 1699, although Governor William Berkeley had received instructions to choose a new site for the town (though retaining the name) more than fifty years earlier. See "Instructions to William Berkeley, 1642," *Virginia Magazine of History and Biography* 2 (1895): 284–85. See also William Waller Hening, ed., *The Statutes at Large; Being a Collection of all the Laws of Virginia, From the First Session of the Legislature in the Year 1619*, 13 vols. (Charlottesville: Univ. Press of Virginia, 1969), 2:135; Jones, *Present State*, 196; and Reps, *Tidewater*, 656.

9. Thomas, Lord Culpeper, "Speech of Governor Lord Culpeper," *Virginia Magazine of History and Biography* 14 (Apr. 1967): 364.

10. Riley, "Town Acts," 310. See also Rainbolt, "Absence of Towns," 50–65; Edward F. Heite, "Markets and Ports," *Virginia Cavalcade* 16 (1966): 29–41; Chernichowski, "Legislated Towns," passim; O'Mara, "Urbanization," 237–72; and Reps, *Tidewater*, 65–91.

11. Hening, *Statutes* 2:471–78; and Stephenson and McKee, *Virginia in Maps*, 49.

act.[12] The Assembly passed a second act in 1691 and a third in 1706, but these failed as well, and the Board of Trade, whose members feared the rise of manufacturing competition, insisted they be repealed. A few of the ports, including Yorktown, Gloucester, Elizabeth Town, Hampton, and Urbanna, succeeded, but the ultimate failure of mass town legislation in Virginia was complete by 1711, when a fourth act did not even gain enough support to pass the House of Burgesses.[13] Writing in 1724, Hugh Jones bemoaned the fact that "neither the interest nor inclinations of the Virginians induce them to cohabit in towns."[14]

Town legislation and other government initiatives, which also failed in Maryland, North Carolina, and South Carolina, did not signify an end to government participation in urbanization.[15] On the contrary, these efforts set a precedent for government authority. During the eighteenth century, Virginia's government chartered and incorporated towns on an individual basis as specific needs required or in answer to legislative petitions from individuals. Throughout this process, public officials often played important roles in acquiring town sites, developing plans, regulating lot sales, establishing building requirements, and appointing trustees. As the people of Virginia began to spread into the western reaches of the colony, public officials remained actively involved in the urbanization process, whether the towns were established through private initiative, to meet a demand for trade, or to serve as administrative centers.

Location was a key factor that distinguished later town formation from the early attempts at mass legislation. While some urban activity continued in the tidewater region during the eighteenth century, the majority of Virginia's new towns rose in the backcountry, a region whose geography differed sharply from the low-lying Coastal Plain with its navigable rivers. It consisted of a vast mosaic of forest and savannah that extended southward from the Delaware Valley and the headwaters of Chesapeake Bay, stretching southward through the Piedmont. The land was rolling and rich, made up of limestone and clay soils. The plateau was watered by swift, shallow streams and narrow rivers, not suited for extensive navigation but excellent for supporting a wide range of plant life from tall grasses to towering forests. The backcountry had a temperate climate

12. W. Noel Sainsbury et al., eds., *Calendar of State Papers, Colonial Series*, 40 vols. (London: Public Record Office, 1860–1938), 11:152.

13. Hening, *Statutes* 3:53–69, 108–9, 404–19; Sainsbury et al., 13:473, 611, 666, 24:538–39; H. R. McIlwaine, Wilmer Lee Hall, and Benjamin Jennings Hillman, eds., *Executive Journals of the Council of Colonial Virginia*, 6 vols. (Richmond: Virginia State Library, 1925–67), 3:576–77; John Pendleton Kennedy and H. R. McIlwaine, eds., *Journals of the House of Burgesses of Virginia*, 13 vols. (Richmond: Colonial Press, E. Waddey, 1905–15), 2:444, 4:324.

14. Jones, *Present State*, 73.

15. Goldfield, "Pearls," 13–14. In addition to the Proprietors' attempts to create towns, North Carolina also tried to stimulate town growth through the use of borough representation. See Francis Nash, "The Borough Towns of North Carolina," *North Carolina Booklet* 4 (Oct. 1906): 83–102; Mary Phlegar Smith, "Municipal Development in North Carolina, 1665–1930: A History of Urbanization" (Ph.D. diss, Univ. of North Carolina, 1930), 25–49; and Mary Phlegar Smith, "Borough Representation in North Carolina," *North Carolina Historical Review* 7 (Apr. 1930): 177–89. For Maryland's urban development see Reps, *Tidewater*, 232–66.

and plentiful rainfall.[16] The region had no distinct boundary, but it began roughly at the fall line, where the falls in the many rivers made unbroken navigation impossible, and ran to the mountains.

Colonists looked to the backcountry and saw great promise. In 1705 Francis Makemie wrote to Virginians with excitement, saying that "the best, richest and most healthy part of your Country is yet to be inhabited, above the Falls of every River, to the Mountains."[17] Yet the region remained essentially unexplored until Lieutenant Governor Alexander Spotswood and his Knights of the Golden Horseshoe made an expedition into the region in 1716.[18] Exploration had been done earlier in the colonial period, most notably by John Lederer in 1669–70, but for the most part, early accounts of the backcountry often were based on limited personal experience or consisted of generalizations about the whole region based on knowledge of a particular area.[19] Still, such descriptions created an image of a fertile land, which influenced settlement. The dominant theme of this literature was praise for the abundance of land and opportunity, the temperate climate, plant life, and wildlife. William Byrd II, for example, based on knowledge he gained from trips with the party surveying the border of Virginia and North Carolina, promoted the attributes of the backcountry and called the land "Eden."[20] Fueled by some basis in fact, the backcountry became legendary for its fabulous resources and the promise it held for settlers.

Initially the push for backcountry settlement came from the east. By the latter part of the seventeenth century, most of the forest in the Tidewater had been cleared and much of the best land claimed. Europeans began to move beyond the protection of forts set up along the fall line and venture into territory still occupied by Indians. After Bacon's Rebellion, the push for settlement began in earnest, aided by Lieutenant Governor Spotswood, who opened up the territory in 1710. Spotswood developed promotional schemes, promising tax and quitrent exemptions for ten years to colonists who took up land in two new counties created by an act in 1720.

As settlers moved into the Virginia backcountry, distinct geographic regions developed different settlement patterns. The Piedmont was one of the

16. Carl Bridenbaugh, *Myths and Realities: Societies in the Colonial South* (Baton Rouge: Louisiana State Univ. Press, 1955), 120.

17. Makemie, "Plain & Friendly," 257; and Harry Roy Merrens, *Colonial North Carolina in the Eighteenth Century: A Study of Historical Geography* (Chapel Hill: Univ. of North Carolina Press, 1964), 39–43.

18. For brief accounts of the Knights of the Golden Horseshoe, see Warren R. Hofstra, *The Planting of a New Virginia: Settlement and Landscape in the Shenandoah Valley* (Baltimore: Johns Hopkins Univ. Press, 2004), 60–62; and David Hackett Fischer and James C. Kelly, *Bound Away: Virginia and the Westward Movement* (Charlottesville: Univ. Press of Virginia, 2000), 101–3.

19. See John Lederer, *The Discoveries of John Lederer*, ed. William P. Cumming (Charlottesville: Univ. Press of Virginia, 1958).

20. See William Byrd II, *William Byrd's Histories of the Dividing Line Betwixt Virginia and North Carolina*, ed. William K. Boyd (Raleigh, NC: Edwards and Broughton, 1929); and William Byrd II, *William Byrd's Natural History of Virginia or the Newly Discovered Eden*, ed. Richard Croom Beatty and William J. Mulloy (Richmond, VA: Dietz, 1940).

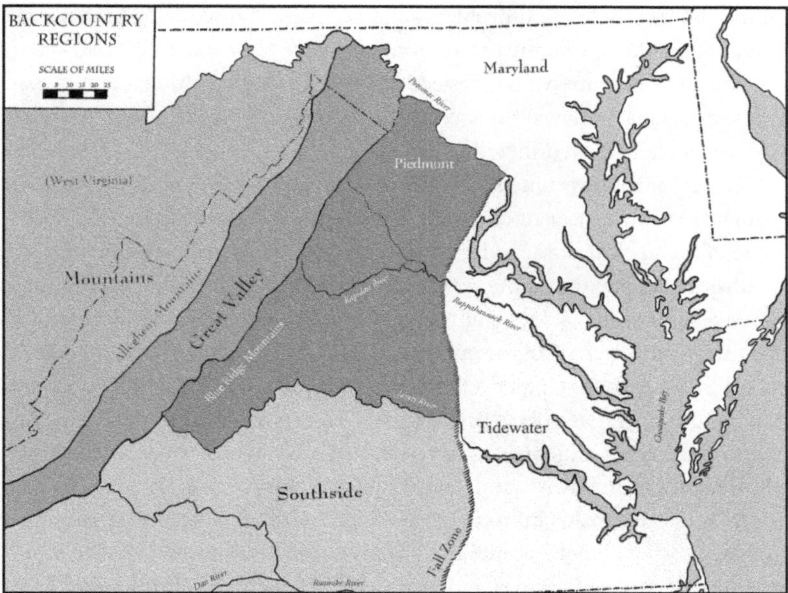

Backcountry regions. Map by the author.

largest regions, consisting of the area north of the James River stretching from the Tidewater to the Blue Ridge, including a portion of Thomas, Lord Fairfax's Northern Neck tract (discussed below). Its proximity to the Tidewater made the Piedmont a natural frontier for settlement, its fertile lands and rich valleys attracting freed indentured servants who began to occupy the land in the late seventeenth century. However, the squatters had no legal claims to the land, and wealthy Tidewater planters soon took control of the region, shaping its future development. Not surprisingly, just as in the Tidewater, family connections and kinship groups were very important to the settlement of the Piedmont, and the gentry worked to keep down land speculation and absentee landlords. They also introduced slavery in the region very early, and people of African descent soon made up between 40 and 45 percent of the population.[21]

Land south of the James, stretching from the fall zone to the Blue Ridge Mountains, is geographically part of the Piedmont. However, early in the seventeenth century the Southside developed its own unique character, identity, and settlement pattern. The territory included about nine thousand square miles. It had fertile soils and many rivers watered the region. However, with the exception of the James and Appomattox, Southside rivers did not flow into the Chesapeake Bay, limiting Southside settlers' economic opportunities and slowing the region's development. The Southside had Virginia's longest growing

21. Fischer and Kelly, *Bound Away*, 94–101.

season, but transportation problems and remoteness discouraged settlement. Just as in the Piedmont, the earliest residents were poor squatters, followed by members of the gentry who invested heavily in land speculation. Landed families were unable to repeat the success they had had in the Piedmont, however, and few actually moved there.

The colonial government actually discouraged settlement in the territory before 1738 out of fear of causing conflict with Indians in the area, and because of the unclear border with North Carolina. As a result, settlement in the Southside stagnated until the second quarter of the eighteenth century when the Assembly passed an act granting tax incentives and other inducements to encourage settlement. Large numbers of Virginians from the area around Richmond then began moving into the territory. But the small size of land patents and an administrative policy that required colonists to take up poor land as well as good hampered settlement. As a result, large numbers of people did not stay. Many moved on into North and South Carolina, and others returned to the Tidewater. Without a steady influx of permanent residents, economic development in the region remained slow until after the American Revolution, when the Southside developed a plantation economy. By the first decade of the nineteenth century enslaved African Americans made up fully two-thirds of the population.[22]

Settlement of the two remaining backcountry regions, the Great Valley and the Mountains, differed from that of the Piedmont and Southside in a number of respects. First, it did not really begin until the 1730s, when large numbers of colonists began immigrating into the region west of the Blue Ridge. Instead of migrating from the Tidewater, these newcomers, who represented a greater variety of religious and ethnic groups than moved into the older regions, came primarily from colonies to the north.

The source of this migration had roots in Europe when large numbers of immigrants crossed the Atlantic, many of them landing in Pennsylvania. The reasons for their coming were economic and political. People arrived in search of economic opportunity, often fleeing from war-ravaged regions of central Europe and the depressed economies of Southern Britain and Ireland. Colonists also sought relief from religious persecution: French Protestants because of the revocation of the Edict of Nantes in 1685, Scots-Irish Presbyterians in defiance of the Penal Act of 1704, and Pietist German Protestants seeking relief from both Catholic- and Lutheran-controlled governments. Ulstermen, Germans, French, and Welsh streamed into Pennsylvania. The influx of people moved toward the southwest into the Lancaster region. By 1740 people had moved beyond southeastern Pennsylvania, seeking to improve their social condition,

22. Ibid., 87–92; Richard R. Beeman, *The Evolution of the Southern Backcountry: A Case Study of Lunenburg County, Virginia, 1746–1832* (Philadelphia: Univ. of Pennsylvania Press, 1984), 14, 24–26; Michael L. Nicholls, "Origins of the Virginia Southside, 1703–1753: A Social and Economic Study" (Ph.D. diss., College of William and Mary in Virginia, 1972), 14, 29–31, 34–35, 37; and Farmer, *In the Absence*, 34–37.

hastened on by a variety of factors: land prices, problems of tenure, and lack of opportunity. Increasingly, Indians refused to sell land in western Pennsylvania, and colonial wars and the accompanying Indian troubles also provided incentive for further migration. The area to the immediate south did not offer much opportunity because of a border dispute with Maryland, during which land offices remained closed, leaving prospective settlers with no access to land patents or clear titles. Colonists naturally looked still further south, and a wave of Marylanders moving out of the soil-depleted Eastern Shore and escaping the chaos of the disputed borderlands joined the migration.[23] A 1749 court statement described the exodus: "Hearing by the hunters and traders, the common-finders out of the backlands, that the lands in the Colony of Virginia were rich and good, they were inclined to bear the burdens of danger and hardships in hopes to provide not only for themselves but to prevent, as much as in them lay, the slavery of their posterity."[24]

With some exceptions, especially during the French and Indian War, a steady flow of immigrants poured into the Great Valley of Virginia from 1730 through the end of the colonial period. By far the majority of them came into the Valley by crossing the Potomac River at ferry sites such as Shepherdstown, Williamsport, and Harper's Ferry; however, a small number did enter through natural gaps in the Blue Ridge Mountains. The wave of migration first came to the Shenandoah Valley, the northern portion of the Great Valley including the modern counties of Jefferson and Berkeley in West Virginia, and Frederick, Shenandoah, Rockingham, Augusta, and Rockbridge Counties in Virginia. The widespread availability of good farmland and the chance to "gain a comfortable livelihood," attracted settlers according to Andrew Burnaby.[25] Furthermore, Virginia government officials encouraged settlement of the Valley to create a buffer zone between Indian areas and the Tidewater, even though there were few permanent Indian settlements in the Valley to discourage European colonization. Virtually empty in 1730, the Great Valley experienced an astounding population boom, reaching an estimated 21,000 inhabitants (20,000 white and 1,000 black) by 1763, which grew to 53,000 people (48,000 white and 5,000 black) by 1776.[26]

23. Fischer and Kelly, *Bound Away*, 105–26; James T. Lemon, *The Best Poor Man's Country: A Geographical Study of Early Southeastern Pennsylvania* (Baltimore: Johns Hopkins Press, 1972), 42, 43, 67, and 71; and Robert W. Ramsey, *Carolina Cradle: Settlement of the Northwest North Carolina Frontier, 1747–1762* (Chapel Hill: Univ. of North Carolina Press, 1964), 12–20, 100–101. For a detailed study of the movements of Pennsylvanians, see Lemon, *Best Poor Man's*, 71–97.

24. As quoted by Klaus Wust, "The Story of Colonial Strasburg," in E. E. Keister, *Strasburg, Virginia, and the Keister Family* (Strasburg, VA: Shenandoah, 1972), 8.

25. Burnaby, *Travels*, 44.

26. Freeman H. Hart, *The Valley of Virginia in the American Revolution, 1763–1789* (Chapel Hill: Univ. of North Carolina Press, 1942), 6–7. For occupation and settlement of the Shenandoah Valley see Mitchell, *Commercialism*, 15–58; Robert D. Mitchell, "The Upper Shenandoah Valley during the Eighteenth Century: A Study in Historical Geography" (Ph.D. diss., Univ. of Wisconsin, 1969), 49–132; and Warren R. Hofstra, "Land, Ethnicity, and Community at the Opequon Settlement, Virginia, 1730–1800," *Virginia Magazine of History and Biography* 98 (1990): 426–29.

But the Shenandoah Valley was not always the terminus for immigrants. People continued through to the largely unpopulated regions of the Roanoke River Valley, the southern portion of the Great Valley. The Valley also served as a migratory corridor, leading settlers through the Rockbridge Gap into the Southside and on into North Carolina along the Great Wagon Road.[27]

The Allegheny Mountains, part of the Appalachian Mountain range, steeply rose to form the western wall of the Shenandoah Valley. The escarpment reached heights of between fifteen and sixteen hundred feet above sea level. Unlike the Blue Ridge range to the east, the Alleghenies had relatively few natural gaps, mostly located in the northern part of the colony. More intrepid settlers crossed the gaps and settled among the irregular ridges in fertile narrow valleys or on an occasional wide plateau. The Appalachian Plateau in the southwestern part of the colony stood even higher, averaging two thousand feet, and most colonists simply avoided settling in the region, preferring to make their way into Kentucky and Tennessee via the Cumberland Gap.

When newcomers to the Virginia backcountry settled in each of the four regions, they could obtain land through patents. A settler chose a piece of land and then was required by law to have the tract surveyed and officially recorded. Government officials instructed county surveyors, who had to be accredited by the College of William and Mary, as to what sizes and shapes the tracts could take, in an effort to prevent settlers from patenting only the best lands in a given area. For example, surveyors were supposed to create tracts using only lines oriented north-south or east-west, and to limit water frontage proportionally to the size of the rest of the parcel. But in practice, the system was subject to corruption and inaccuracy, and as a result, land affairs were often in a state of chaos. The confusion arose from a number of spheres. Surveyors routinely ignored their instructions and laid out irregularly shaped grants. Poor measuring techniques were commonplace, as surveyors made obscure references to impermanent features, leaving boundaries unclear. Surveyors wielded a great deal of power in Virginia and rewarded friends or punished enemies by exaggerating or understating the size of holdings and by controlling when or if a patent would be recorded.[28]

People could patent land in a number of ways. Under the headright system instituted in the seventeenth century, the head of a household could claim a minimum of fifty acres for himself and was guaranteed similar claims for other people he brought with him, whether they were family members, servants, or other settlers. By 1715 the treasury right largely superceded the headright system. Under this arrangement, a settler chose a tract of land, had it

27. Mitchell, "Upper Shenandoah," 113.

28. See Sarah S. Hughes, *Surveyors and Statesmen: Land Measuring in Colonial Virginia* (Richmond: Virginia Surveyors Foundation: Virginia Association of Surveyors, 1979), 107–27. For a case study of backcountry land settlement and its implications see Turk McCleskey, "Rich Land, Poor Prospects: Real Estate and the Formation of a Social Elite in Augusta County, Virginia, 1738–1770," *Virginia Magazine of History and Biography* 98 (July 1990): 449–86.

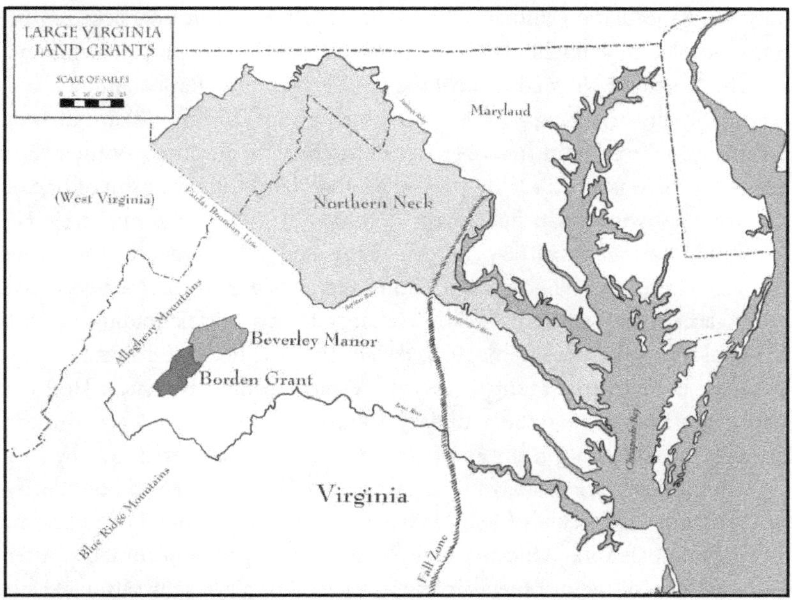

Large Virginia land grants. Map by the author.

surveyed by the county surveyor, and then applied to Virginia's receiver general in Williamsburg for the patent. After the French and Indian War, another type of patent, the military right, was available for men who served in the county militia units.[29] The sizes of land holdings varied but were generally small. Most grants were less than six hundred acres—three hundred being typical. A few individuals accrued large land holdings for speculative ventures, though the government made efforts to limit the number of extensive grants. Nevertheless, land speculation did occur in the backcountry, with speculators experiencing varying degrees of success in disposing of their holdings.[30]

In the 1730s a few men and their associates obtained large land grants in the backcountry. Orange County burgess William Beverley and Benjamin Borden Sr., who had traveled to Virginia as an agent for Lord Fairfax, each received tracts of land in the upper Shenandoah Valley (modern Augusta and Rockbridge counties), Beverley receiving 118,491 acres and Borden 92,100. James Patton, who served as Beverley's land agent, got 100,000 acres of his own in southwest Virginia. But these men did not hamper backcountry settlement because they were obliged to follow the same stipulations as other grantees and had to find settlers to buy or rent their lands. As a result, they actively recruited settlers, serving almost as immigration agents for the backcountry.[31]

29. Mitchell, *Commercialism*, 64.

30. Hughes, *Surveyors*, 84; Bridenbaugh, *Myths*, 138–39; and Merrens, *Colonial*, 25–26.

31. McCleskey, "Rich Land," 459, 463, 465, 467; Fischer and Kelly, *Bound Away*, 113, 126; Mitchell, "Upper Shenandoah," 63–73; and Mitchell, "Settlement," 73. For a detailed account of the shenanigans Beverley went through to acquire Beverley Manor, see Mitchell, *Commercialism*, 62n13.

Such land speculation influenced the rate of settlement in the backcountry, but a speculator did not hold the largest private tract. It was a proprietary grant.

The Northern Neck consists of the land between the Rappahannock and Potomac rivers stretching west through the colony into the mountains. Charles II first made the grant in 1648/49 to seven patentees in gratitude for their support while he was in exile.[32] By 1681 Alexander, Lord Culpeper, son of one of the original owners, had purchased the rights of the other proprietors. He confirmed the patent in 1688 and passed the land to his daughter, Catherine Fairfax, at his death. When her son Thomas came of age, Catherine persuaded him to accept the Northern Neck in exchange for his Fairfax holdings so that she could save the heavily mortgaged Culpeper estates. Beginning in 1736, Thomas, Lord Fairfax spent three years exploring his new lands. He then returned to England to settle boundary disputes with the Virginia government through the courts. With the assistance of an impressive map drawn by surveyor John Warner, Fairfax won the case in 1745. The confirmed boundaries left Fairfax in possession of 5,282,000 acres, stretching across the Piedmont, the Shenandoah Valley, and the Blue Ridge and Allegheny Mountains. After the resolution of the dispute, Fairfax moved to Virginia, finally settling at his Greenway Court estate in the Shenandoah Valley in 1748. He opened a land office, which issued grants in the western part of the Northern Neck under ninety-nine-year leases starting in 1752. The grants were made separately from government patents until just after Fairfax's death in 1781.[33]

Fairfax's administration of the Northern Neck began after the Shenandoah Valley already had a sizeable population. Indeed, the crown had made other grants in the region, including an 80,000-acre tract to Isaac and John Vanmeter. Alsatian immigrant Yost Hite and some partners purchased the land, divided it into smaller tracts and sold them to other settlers. While Fairfax lived in London, he agreed to respect the grants, including those that stood within his proprietorship. However, when he arrived in Virginia, Fairfax proclaimed that all settlers on the Hite lands—some five hundred tracts—were squatters and owed quitrents. Hite promptly filed a lawsuit, but through his connections, Fairfax drew out the case. The court finally rendered a verdict favoring the Hites in 1786, by which time Lord Fairfax had died. The lawsuit had left settlers in doubt of the legitimacy of their holdings for thirty-seven years.[34]

32. While most of Europe began changing to the current Gregorian calendar (referred to as New Style) in the sixteenth century, Great Britain continued to use the Julian calendar (Old Style) until 1752. That meant that British territories were eleven days behind other European nations in reckoning dates. Confusing things even more, the new year began March 25 on the Julian calendar. The years of dates before 1752 that fall between January 1 and March 25 will be indicated with a slash to help alleviate some confusion.

33. Fischer and Kelly, *Bound Away*, 85–86; Mitchell, "Upper Shenandoah," 58–63; Samuel Kercheval, *A History of the Valley of Virginia* (Winchester, VA: Samuel H. Davis, 1833), 209–11; and Frederic Morton, *The Story of Winchester in Virginia* (Strasburg, VA: Shenandoah, 1925), 28–30. Until 1690, grants made in the Northern Neck were recorded in the Virginia Colonial Records. From 1690 to 1782 they were filed at the proprietary office. Northern Neck grants may be found at the Library of Virginia in Richmond.

Although frustrating to the landowners, the effect of the Fairfax proprietorship on the course of settlement in the backcountry was not major, in spite of the fact that proprietors were not held to the same requirements as other landholders. The headright system did not apply, nor did requirements for the number of settlers. However, Fairfax positioned himself to make attractive offers to prospective settlers that land speculators could not match. He made several large grants to Tidewater families in the eastern third of Frederick County, which they did not take up in earnest until after the revolution. In the rest of the county, however, the Hite faction brought a different settlement pattern favoring small farms and market towns without connections to the Tidewater. The Northern Neck also created a division of the Shenandoah Valley along the Frederick and Augusta County border, with Tidewater influence stronger in the north and the influence of the middle colonies stronger in the south. Certainly the existence of a separate land administration in Virginia caused discontent and some instability, but then both land systems had problems. Still, land in the Great Valley was plentiful, and if a settler met with problems acquiring property, he always had the recourse of taking possession of a tract, fighting any officials who intruded, and waiting for the matter to be straightened out in court.[35]

While geography shaped town development in the backcountry by influencing settlement patterns, it also helped influence the location and nature of towns through its effect on trade in the region. The size and courses of rivers, for example, created problems in the shipment of goods. Trade in the Piedmont depended on roads leading to fall-line towns, where goods could be loaded on boats and shipped downriver to the coast. The James River served as the major artery for Southside trade because the smaller rivers in the region were not navigable for long stretches and flowed south toward the Albemarle Sound in North Carolina and away from Virginia's ports. The mountain range that separated the Great Valley from the coast hampered the marketing of goods in the Valley. Furthermore, social, linguistic, and religious ties of the settlers to Pennsylvania directed a lot of the area's products to Philadelphia. Towns in the mountains depended on links to towns in the Valley to get their goods to market. Geography necessitated building and maintaining a good network of roads, and to help the flow of goods and direct trade along east-west routes, administrative officials on the local and regional levels frequently lobbied for their construction. County officials provided for opening roads to courthouses, mills, and stores, while the Virginia Assembly granted petitions to establish or improve roads and for the operation of ferries, in an effort to increase the amount of intracolonial trade.[36]

34. (Previous page) Hofstra, *Planting*, 94–99; Mitchell, "Upper Shenandoah," 61–63; and Morton, *Story of Winchester*, 30–31. A copy of the suit can be found in Katherine Glass Greene, *Winchester, Virginia, and Its Beginnings, 1743–1814* (Strasburg, VA: Shenandoah, 1926), 38–39.

35. Robert D. Mitchell, "'Over the Hills and Far Away': George Washington and the Changing Virginia Backcountry," in Warren R. Hofstra, ed., *George Washington and the Virginia Backcountry* (Madison, WI: Madison House, 1998), 71; and Mitchell, "Upper Shenandoah," 58–63.

36. Fischer and Kelly, *Bound Away*, 88; Hart, *Valley*, 20–23; and Goldfield, "Pearls," 14–15.

By the third quarter of the eighteenth century, an incredible population growth in the backcountry, the development of trading patterns, and advances in transportation systems had laid the groundwork for a boom in town development. New towns gave their inhabitants a sense of security on the frontier. They provided settlers with a wide range of social and economic services. Government administrations and courts grew to meet the demands of justice and order in the backcountry. Market centers developed to provide commercial opportunities and increase trade. Towns functioned as way stations for newcomers as they traveled into the region, and they provided familiar surroundings for members of a vast array of religious and ethnic groups. Just as government officials had predicted from the earliest days of British settlement, towns brought an element of civilization into the backcountry.[37]

The most common location for an urban center in colonial Virginia was the site of the county court. These were administrative centers where officials meted out justice, recorded land transactions, oversaw the construction of roads, issued licenses, and implemented new laws. Because of an almost obsessive preoccupation with locating the court near the geographic center of its district, the creation of a new county often meant that two new courthouses had to be built—one in the new county and one in the old. The choice of sites fell to newly appointed justices and was frequently the source of debate, chicanery, and outright corruption as powerful men in the community, often the justices themselves, vied for the privilege of locating the court on their property. As a result, during the process of debate, the court moved from house to house while the justices failed to either choose a site or allocate funds for construction. The delay, sometimes lasting years, caused difficulties in record keeping and created animosity among county citizens as the court shifted locations. For the winner, capturing the courthouse could be very lucrative, immediately increasing the value of the adjacent land and creating income opportunities through the establishment of stores, taverns, and ordinaries (private houses with at least one public room), or through the sale of town lots.[38]

After choosing a site, the justices arranged for the construction of a courthouse, a jail, and other service structures. A building committee made up of court officials and local freeholders set the general guidelines for the structures, designating their dimensions, layout, and building materials, and often specifying certain features such as windows, a platform, or an attorney's bar. Some courts commissioned plans, met with local builders, and asked for bids. Once the committee awarded the building contracts, an undertaker or general contractor paid the court a bond assuming all of the financial liabilities until the building's completion. Usually a local planter or merchant, the undertaker was often also a justice himself and stood to make a sizeable profit from

37. Mitchell, "Upper Shenandoah," 233–36.

38. Mitchell, *Commercialism*, 88; and Isaac, *Transformation*, 88.

a successfully completed project. The costs of building the courthouse and jail were usually covered by a specially levied tax.[39]

A courthouse complex could remain isolated, coming to life once a month when the court met. Often, enterprising merchants and innkeepers established stores and ordinaries nearby. During court days, the county seat came alive as people arrived to seek justice, record transactions, and conduct trade. If they found the location useful, people built residences at the courthouse and the site grew to have a sizeable population year round. But the life of such a town was tenuous. As backcountry counties continued to be divided, courts frequently changed locales, leaving the town to survive or fail without its primary industry.[40]

Trade was another important impetus for the creation of backcountry towns, and when chartering or incorporating a town, the Virginia General Assembly frequently stipulated that the community be well situated "for inland trade."[41] Urban centers functioned to provide their surrounding areas with goods and services. Similarly, they worked in tandem with other towns to develop trading networks that linked western communities with distribution centers at the fall line and seaports. These systems made the transportation of agricultural goods more profitable and provided settlers with access to imported products. Trading towns created market opportunities for craftsmen, merchants, and fledgling industries. Communities developed along major transportation routes and operated as service centers for immigrants into Virginia and the Carolinas. As settlers moved into the backcountry, they depended on these towns to provide supplies, shelter, even protection from Indian attack. The success or failure of trade and commercial activities proved a leading factor in the growth or decline of urban centers.[42]

Other incentives for the establishment of backcountry towns included ethnicity, religion, defense, and private initiative. Colonists often immigrated into the backcountry in large groups and settled in compact communities. Members of various ethnic groups settled together as a result of kinship ties, custom, and language. Similarly, congregations of different denominations clustered together for support, and towns grew up around or near churches.

39. For a description of the layout of Virginia courthouses and courthouse complexes see Carl Lounsbury, "The Structure of Justice: The Courthouses of Colonial Virginia," in Thomas Carter and Bernard L. Herman, eds., *Perspectives in Vernacular Architecture, III* (Columbia: Univ. of Missouri, 1989): 214–26; and Marcus Whiffen, "The Early Courthouses of Virginia," *Journal of the Society of Architectural Historians* 18 (Mar. 1959): 2–10.

40. Mitchell, "'Over the Hills,'" 74–75; Mitchell, "Upper Shenandoah," 233; and Eric H. Monkkonen, *America Becomes Urban: The Development of U.S. Cities and Towns, 1780–1980* (Berkeley: Univ. of California Press, 1988), 65–66.

41. For example, see Hening, *Statutes* 7:406, 600, 8:417.

42. Mitchell, "Upper Shenandoah," 234–35; Kenneth E. Lewis, "Economic Development in the South Carolina Backcountry: A View from Camden," in David Colin Crass et al., eds., *The Southern Colonial Backcountry: Interdisciplinary Perspectives on Frontier Communities* (Knoxville: Univ. of Tennessee Press, 1998), 89; and Rutman with Rutman, *Small Worlds*, 250–51.

Often, settlements resulted in times of unrest, when an individual laid out lots on his land to accommodate neighbors gathering together for safety. Other landholders laid out towns as speculative ventures, seeking to exploit the opportunities of a nearby feature, such as a river, road, fort, or mill. Economics, religion, kinship, safety, and chance all helped shape urban development in the Virginia backcountry.[43]

While a few backcountry towns grew almost organically around some central feature, most of the towns in Virginia and throughout the American colonies were planned communities.[44] Colonists brought with them a long tradition of urban planning, which influenced the choice of town sites, urban design, and regulations. Colonial towns were not created in a vacuum. Indeed, many urban designs reflected classical and contemporary theories of town planning. The European design traditions were myriad and rich, bringing in ideas from Greece, Rome, and Renaissance Italy. English experience alone included Roman *castra*, thirteenth-century fortified towns, Elizabethan colonies in Ulster, plans for the rebuilding of London following the Great Fire of 1666, and eighteenth-century innovations such as residential squares, parks, and walks.[45] French and German influences in the townscape of the Virginia backcountry is also evident in the use of such public squares and line settlements—villages that developed along important roads and intersections.[46] The designer of a colonial town was limited only by time, resources, and the extent of his knowledge or experience. Many planners had no training and made impractical choices in dealing with new soils, climates, and resources. But from the beginning of settlement, town planning played an integral role in the

43. Hughes, *Surveyors*, 86; Mitchell, "Upper Shenandoah," 234; and Wellenreuther, "Urbanization," 664–65.

44. Reps, *Tidewater*, 1.

45. Monkkonen, *America*, 66. For background on town planning traditions see John W. Reps, *The Making of Urban America: City Planning in the United States* (Princeton, NJ: Princeton Univ. Press, 1965), 1–25; Reps, *Tidewater*, 1–23; and Sylvia Doughty Fries, *The Urban Idea in Colonial America* (Philadelphia: Temple Univ. Press, 1977), 3–31. For a comparison with English town planning and settlement in Ulster, see Gilbert Camblin, *The Town in Ulster* (Belfast, Northern Ireland: Wm. Mullan & Son, 1951); and Philip R. Robinson, *The Plantation of Ulster* (New York: St. Martin's, 1984).

46. Paul Zucker, *Town and Square: From the Agora to the Village Green* (New York: Columbia Univ. Press, 1959), 64–66, 72, 79, 127, 131–32, 206, 214–19; and Bernard Herman, Thomas Ryan, and David Schuyler, "Townhouse: From Borough to City, Lancaster's Changing Streetscape," in *Architecture and Landscape of the Pennsylvania Germans, 1720–1920*, Guidebook for the Vernacular Architecture Forum Annual Conference, "Architecture and Landscape of the Pennsylvania Germans," Harrisburg, Pennsylvania, May 12–14, 2004, 78–79. Much of the German influence in Virginia came via Pennsylvania. See Wilbur Zelinsky, "The Pennsylvania Town: An Overdue Geographical Account," *Geographical Review* 67 (Apr. 1977): 127–47; Richard Pillsbury, "The Urban Street Pattern as a Culture Indicator: Pennsylvania, 1682–1815," *Annals of the Association of American Geographers* 60 (1970): 428–46; William J. Murtagh, *Moravian Architecture and Town Planning: Bethlehem, Pennsylvania, and Other Eighteenth-Century American Settlements* (Chapel Hill: Univ. of North Carolina Press, 1967); and James T. Lemon, "Urbanization and the Development of Eighteenth-Century Southeastern Pennsylvania and Adjacent Delaware," *William and Mary Quarterly*, 3rd series, vol. 24 (Oct. 1967): 501–42. The Lemon article also appears as chapter 5 in his book *The Best Poor Man's Country*, 118–49. For German influences in towns in Virginia and other colonies generally, see James D. Kornwolf with Georgiana W. Kornwolf, *Architecture and Town Planning in Colonial North America*, 3 vols. (Baltimore: Johns Hopkins Univ. Press, 2002), 1:437–69.

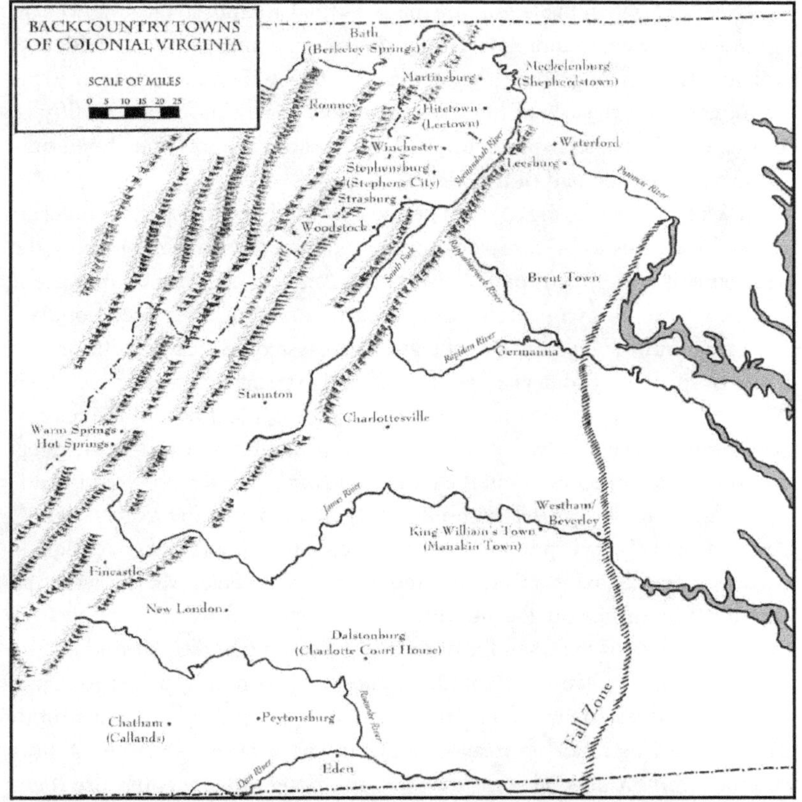

Backcountry towns of colonial Virginia. The stylized mountain ranges are from John Henry, *A New and Accurate Map of Virginia Wherein most of the Counties are laid down from Actual Surveys. With a Concise Account of the Number of inhabitants, the Trade, Soil and Produce of that province. By John Henry* (London: Thos. Jeffreys, 1770). Map by the author.

colonization of the Virginia backcountry, revealing clues to the heritage, experience, and creativity of its inhabitants.[47]

At first, colonists living in backcountry settlements enjoyed only the barest essentials. But with the easing of possible Indian threat, the development of some industry, and the rise of trade, settlers began to rely more heavily on European traditions and expectations of town development.[48] The presence of roads or trading routes as well as rivers or streams for transportation and power influenced site selection. In the rolling plains of the Piedmont, colonists often sought out hills or ridges to lay out their communities. In more mountainous regions, settlers showed preference for valleys that provided level expanses for their towns. Town founders throughout the backcountry took special care to locate settlements near a plentiful supply of water.[49]

47. Carl Feiss, "Early American Public Squares," in Zucker, *Town and Square,* 237; and John W. Reps, *Town Planning in Frontier America* (Princeton, NJ: Princeton Univ. Press, 1969), 3.

48. Reps, *Town Planning,* 4.

49. William Garner Roberts Jr., "Determinants of Physical Characteristics of the Eighteenth-Century North Carolina Town," M.A. thesis, Univ. of North Carolina, 1963, 23.

After 1711, when the legislature made its final attempt to create towns on a grand scale, town founding in Virginia became a matter of private initiative. Individuals or small groups, hoping to capitalize on increased trade or earning money from the sale of lots, laid out towns consisting usually of fifty or sixty acres. When these speculators actually laid out the lots, they hired official surveyors about half of the time.[50]

Town plans during the colonial period consisted of either written descriptions of what was to be constructed or graphic representations showing the arrangement and dimensions of streets, lots, and the location of important features or structures. One town design feature that quickly gained popularity throughout the colonies was the grid road system, which was efficient in its use of space, easy to devise and lay out, and extremely cost effective. Town founders often laid out roads in repetitive patterns, regardless of the natural topography. However, it was possible to vary the intervals or widths of streets and to include open squares in the design, allowing planners to avoid intruding on geographic features without totally abandoning the grid pattern.[51] Designers usually incorporated only one square in a town's design, designating it as a market, park, militia ground, or a grazing field. Alternatively, the square might emphasize the importance of a central feature.[52] Planners reserved the edges of the town for noisy and odious industries. Beyond lay the common land for livestock, wood supplies, and gathering places for large meetings.[53] Occasionally, a founder created outlots—larger tracts adjacent to the town—giving residents areas to plant gardens or raise cash crops. Outlots were uncommon in American town design, though planners did use them occasionally. However, they were common in Europe. Often they were incorporated into towns in areas where residents needed a margin of self-sufficiency in case of conflict. The English, for example, used outlots in the plantations they established in Ulster.[54] Backcountry Virginia towns rarely included all of these components, but they tended to reflect the same common European traditions of land distribution, building practices, and urban governance. Of the twenty-five attempted towns, for example, seventeen (and possible more whose plans have been lost) used a grid system of roads, five had a system of outlots, and five incorporated some form of square into their designs. In the backcountry, where towns were being built free of firm guidelines and repressive political forces, new and unusual forms appeared in response to new situations.[55]

50. Hughes, *Surveyors*, 134–35; and Wellenreuther, "Urbanization," 662.

51. Roberts, "Determinants," 24–25, 30; James Elliot, *The City in Maps: Urban Mapping to 1900* (London: British Library, 1987), 55; Russo, *American Towns*, 48; and Reps, *Tidewater*, 230, 296.

52. Feiss, *Early American*, 238, 240–42.

53. Monkkonen, *America*, 59; and Roberts, "Determinants," 29.

54. Hofstra, *Planting*, 193. In colonial America, this defensive reasoning may have been why James Edward Oglethorpe used outlots in his plan for the city of Savannah, founded in 1733 in part to defend the other English colonies from Spanish attack. See Reps, *Making*, 185–92.

55. Monkkonen, *America*, 36–37, 42–43; Warren Boeschenstein, *Historic American Towns along the Atlantic Coast* (Baltimore: Johns Hopkins Univ. Press, 1999), 7–8; and Reps, *Making*, 1.

Urban development in the Virginia backcountry was not a dramatic movement but rather a slow, steady progression of events. Colonial officials failed in their attempts to legislate Tidewater towns into existence. In the backcountry, the rise in population, improvements in transportation, increased trade, and industrial development established a firm basis for urban growth. At the end of the colonial period, less than 5 percent of Virginia's population was urban.[56] In the Piedmont, Southside, Great Valley, and Mountains of Virginia, there were only seven attempts to found towns before 1750, but by 1776 there had been twenty-five. Not all of these attempts succeeded, but the desire to create civilization and make money in the wilderness kept people trying. At the heart of all of these efforts, individuals or small groups of people used towns to help speed settlement in the Virginia backcountry.

56. Ernst and Merrens, "'Camden's turrets,'" 567; and Monkkonen, *America*, 5.

Chapter 2

The Piedmont

Virginia's Piedmont was the first western frontier after the settlement of the Tidewater. Its vast, rich lands beckoned poor settlers looking for inexpensive property, as well as members of the landed gentry, who sought to expand their vast holdings of wealth and power. Settlement proceeded in the Piedmont along two important river valleys. Near the turn of the eighteenth century, William Randolph, a younger son of an important English family, settled in the James River Valley. With his Virginia-born wife, Mary Isham, he founded a dynasty that dominated much of the land in the region. They were joined by members of the existing Virginia gentry, people with names like Carter, Page, and Walker, who moved into the valley and intermarried with the Randolph clan. This effectively recreated the importance of family connection that had dominated the Tidewater. But colonization of the Piedmont did not entirely replicate the Tidewater experience. Indeed, the lands along the Rappahannock were opened up through the efforts of an individual. Lieutenant Governor Alexander Spotswood looked to the west with ambitions of breaking into the gentry-dominated Virginia society. By the second decade of the eighteenth century he found the Randolphs already dominating the James River, so through careful maneuvering, he managed to build up large holdings of his own further north. Firmly in control of political power in the region,

Spotswood and the Virginia gentry created a climate of development that discouraged land speculators and absentee landlords and encouraged settlement through tax initiatives. Under their tutelage, the Piedmont prospered, creating a kind of Tidewater culture shaped by the healthy climate of the region. By the middle of the eighteenth century, the Piedmont surpassed the Tidewater to become Virginia's dominant region both economically and culturally.[1] It was only natural that towns would grow and prosper in such an environment. Not all of the attempts to establish towns in the region were successful, but people tried to found six Piedmont towns that illustrate the various catalysts—social, economic, and geographic—that led to urban development in the colonial period.

The earliest attempts to create Piedmont towns stemmed from a shift toward religious and ethnic toleration in Virginia that began during the waning years of the seventeenth century. The repressive nature of Virginia's early government began to break down following Bacon's Rebellion, encouraged by a new era of toleration that was emerging in England. Virginia politicians grudgingly began to allow religious dissenters greater standing in the colony, even passing a law granting European Protestants citizenship after a seven-year residency. The new political climate led a number of people with diverse religious and cultural backgrounds to settle in the region, as Germans of many different religious persuasions, Ulster Scot Presbyterians, Quakers, and many others began to move to Virginia.[2] After the revocation of the Edict of Nantes in 1685, Virginians worked hard to attract French Protestants to their shores. Governor Francis, Lord Howard of Effingham tried to recruit Huguenots with land offers and tax initiatives, though with little success.[3] But the Virginia government was not alone in trying to attract French settlers; so were private landholders.

Brent Town

Nicholas Haywood was a London merchant and something of a land speculator who purchased a plantation on the banks of the Potomac River. He had connections in Virginia. His father had been a merchant there, and his brother Samuel was the clerk of court for Stafford County. Samuel was also a close friend of planter, merchant, and lawyer William Fitzhugh, whose home, Bedford, bordered Haywood's new plantation. Haywood's plan was to settle the land with French Huguenots. Fitzhugh learned of the scheme in May of 1686 and offered to purchase Haywood's property, claiming the tract was too small

1. Fischer and Kelly, *Bound Away*, 95–101; and L. Scott Philyaw, *Virginia's Western Visions: Political and Cultural Expansion on an Early American Frontier* (Knoxville: Univ. of Tennessee Press, 2004), xvi–xvii.

2. Fischer and Kelly, *Bound Away*, 103–5; and Philyaw, *Virginia's Western Visions*, 10.

3. Durand de Dauphiné, *A Huguenot Exile in Virginia, or Voyages of a Frenchman Exiled for His Religion, with a Description of Virginia and Maryland*, ed. Gilbert Chinard (1687; New York: Press of the Pioneers, 1934), 143–44.

for Haywood's scheme. In exchange for the Potomac plantation, Fitzhugh offered to sell him a larger tract, "convenient and good Land enough [to] seat 150 or 200 familys."[4] Haywood declined but realized that Fitzhugh was probably correct in his assessment. Haywood knew he would be able to get a better deal from the cash-strapped proprietor of the Northern Neck, Alexander, Lord Culpeper.

Culpeper had bought out the other Northern Neck proprietors in 1681 and discovered it was not as profitable a move as he had anticipated. So when Haywood approached him with the proposal to pay cash for thirty thousand acres of land in Stafford (modern Fauquier) County, Culpeper jumped at the chance. The deal went through on January 10, 1686/87. Haywood formed a partnership with his brother-in-law Richard Foote and merchant Robert Bristow, who had left Virginia for London following Bacon's Rebellion. George Brent became the company's resident partner. He was an important partner, serving the colony as Stafford County surveyor and council receiver general north of the Rappahannock River. He was also William Fitzhugh's law partner and did work for Lord Culpeper.[5]

To assure royal blessing for the scheme, Haywood petitioned James II for a grant offering religious toleration for the settlers. James's warrant, issued February 10, 1686/87, informed Governor Howard that because the partners

> do speedly designe to build a Towne with convenient fortifications, and doo therefore pray that for the encouragement of Inhabitants to settle in the said Towne and plantation . . . wee do accordingly give and grant unto the Pet'rs and to all and every the Inhabitants which are now or hereafter shall be settled in the said Towne and Tract of Land belonging to them as is above mentioned, the full exercise of their Religion without being prosecuted or molested upon any penall laws or other account for the same.[6]

The town mentioned in the warrant was to be called Brenton, although it soon became known locally as Brent Town.

George Brent got to work on the project even before the king issued his warrant. In 1686 he met Durand de Dauphiné, a French Protestant traveling through Virginia who was staying with Fitzhugh. Dauphiné had left France and settled briefly in Charleston after Louis XIV revoked the Edict of Nantes. He traveled through the Chesapeake before returning to Europe and publishing an account of his adventures. Brent learned that Dauphiné was in the

4. William Fitzhugh to Nicholas Haywood, May 1686, in "Letters of William Fitzhugh," *Virginia Magazine of History and Biography* 1 (1893–94): 48; Fairfax Harrison, *Landmarks of Old Prince William: A Study of Origins in Northern Virginia* (Richmond, VA: Old Dominion, 1924), 177; and H. C. Groome, *Fauquier during the Proprietorship* (Richmond, VA: Old Dominion, 1927), 22.

5. W. B. Chilton, ed., "The Brent Family," *Virginia Magazine of History and Biography* 17 (1909): 308–9; Harrison, *Landmarks*, 178; Groome, *Fauquier*, 22–23; and Philyaw, *Virginia's Western Visions*, 10–11.

6. James II, Proclamation, Feb. 10, 1686/87, in Chilton, "Brent Family," 17:309–10.

neighborhood and tried to convince him to help promote Brent Town. He assured Dauphiné that the partners "were very honest men" who "would offer lands at a reasonable price to any Frenchman wishing to come, & even advance money to help build houses for those who had no funds, as well as corn for their subsistence during the first year."[7] Apparently the presentation impressed Dauphiné, because when he published an account of his travels, he included a circular published in French advertising the project.[8]

Brent began developing the site by laying the Brent Town road from the Potomac to the town on the banks of Town (or Brent Town) Run. Unfortunately, no map of the town survived, but the plan called for an agricultural community designed along lines developed in Europe during the medieval period. Brent Town's residents would reside on one-acre town lots within the village and have outlying tracts of one hundred acres each for farmland. The circular that Dauphiné published with his book in 1687 mentions the proprietors' offer to assist with building houses "in size 26 to 28 feet long and 14 to 16 feet wide," giving an idea of typical house dimensions in the community.[9] Although the town site stood just west of the fall zone, there were still occasional clashes with Indians in the area during the seventeenth century. Brent built a block house on the south side of the creek overlooking an old Indian trail to provide protection for the settlers, and the fortification quickly became an important outpost. Apparently the town was actually laid out. In broadsides Brent circulated around the French refugee community in London, Haywood referred to "the town that they have begun to build," and at his death in 1694, Brent bequeathed his son Henry 606 acres of land in Brent Town, "six acres in the town and six hundred in the country, being lots to be laid out together, both in town and country."[10]

Haywood, Brent, and the other partners soon learned that they were not the only people trying to lure Huguenot colonists to the New World, and despite their best advertising efforts, they attracted few settlers. Carolina's eight Lords Proprietors had been particularly active in their recruiting efforts, flooding French port towns with advertisements, so that French emigrants arrived in London with "nothing but Carolina in their minds."[11] Representatives from Pennsylvania and Massachusetts plied their own broadsides, and there were other Virginia entrepreneurs interested in Huguenot settlers, including William Fitzhugh, who tried to establish a settlement called Ravensworth on the land adjacent to Haywood, and later the first two William Byrds (see chapter 3).[12]

7. Dauphiné, *Huguenot Exile*, 159.

8. Virginia Writers' Project, *Prince William: The Story of Its People and Its Places*, 4th ed. (Manassas, VA: Bethlehem Good Housekeeping Club, 1961), 21. A translation of the circular can be found in Harrison, *Landmarks*, 180–81.

9. As quoted in Harrison, *Landmarks*, 181.

10. Ibid., 180; "Will of George Brent of Woodstock," in W. B. Chilton, "Brent Family," *Virginia Magazine of History and Biography* 18 (1910):96; and Groome, *Fauquier*, 24.

11. Harrison, *Landmarks*, 181.

12. William Fitzhugh to Nicholas Haywood, July 10, 1690, in "Letters of William Fitzhugh," *Virginia Magazine of History and Biography* 3 (1895–96): 8; and Harrison, *Landmarks*, 186–89.

Through the services of ship captains and Dauphiné, Haywood enrolled some individuals and families to sail for Brent Town. Still, the large groups he hoped to recruit remained elusive. He was particularly disappointed when one group he had spent a great deal of time courting chose to go to South Carolina instead. Haywood and his associates were losing the propaganda campaign, and without settlers, Brent Town was doomed.[13]

Since it seemed apparent that no large group of French refugees was forthcoming, Brent decided to take a new tack. After the Glorious Revolution in 1688, he believed that he might be able to lure English Catholics to Virginia. Catholic themselves, Brent's family had settled in Maryland, then relocated to Virginia, where the Brents had prospered. George himself held a number of government positions and was the only Catholic to serve in the House of Burgesses.[14] Since there was already a royal warrant in place granting religious liberty, he had every reason to believe his plan might succeed. But as if the change in the English government and the potential for religious persecution were not enough to cause problems for Brent Town's proprietors, Indian activity in the backcountry was on the rise. "Capt. Brent intimates though not plainly expresses, by being a Refuge and Sanctuary for Roman Catholicks and I dare say let it be increased by whom it will," William Fitzhugh wrote Haywood April 1, 1689, "our government will give it all the Indulgences that can be reasonably required by reason of its convenient Scituation for a Watch and Defence agst Indian Depredations and Excursions; neither do I believe that perswasion will be hindered from settling any where in this country, especially there where being Christians they may secure us against the Heathen."[15] Fitzhugh promised to assist in any way he could:

> What encouragement my poor Endeavours or Interest can give to your pleasing Establishment at Brenton . . . gives me the present opportunity not only to assure the people but also to satisfie the Government that were full encouragement given & Immunity granted to that Town which might be conducive to draw Inhabitants thither, the county would be indifferent secure from future alarms and it would be a sure Bulwark against reall dangers, because either by them or within them must be the Indian Road; a good company of Men there settled would be immediately called, either to keep off the Enemy at his first approach or cut him short in his Return.[16]

Meanwhile, other people worked to assure the safety of Brent Town's inhabitants. In 1694 the Governor's Council reported, "Upon reading a Letter from Capt Geo: Mason to his Excelly Accquainting his Excelly that the Rangers

13. Harrison, *Landmarks*, 181–82.

14. Chilton, "Brent Family," 17:309, 311.

15. William Fitzhugh to Nicholas Haywood, Apr. 1, 1689, in "Letters of William Fitzhugh," *Virginia Magazine of History and Biography* 2 (1895): 275. That particular Indian scare was a false alarm caused by panicking settlers when some Maryland Indians arrived in the backwoods of Stafford for their annual hunting trip. See Harrison, *Landmarks*, 129.

16. Fitzhugh to Haywood, Apr. 1, 1689, in "Letters of William Fitzhugh," 2:275.

fouer miles in the Woods back of the Inhabitants found a Negro Killed Supposed by Indians as also that he canot perswade the Inhabitants of Brent Towne to retyrne to their habitations again." The Council decided to beef up ranger patrols and ordered them to "take perticular Care of Brent Towne not to be deserted nor hurt by any Indian or Other Enemy's, and that the Magistrat's have Notice, if possible to find out who Murthered the Negro."[17]

Despite the Council's efforts, it was apparent that the Brent Town project had failed. As early as July 1690 Fitzhugh noted that the "Brenton design wants people," and that "Captain Brent's utmost endeavours will make a thin supply here."[18] A year later he wrote Haywood, "I truly condole your unsuccessful (though chargeable and vigorous) proceeding about Brenton the unsteadiness of the times Since the first undertaking has been a great hindrance thereto, When or Whether they will end, for your advantageous perspect and Interest in that concern, I believe is uncertain."[19] In 1694 George Brent, the associates' partner in America, died, sealing Brent Town's fate.

Brent Town became a mere place name, appearing briefly during survey disputes in the first quarter of the eighteenth century and on various deeds. The land was divided and passed to the heirs of the original partners. For a brief moment in 1742 it appeared that the town might be reborn when the Governor's Council discussed choosing the site for the Prince William County Courthouse. But when the Council decided against the move, Brent Town once again faded into obscurity; its primary legacy was a number of French surnames left by the few settlers Haywood was able to persuade to venture into the Virginia backcountry.[20]

Germanna

While colonial governments and landowners busily sought colonists on the continent, they by no means limited their activities to France. Because of their history of religious turmoil in the aftermath of the Thirty Years War and the constantly changing political situation in Central Europe, the German states furnished a number of potential candidates for immigration to Virginia. And some continental Europeans headed across the Atlantic of their own volition, searching for new lands where they could escape the uncertainties of life at home.

One such individual was Swiss merchant François Louis Michel. Intrigued by Virginia's attempts to lure the Huguenots to the New World, Michel decided to explore the possibilities of trade and settlement with the idea of plant-

17. McIlwaine, Hall, and Hillman, *Executive Journals,* 1:315.

18. William Fitzhugh to Nicholas Haywood, July 10, 1690, in "Letters of William Fitzhugh," *Virginia Magazine of History and Biography* 3 (1895–96) 3:8–9.

19. William Fitzhugh to Nicholas Haywood, May 20, 1691, in "Letters of William Fitzhugh," *Virginia Magazine of History and Biography* 3 (1895–96): 259.

20. "Journals of the Council of Virginia in Executive Sessions, 1737–1763," *Virginia Magazine of History and Biography* 15 (1907–8): 384; Harrison, *Landmarks,* 183–86, 189–90; and Groome, *Fauquier,* 27–29.

ing a Swiss colony in America. Arriving in 1702, he spent five months exploring the colony. He spent some time in Manakin Town (see chapter 3) and visited with Swiss settlers in Gloucester County along the Mattaponi River. Favorably impressed, he made a second trip in 1703.[21] Then Michel returned to Switzerland, where he convinced a number of businessmen to form a joint-stock company headed by an apothecary from Bern named Georg Ritter. In March 1705/6 Ritter and Company petitioned Queen Anne for a land grant in Virginia, asking for one hundred acres of land per settler, building materials, six years of tax exemptions, assistance with transportation costs, and the rights of free trade and freedom of worship.[22] While the government considered the petition, Michel returned to Virginia in 1707. There he mapped the areas between the Potomac and the Shenandoah rivers, including the Massanutten mountain range, where he believed he had discovered silver. His encouraging reports to Bern only increased the company's interest. It continued to press the government to act on the petition, suggesting that the French government might soon encroach on the territory. Finally, in 1709, the British government granted the company the right to settle in Virginia and ordered that the governor "doe upon the said Petitioners Arrival there, forthwith Allot unto them certain Lands on the South-west Branch of Potomac."[23] But the order had come a little late.

While Ritter and Company's request for land in Virginia worked its way through the bureaucratic wheels of government, the company's efforts attracted the attention of Baron Christoph von Graffenried, a very energetic Swiss nobleman, who also happened to be deeply in debt. Excited about the project and thinking it might be financially lucrative, Graffenried joined the outfit, and in 1709 escaped his creditors by traveling to Virginia to assist Michel in negotiating the land deal. Explorer John Lawson, working in the capacity of official surveyor of Carolina's eight Lords Proprietors, persuaded the men to locate their colony in North Carolina, promising excellent terms including transportation. The next year, Graffenried led a group of German and Swiss settlers to the Cape Fear River and established the town of New Bern. He thought that the company would be able to exploit Michel's silver mines later, but many of the immigrants died in an Indian attack in 1711. Tuscarora Indians held Graffenried hostage for several months until Virginia's new lieutenant governor, Alexander Spotswood, successfully negotiated his release.[24]

21. See François Louis Michel, "Report of the Journey of François Louis Michel from Berne, Switzerland, to Virginia, October 2, 1701–December 1, 1702," trans. and ed. William J. Hinke, *Virginia Magazine of History and Biography* 24 (1916): 1–43, 113–41, 275–303.

22. Michel, "Report," 298–99.

23. "First Memorial of Michel and Graffenried, July 11, 1709," in Charles E. Kemper, ed., "Documents Relating to Early Projected Swiss Colonies in the Valley of Virginia 1706–1709," *Virginia Magazine of History and Biography* 29 (1921): 11; "Copy of an Order of Councill of the 22nd August 1709 Upon a Letter to the Earl of Sunderland About Settling a Colony of Switzers in Virginia &c.," in Kemper, "Documents," 17; and Klaus Wust, *The Virginia Germans* (Charlottesville: Univ. Press of Virginia, 1969), 17–19.

24. Wust, *Virginia Germans*, 19.

Spotswood, who served as lieutenant governor from 1710 to 1722, was one of the first British colonial officials to fully recognize the importance of westward settlement. During his tenure in office, he recommended establishing a trading company with the Indians, and he worked to pacify the backcountry by building a system of forts and settling allied Indian tribes in buffer zones to prevent attack from more hostile groups. He sent out a number of survey teams to explore the frontier, and in 1716 he personally led an expedition into the Virginia backcountry, dubbing his group the Knights of the Golden Horseshoe.

Spotswood was also something of an opportunist. In conversations with Graffenried, Spotswood learned of Michel's silver mines. Although he doubted there was any silver in the Virginia mountains, some of his early survey teams had discovered iron ore deposits. Since the Board of Trade had issued an order against mining iron in the colonies, he disguised his efforts to develop the iron deposits using the silver as cover. Before he led his ill-fated colonists to North Carolina, Graffenried had arranged with Michel to start negotiating with miners. Michel formed a contract with mining expert Johann Justus Albrecht, who began to assemble equipment and men. Albrecht traveled to Nassau-Siegen where he located miners through the assistance of local ministers in exchange for future contributions once the mines became profitable. Although he heard nothing from Graffenried, in 1713 Albrecht assembled his party and headed for England.[25]

Meanwhile, back in Virginia, Graffenried decided there were no silver mines, and in 1713 he left America deeper in debt than ever before. When he arrived in London, Graffenried was shocked to find Albrecht, forty-odd German miners, and a Reformed minister waiting to sail for Virginia. "This caused me not a little pains, worry, vexation and expense," Graffenried wrote, "since this people had come there so blindly, thinking to find everything necessary for their support and their transportation to the American mines."[26] Graffenried had sent several letters to Michel explaining the situation in Virginia, but Michel either failed to pass the word to Albrecht, or the miners chose to go anyway. Graffenried urged the miners to return home, "but this seemed so hard for them they preferred to hire themselves out for four years as servants in America than to return."[27] The baron scrambled to find them work to survive through the winter, for there were no ships until spring. He contacted Spotswood's agent, Nathaniel Blakiston, and merchant Micajah Perry, who agreed to cover the transportation costs at the lieutenant governor's expense. Then Graffenried wrote Spotswood, "telling him that the little colony should be appointed to the land which we had together in Virginia not far from the place where min-

25. Ibid., 19–20; and Elizabeth Chapman Denny Vann and Margaret Collins Denny Dixon, *Virginia's First German Colony* (Richmond, VA: n.p., 1961), 9–11, 13–14.

26. Christoph von Graffenried, *Christoph von Graffenried's Account of the Founding of New Bern*, ed. Todd H. Vincent (Raleigh: North Carolina Historical Commission, 1920), 257.

27. Ibid., 257–58.

erals were found and, as supposed, the traces of a mine, where they could settle themselves according to the wise arrangements and under the helpful supervision of the governor."[28] His experiences in America left Graffenried feeling "sorry for the poor miners who have left a certain thing they had in Germany to go to find the uncertain in America. In place of a good vocation that they had, they have nothing at present except what they can gain from some cleared land where they are obliged to live very modestly."[29]

The group arrived in Virginia in April 1714. Far from being upset with the prospect of unexpected settlers, Spotswood was delighted and set about to exploit the situation. He announced to the Governor's Council that "sundry Germans to the number of forty two men women & Children who were invited hither by the Baron de Graffinried are now arrived, but that the Said Baron not being here to take care of their Settlement The Governor therefore proposed to settle them above the falls of Rappahannock River to serve as a Barrier to the Inhabitants of that part of the Country against the Incursions of the Indians."[30] The Council agreed to build a fort, clear a road to the site, provide weapons, and provision the group for a year all at government expense. The Council classified the settlers as rangers, thereby exempting them from government levies.

When Spotswood presented his proposal to the Council, he did it under the guise of creating a buffer zone between hostile Indian groups and the Tidewater, a deception he continued in a report to the Lords of Trade, July 21, 1714: "I continue, all resolv'd to settle out our Tributary Indians as a guard to ye Frontiers, and in order to supply that part, w'ch was to have been covered by the Tuscaruros, I have placed here a number of Prodestant Germans, built them a Fort, and finish'd it with 2 pieces of Cannon and some Ammunition, which will awe the Stragling partys of Northern Indians, and be a good Barrier for all that part of the Country."[31] Further along he casually mentioned, "They are generally such as have been employed in their own country as Miners, and say that they are satisfyed there are divers kinds of minerals in those upper parts of the Country where they are settled, and even good appearance of Silver Oar," and asked for permission to allow them to mine it, before continuing to other matters in his report.[32]

Spotswood settled the twelve German families thirty miles west of the fall zone in a town he named Germanna in honor of their point of origin. It was located in Essex (later Spotsylvania and now Orange) County in a bend in the south branch of the Rappahannock (modern Rapidan) River, a dozen miles

28. Ibid., 258; Wust, *Virginia Germans*, 20; and Groome, *Fauquier*, 116.

29. Graffenried, *Christoph von Graffenried's*, 386.

30. McIlwaine, Hall, and Hillman, *Executive Journals* 3:371.

31. Alexander Spotswood, "To the Lord Comm'rs of Trade: July 21st, 1714," in *The Official Letters of Alexander Spotswood*, ed. R. A. Brock, 2 vols. (Richmond: Virginia Historical Society, 1882–85), 2:70; and Wust, *Virginia Germans*, 21.

32. "To the Lord Comm'rs of Trade: July 21st, 1714," in Spotswood, *Official Letters* 2:70–71.

before it ran into the Rappahannock proper. It was a defensive location, far different from the vast open farmlands Michel and Graffenried had foreseen for their colony. William Byrd II explained that the river wound "in the form of a horseshoe about Germanna, making it a peninsula containing about four hundred acres."[33] John Fontaine, a Huguenot soldier who served in the British army passed through the village in 1715, a year after the settlers arrived. He found a palisade consisting of "stakes stuck in the ground, and laid close to one another, and of substance to bear out a musket-shot" protecting nine houses, "built all in a line; and before every house, about twenty feet distant from it, they have small sheds built for their hogs and hens, so that the hog-sties and houses make a street. The place that is paled is in a pentagon, very regularly laid out; and in the very centre there is a blockhouse, made with five sides, which answer to the five sides of the great inclosure; there are loop-holes through it from which you may see all the inside of the inclosure. This was intended for a retreat for the people, in case they were not able to defend the palisadoes, if attacked by the Indians."[34] The site also had another advantage: it was only a dozen miles from the iron ore deposits.

Once he settled the Germans on the Rapidan, Spotswood had to deal with a small problem. He did not own the land. So in October 1716, the clerk of the Governor's Council, William Robinson, patented a 3,229-acre plot that included Germanna, and a month later, he transferred the property over to Spotswood, who in turn leased it to the settlers.[35]

Spotswood made every effort to help get Germanna's inhabitants settled. He convinced the House of Burgesses to pass an act exempting the miners from all taxes for seven years, as long as they remained in the community. Another act created a separate parish for them and allowed them the right to choose their own minister. Reformed minister Johann Heinrich Hager, who was just shy of seventy when they arrived in 1714, came out of retirement to serve as the group's minister. During the first years, since there were few structures in the community, Germanna's residents had to be creative in locating worship space. Fontaine explained, "They make use of this block-house for divine service. They go to prayers constantly once a day, and have two sermons on Sunday. We went to hear them perform their service, which was done in their own language, which we did not understand; but they seemed to be very devout, and sang the psalms very well."[36] The special privileges the lieutenant governor obtained applied not only to the original Germanna settlers but also to any new "German or Foreign Protestants" who settled in the community.[37]

33. William Byrd II, "A Progress to the Mines in the Year 1732," in *The Prose Works of William Byrd of Westover: Narratives of a Colonial Virginian*, ed. Louis B. Wright (Cambridge, MA: Belknap Press of Harvard Univ. Press, 1961), 361; Groome, *Fauquier*, 117; and Wust, *Virginia Germans*, 21.

34. John Fontaine, *Memoirs of a Huguenot Family*, ed. Ann Maury (New York: Putnam's, 1907), 268.

35. Leonidas Dodson, *Alexander Spotswood: Governor of Colonial Virginia, 1710–1722* (Philadelphia: Univ. of Pennsylvania Press, 1932), 277–78.

36. Fontaine, *Memoirs*, 268; and Wust, *Virginia Germans*, 21.

37. Groome, *Fauquier*, 126; and Wust, *Virginia Germans*, 21–22.

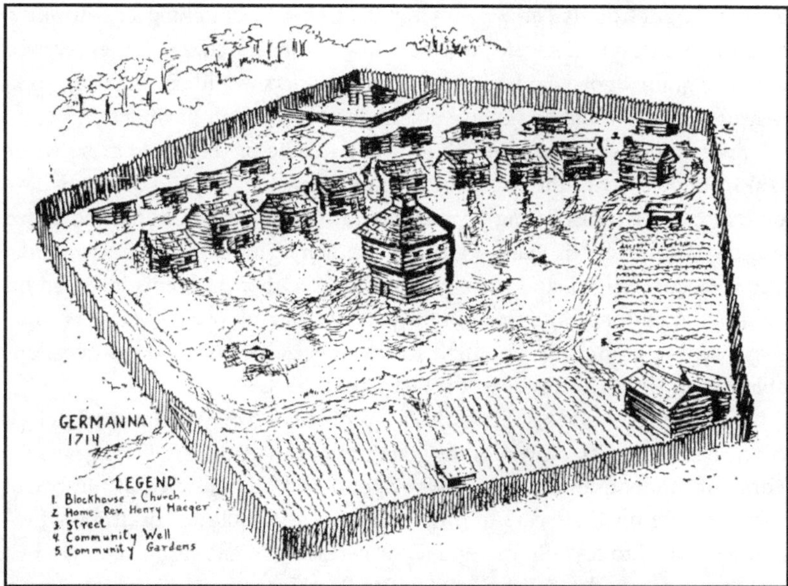

Germanna, 1714. Drawing by Charles Herbert Huffman based on the description by John Fontaine. Courtesy of the Memorial Foundation of the Germanna Colonies in Virginia.

Despite the special treatment the colonial government gave the Germanna colonists, life was difficult. During the first year, the citizens of Germanna built their houses and outbuildings, laid out a road, and constructed a bridge over a stream on the approach to the town. Work in the mines was delayed while Spotswood continued to request permission to commence operations but finally began in the spring of 1715. Although Spotswood provided money for provisions out of his own pocket for the first two years, food was in short supply. When Fontaine and his two colleagues passed through that summer, they stayed at Reverend Hager's home. There the men "found nothing to eat, but lived on our small provisions." Fontaine observed, "The Germans live very miserably. We would tarry here some time, but for want of provisions we are obliged to go. We got from the minister a bit of smoked beef and cabbage, which were very ordinary and dirtily dressed." The Germans' distress so moved the members of the group that they "made a collection between us three of about thirty shillings for the minister" before they left.[38]

Germanna brought Spotswood a great deal of unwanted attention as his adversaries sought to make political capital out of the way the lieutenant governor had built his town. From the very beginning of the project he had been involved in underhanded dealings. In his correspondence with Blakiston about obtaining royal approval for the mining project, Spotswood repeatedly stressed the necessity of keeping the negotiations as quiet as possible. He had hoped to get

38. Fontaine, *Memoirs*, 268–69; and Vann and Dixon, *Virginia's First*, 20.

a private grant from the crown but doubted it possible, thinking a grant would be forthcoming only if it were presented as benefiting the colony. If they received a private grant, Spotswood said he and any partners would pay Blakiston's expenses so there would be no question about government payments.[39]

Spotswood was concerned about the outcome of the affair, as he wrote Blakiston that "I run the risque of the same Censure, as you say others have undergone, for transporting Forreigners into these parts," though he added stoically, "however, 'tis vain to look on the worst side of a business wherein one is so far engaged, and must go through."[40] Other problems included his failure to mention to the Council his part in bringing over the settlers when they voted to grant the Germanna settlers special benefits and the questionable way in which he obtained the Germanna tract.

Finally, Spotswood's political rivals—probably led by William Byrd II, who felt he had been passed over for the governorship—sent a list of charges to the Lords of Trade, questioning the way Spotswood had handled a number of issues during his first years in office. Some of the "queries" dealt with Germanna. Called to task, Spotswood felt it necessary to answer the charges in a lengthy response dated February 7, 1715/16. His answers were not exactly deceitful, but they certainly were not entirely forthcoming either, and he couched them in such a way as to portray himself in the best possible light. For example, he blamed Graffenried for the Germans' arrival and claimed that when they arrived it was "both in Compassion to those poor Strangers, and in regard to the safety of the Country" that he located them in Germanna, "where I built them Habitations and subsisted them until they were able, by their own Labour, to provide for themselves and I presume I may, without Crime or Misdemeanour, endeavour to put them in an honest way of paying their Just Debts."[41] He failed to mention his intent to use the miners to develop an iron industry of dubious legality, using silver mining as a cover story. When John Fontaine returned to Germanna in August 1716 to rendevous with Spotswood and the other members of the Knights of the Golden Horseshoe expedition, he surveyed the mining operation and observed even then, "The Germans pretend that it is a silver mine."[42]

Another charge against Spotswood dealt with his land purchase—why he patented a large tract of land when others had been prevented, why he had done it surreptitiously, and why he had not granted land to the German settlers outright instead of leasing it to them. In his response, Spotswood argued that he had instituted a new policy requiring Council approval for large grants in order to prevent people from holding the tracts and robbing the crown of

39. "To Colo. Blakison: August 17th, 1713," in Spotswood, *Official Letters* 2:33; and Dodson, *Alexander Spotswood*, 230.

40. "To Colo. Blakison: March 15th, 1713," in Spotswood, *Official Letters* 2:66.

41. "To ye L'ds Comm'rs of Trade and Plantations," [Feb. 7, 1715/16], in Spotswood, *Official Letters* 2:196.

42. Fontaine, *Memoirs*, 282.

the quit rents. "And as I don't know that his Majesty has in any of his Instructions restrained a Governour from taking up Land to his own use, as well as any other of his Subjects," Spotswood continued, "I hope it will not be accounted any breach of my Duty, if, for the Security of the Frontiers of Government and for the Settlement of a number of indigent people I have been at the expense of Surveying and purchasing Rights and Patenting a tract of land to which no other person had any pretensions." Although buying the land "in a borrowed Name may carry with it some colour of Fraud," he explained that since a governor had to sign each patent, it was necessary to use someone else, a practice followed by previous governors. He claimed that his rents were very inexpensive and explained to the lords that the German settlers would not have been able to afford to buy any land outright. He had not placed them into five years of servitude but instead lent them money. He ended his response guilefully, with a suggestion for the man who submitted the complaints:

> And since, in this point, he is forced to be silent in the only thing which could give ground for his charge of oppressing those People, I hope your Lordships will be of Opinion that my taking up Land and building houses for people who were not able to take it up or build for themselves; my advancing Money for their Transportation and subsistence, when they must have been sold, (according to the Custom of this Country,) into servitude or have famished, and at last my allowing them to Live at such easy Rents, is far from what the Queriest would here charge me with. If he has a mind to extend his Charity to those poor Strangers beyond what I have done, or believes I reap any great advantage by this tract of Land, I shall very readily yield him up the Property thereof, together with all the profits I have made by those People; provided, he barely reimburse what I can fairly make appear to have been expended on that Account.[43]

Spotswood's responses seem to have silenced his critics for a time, and he returned to the business of running the colony and developing his town.

Germanna got an infusion of settlers in 1717. This second group consisted of seventeen Lutheran families from the Alsace/Palatine/Hesse regions of Germany who had planned to settle in Pennsylvania. When they were scheduled to set sail from London, their ship's captain was thrown into debtors' prison, delaying the departure for several weeks. The passengers ate most of their provisions before they even left port, and several people died of starvation during the voyage. Instead of landing in Pennsylvania, the prevailing winds sent the ship to Virginia, where the captain refused to release his passengers until someone paid him. Aware that the first settlers had almost repaid their debt to him, when Spotswood decided to pay this group's passage, he handled the situation differently. He paid the cost of their voyage, and in return they contracted to work for him for eight years. All was not well after they arrived in

43. "To ye L'ds Comm'rs," in Spotswood, *Official Letters* 2:216–18.

Germanna. Eighty new residents strained the citizens' resources, and there may have been some religious disputes between the two groups.[44]

Discontented with their life in Germanna, the German colonists sought ways to escape Spotswood's paternalism. Their primary object was purchasing land of their own. There was plenty of available land nearby, but as aliens, they were barred from passing any land they might purchase to any heirs. Three members of the first group, John Fishburn, John Hoffman, and Jacob Holtzclaw became naturalized citizens. In 1718 they petitioned for a Northern Neck grant from Lord Fairfax. It was a 1,805-acre tract in modern Fauquier County that the three men held in trust for twelve families. In 1719, after they met their financial obligations to Spotswood, the members of the 1714 group moved nineteen miles up an Indian trail to an area that quickly became known as Germantown. Despite its name, it was not really an urban area. Indeed, at the end of the century, Moravian bishop John Frederick Reichel passed through Germantown and quipped, "[W]hen one is in the town one asks where the town is."[45] According to another Moravian minister, Matthias Gottlieb Gottschalk, Germantown was a community more "like a village in Germany, in which the houses are far apart."[46] In fact there really was no village at all; the families divided the land into twelve strips of land of 150 acres each and lived separately.

Striking out on their own was not easy for the 1714 settlers. They had to start by clearing enough land to provide themselves with food. Later they produced tobacco, though getting their crop to market in Falmouth was difficult because of the distance and the bad roads. Over the years, other amenities emerged, such as a blacksmith shop and a mill. The settlers erected a school, headed by John Jacob Holtzclaw. They also had a church building, something they had never enjoyed in Germanna.[47]

Reverend Hager moved his family to Germantown to continue his duties as pastor despite his increasing age. Knowing the community could ill afford to construct a church, he wrote a moving appeal to congregations in Germany for financial assistance and a younger minister to assist him in his duties. Jacob Zollikoffer, a Swiss merchant who lived near Germanna, carried the "memorial" to London and then to Germany. Zollikoffer persuaded local clergymen to endorse the appeal, and newspapers carried accounts of his efforts. Zollikoffer

44. B. C. Holtzclaw, "The Second German Colony of 1717, Other Germanna Pioneers, the So-Called Third Colony of 1719, and Later Comers to the Hebron Church Community," *Germanna Record* 6 (1965): 4; Arthur Leslie Keith, "The German Colony of 1717," *William and Mary Quarterly*, 1st series, vol. 26 (1917–18): 79; and Groome, *Fauquier*, 122.

45. John Frederick Reichel, "Travel Diary of Bishop Reichel, Mrs. Reichel, and Their Company from Lititz, Pa. To Salem, N. C., 1780," in Newton D. Mereness, ed., *Travels in the American Colonies* (New York: Macmillan, 1916), 593; and Wust, *Virginia Germans*, 22. Because the Northern Neck land office was closed, the grant was not registered until 1724. See B. C. Holtzclaw, "Germantown Revived," *Germanna Record* 2 (1962): 11–12.

46. Matthias Gottlieb Gottschalk, "Moravian Diaries of Travels through Virginia," eds. William J. Hinke and Charles E. Kemper, *Virginia Magazine of History and Biography* 11 (1903–4): 233.

47. Wust, *Virginia Germans*, 23–24; and Van and Dixon, *Virginia's First*, 36.

returned in 1720, laden with donated German books and money, enabling the community build their church. However, no minister arrived to assist Hager. Even the Society for the Propagation of the Gospel in Foreign Parts did not send a missionary, though it did provide twenty-five copies of the *Book of Common Prayer* printed in German. Hager continued to serve as the community's only minister until his death in 1738 at the age of ninety-four. Relieved to be out from under Spotswood's domination, the settlers set about building their new lives, and ultimately the community prospered. In 1724 Hugh Jones reported that the people of Germantown "thrive very well, and live happily, and entertain generously."[48]

Meanwhile, things were still far from well in Germanna. Spotswood breathed some life back into his town when the legislature created a new county named in his honor in 1720. A section of the act recognized that "[b]ecause foreign Protestants may not understand English readily, if such shall entertain a minister of their own they and their titheables shall be free for ten years, from the said first of May, 1721."[49] The act included a provision for building a church, which Spotswood began in 1724 but was still only "almost compleated" in 1726.[50] Most importantly, however, the act allowed Spotswood to choose the site for the Spotsylvania County courthouse, though he had to "imploy" the workmen and provide the materials for the courthouse, the jail, and the stocks and pillory.[51] Naturally, he chose Germanna. But despite capturing a county court and all of the business it could generate, Germanna still did not prosper and soon faced another crisis.

After years of political maneuvering, Spotswood's political rivals succeeded in having him replaced as lieutenant governor in 1722. Finding himself a private citizen, Spotswood focused more of his attention on his landholdings. He was hit by an unexpected blow in 1724, when the remaining citizens of Germanna, the members of the second group of settlers announced their intention to leave, believing they had fulfilled the terms of their indentures. Spotswood was furious, immediately ordered their arrest, and instituted court proceedings to keep them in his service for another year. The details of the dispute are muddled; the Germans may have been reluctant to make their real complaints against the former governor while he wielded all of his power and influence to keep them in Germanna. However, they did petition the Council, complaining that "Colonell Spotswood hath arrested above 25 of us, wee not knowing wherefore we are arrested," that they had repeatedly asked Spotswood for a copy of their contract, and had "desired the Justices of Spotsylvania Court to assist us and to be our witnesses that the Colonell will not deliver the above mentioned covenant, but they refuse to have anything to do

48. Jones, *Present State,* 91; and Wust, *Virginia Germans*, 24.

49. Hening, *Statutes* 4:78.

50. George Carrington Mason, "The Colonial Churches of Spotsylvania and Caroline Counties, Virginia," *Virginia Magazine of History and Biography* 58 (1950): 448–49.

51. Hening, *Statutes* 4:77.

with it."[52] The Council ordered "in regard of the Pet[rs] poor Condition, and their Ignorance of the Laws of this Colony," that the King's deputy attorney should represent them at their trial.[53] Spotswood won the court case and the Germans had to remain for another year, but that only delayed the inevitable. As soon as their year was over, the 1717 group left Germanna, settling on crown lands in modern Morgan County.[54] By 1725 Germanna stood deserted.

Spotswood was not in Virginia to witness the evacuation, having traveled to England to settle some questions about tax and land issues, including the legality of his personal land patents. While he was there, he married and fathered two children. He brought his new family with him back to Virginia when he returned in 1729. During his absence, Spotswood had left his cousin John Graeme in charge of his affairs. It was not a wise choice. When he returned, Spotswood not only had to try to revive his derelict town, he discovered other problems. With the "neglect and severity" of Graeme's "wretched management," Spotswood found "above eighty of his slaves were lost while he was in England and most of his cattle starved. That his furnace stood still great part of the time, and all his plantations ran to ruin."[55]

Spotswood immediately went to work trying to rebuild his holdings. He built a home at Germanna where he could oversee operations at the ironworks and develop new ones. He brought new colonists and slaves onto his lands to work the plantations and to mine the ore, make charcoal, and process the iron. Over the course of the winter months, he produced pig iron to haul to the small river port of Massaponax for export. In 1732 he built an air furnace near the port and began casting iron products. Spotswood claimed that by developing the new industry he was helping Virginia by diversifying its economy into areas beyond tobacco production, and he was helping Britain by cutting down on foreign iron imports. It did not hurt that he made himself wealthy in the process as his businesses prospered.[56]

Despite these economic successes, Spotswood could not rebuild Germanna. Since Spotswood's land surrounded Germanna for eight to ten miles in any direction, the court was inconveniently located for most of Spotsylvania County's inhabitants. And just as he had delayed building the parish church, Spotswood never built a courthouse. Instead, the justices met at a room in his house. In 1726 the Assembly began the process of choosing a new county seat and six years later moved the court to Fredericksburg. The court last met at Germanna June 6, 1732.[57] It was the death knell for the town.

52. "Complaint by Germans Against Governor Spotswood," *Virginia Magazine of History and Biography* 6 (1898–99): 385; and Wust, *Virginia Germans*, 24.

53. McIlwaine, Hall, and Hillman, *Executive Journals*, 4:65.

54. Wust, *Virginia Germans*, 23–24.

55. Byrd, "Progress to the Mines," 358.

56. Ibid., 357; James Roger Mansfield, *A History of Early Spotsylvania* (Orange, VA: Green, 1977), 32–33; and Vann and Dixon, *Virginia's First*, 28–29.

57. Hening, *Statutes* 4:364–65; Dodson, *Alexander Spotswood*, 294; and Mansfield, *History*, 47.

When William Byrd II traveled to Germanna to tour Spotswood's ironworks in September 1732, just three months after the court moved, he noted, "This famous town consists of Colonel Spotswood's enchanted castle on one side of the street and a baker's dozen of ruinous tenements on the other, where so many German families had dwelt some years ago, but are now removed ten miles higher, in the fork of Rappahannock, to land of their own." County residents had not been content with just moving the court, but had their sights on Germanna's church as well: "There had also been a chapel about a bowshot from the colonel's house, at the end of an avenue of cherry trees, but some pious people had lately burnt it down, with intent to get another built nearer their own homes." Germanna had become such a desolate place that Spotswood's wife Ann kept animals that "cheered this lady's solitude." Among her pets was "a brace of tame deer" that "ran familiarly about the house." During Byrd's visit, one of the deer caught its reflection in a pier mirror, "made a spring over the tea table that stood under it and shattered the glass to pieces and, falling back upon the tea table, made a terrible Fracas among the china."[58]

Germanna was practically a ghost town when Byrd saw it in 1732. The Spotswoods had two more children, and although the family continued to live in the area, over time they left the Germanna house, which fell into ruin. Soon all that remained of Germanna was its name. Only thirty years passed between the time François Louis Michel first arrived in Virginia exploring the possibilities of establishing a colony and Byrd's visit to Spotswood's derelict town. Baron von Graffenried's colorful personality and Governor Spotswood's ambition had led the project into areas Michel could never have conceived. In his rush to develop his ironworks, Spotswood had unwittingly sacrificed Germanna. By emphasizing the development of the mining operation to the detriment of the colonists' interests, he angered them to the point they were unwilling to stay on his land. Although he tried to salvage the town, ultimately it was less important to him than his iron. Still, the German colonists had accomplished the two goals that Spotswood had presented to the Council in 1714: they had provided security against Indian attacks in the colony, and they had pushed the limits of the frontier beyond the falls and into the backcountry.[59]

Waterford

The earliest successful town in Piedmont Virginia was unique for a variety of reasons. Unlike Brent Town or Germanna, no individual or group of people set out to establish it. There was no great design scheme for the town; one simply evolved naturally based on the lay of the land. And while European refugees did not settle the town, religion was the center of this community. The settlers were members of the Society of Friends, familiarly known as

58. Byrd, "Progress to the Mines," 355–56.

59. John J. Wayland, *Germanna: Outpost of Adventure, 1714–1956* (Staunton, VA: Memorial Foundation of the German Colonies in Virginia, 1956), 19; and Wust, *Virginia Germans*, 25.

Quakers, who left the Delaware Valley because of the high price and scarcity of land. They named the town they established in Virginia Waterford.[60]

In 1732 a farmer named Asa Moore built a house in Prince William (modern Loudoun) County about ten miles south of the Potomac River. He sited his home on the south branch of Catoctin Creek in a small winding valley. A year later, Amos and Mary Janney left a Quaker community in Bucks County, Pennsylvania, and settled on the opposite side of the creek. Janney may have known the region from survey work he performed for Lord Fairfax. He knew that the region contained rich farmland for wheat and other grains, but without a milling operation, there was little hope of making much of a profit. So, in addition to his home, he constructed a grist and saw mill. He also built a blacksmith's shop. In 1735 and 1736 he purchased about four hundred acres of land surrounding the mill.[61]

The Janneys sent word to friends and relations that good land remained available in the region, and other Quakers began to travel down from Pennsylvania and settle. They either bought adjacent tracts or leased land from Janney. By 1741 a small community had developed at the mill site, consisting of the mill, the blacksmith's shop, and four or five houses. The Janneys held worship meetings in their home, but by that year enough Friends lived in the surrounding community to organize the Friends Preparative Meeting and construct a meetinghouse. The group fell under the care of the Hopewell Monthly Meeting, which had just been organized for Friends living in the Shenandoah Valley. The building served not only as a place of worship but as a place for civic, artistic, and literary activities. The village, known as Janney's Mill or Milltown prospered as more and more Friends migrated to the area each year from Pennsylvania, New Jersey, Maryland, and Great Britain. By 1744 enough people lived in the area for the Meeting to be recognized and split off from Hopewell. Since Fairfax County had just been split off of Prince William, the congregation was known as the Fairfax Meeting.[62]

Amos Janney died in 1747, leaving his lands to his sixteen-year-old son Mahlon, who took control of the property when he came of age in 1752.[63] Mahlon Janney worked to develop his father's village. He replaced the first mill with a larger structure and laid out and sold house lots along the south side of the road leading to the meetinghouse. In 1755 he deeded ten acres of land to the Meeting to provide space for a cemetery and a school. As the town evolved,

60. Fischer and Kelly, *Bound Away*, 109. In the middle of the seventeenth century, Governor William Berkeley attempted to force Quakers and other nonconformists out of Virginia, but the mood of religious toleration after the Glorious Revolution led to Quakers' returning. See Fischer and Kelly, *Bound Away*, 46–47, 104–5, 109–11.

61. Harrison, *Landmarks*, 267; and Asa Moore Janney and Werner Janney, *Ye Meetg Hous Smal: A Short Account of Friends in Loudoun County, Virginia, 1732–1980* (Lincoln, VA: n.p., 1980), 7–8.

62. Harrison, *Landmarks*, 268; Janney and Janney, *Ye Meetg Hous Smal*, 9; and Asa Moore Janney, "The Quaker Settlement at Waterford," in *Waterford Perspectives* (Waterford, VA: Waterford Foundation, 1983), 11.

63. "Loudoun Will Book," Loudoun County Courthouse, Leesburg, VA, A:206.

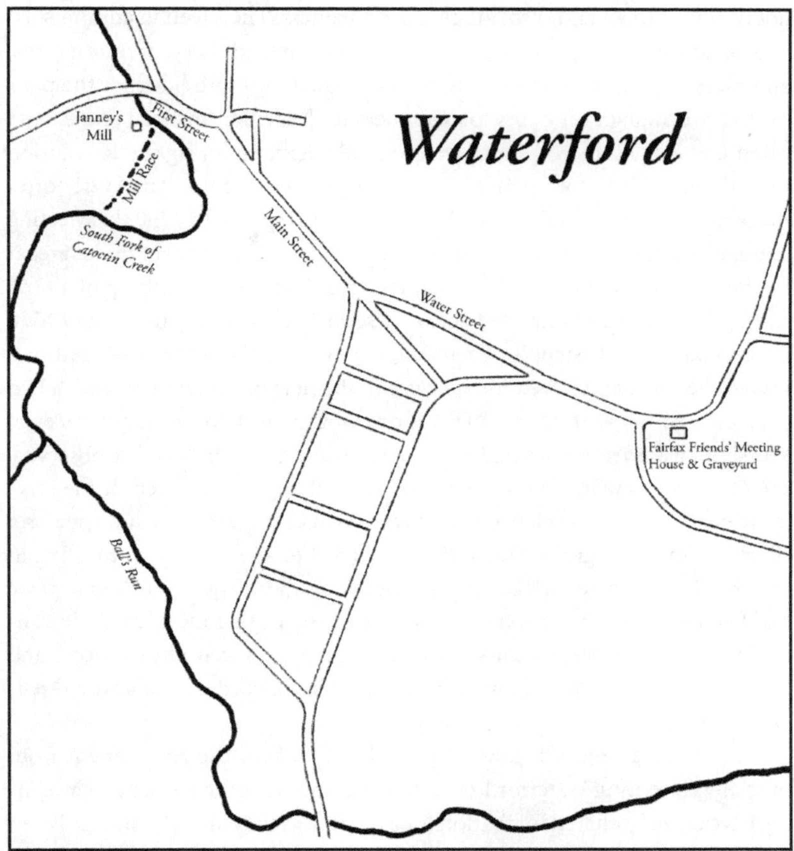

Waterford, Virginia. Although early deeds make reference to an eighteenth-century plat of Waterford, it no longer exists. The gridiron portion of the town was laid out early in the nineteenth century. Map by the author.

Mahlon did not set out regular blocks and a grid street pattern, although there were sections of town laid out that way in early-nineteenth-century expansions. Instead, the village first followed the paths of existing roads as they led into the valley through a gap. Essentially, the town was simply a collection of structures stretching along a street as it meandered between two forks and a crossroads. But as the town expanded, its citizens began to take pride in their community. As a result, around 1750 the citizens renamed Milltown as Waterford, possibly through the influence of Asa Moore or a relative newcomer to the community, a shoemaker named Thomas Moore.[64]

As a Quaker community, Waterford's citizens spent a great deal of time looking after one another's well being. This vigilance included striving to keep

64. Harrison, *Landmarks*, 267; Helen Hurst Marsh, "Early Loudoun Water Mills," *Bulletin of the Loudoun County Historical Society* 1 (1958): 23; and George E. Bentley, "Old Quaker Town," in *Waterford Perspectives* (Waterford, VA: Waterford Foundation, 1983), 13–14. According to local tradition both Asa and Thomas Moore originated from Waterford, Ireland.

liquor out of town and discouraging drunkenness. The Meeting admonished and occasionally repudiated members for dancing, adultery, premarital sex, and marrying outsiders. But Waterford's residents also provided for the poor in their town, paid off debts for members in desperate financial straits, and cared for widows and orphans. Determined pacifists, during the Revolution the citizens of Waterford refused to serve or pay muster fines. And Waterford's residents differed from their neighbors in other respects. In 1790 the Meeting appointed a committee to assist free blacks and welcomed them in the area.[65]

Because of its religious character, Waterford became something of a novelty in the region and attracted curiosity seekers to the town. In January 1776 English adventurer Nicholas Cresswell, who was staying in nearby Leesburg, visited the town and stayed for a service in the new meetinghouse, which had been erected the year before. "This is one of the most comfortable places of Worship I was ever in, they had two large fires and a Dutch stove," he observed. But Cresswell's favorable impression of the building did not include the service itself: "After a long silence and many groans a Man got up and gave us a short Lecture with great deliberation." He tried to attend another meeting in October, "but it were too late, tho' it would have been equally as well as if we had been sooner, for the spirit did not move any of them to speak." He concluded, "Can't conceive what service the people can receive by grunting and groaning for two or three hours without speaking a word. This is a stupid religion indeed."[66]

It may have been this kind of prejudice that kept the government from officially chartering Waterford as a town. Alternatively, the residents may simply have never bothered to petition for a charter, as they already effectively ran their own government through the Meeting. Even without a charter, Janney's mill town continued to grow and prosper after the Revolution. Mahlon Janney continued to lay out and sell new lots, and he extended Main Street in 1800. Finally, the next year, sixty years after residents built their first meetinghouse, the Virginia state government officially chartered Waterford.[67]

Westham/Beverley

Although religion played a principal role in each of the first attempts to establish towns in the Piedmont, trade was the chief factor in founding the next town. During the middle of the eighteenth century, Beverley Randolph, a scion of the Piedmont's founding dynasty, decided to establish a town above the falls of the James River. It was located on the north bank where Westham Creek

65. Asa Moore Janney, "Quaker Settlement," 11–12; and Harrison Williams, *Legends of Loudoun* (Richmond, VA: Garrett and Massie, 1938), 137.

66. Nicholas Cresswell, *The Journal of Nicholas Cresswell, 1774–1777* (New York: Dial, 1924), 138, 163.

67. Samuel Shepherd, ed., *The Statutes at Large of Virginia, From October Session 1792, to December Session 1806, Inclusive, in Three Volumes, (New Series) Being a Continuation of Hening*, 3 vols. (New York: AMS, 1970), 2:270; and Eugene M. Scheel, "An Archaeological Plan for the Waterford Historic District. Loudoun County, Virginia," Vertical File, Thomas Balch Library, Leesburg, VA, 1979.

flowed into the river. The land was part of Westham Plantation, which Randolph inherited from his father, Councillor William Randolph II, in 1742.[68] Randolph realized that the location was a perfect place to establish a trading center.

Typically, backcountry farmers shipped their produce down the James on flatboats or "upon two canoes lashed together" but then were forced to unload their cargo and cart it overland below the falls where it could be reloaded onto eastward bound ships.[69] William Byrd II had tried to take advantage of this trade by establishing Richmond east of the falls in 1733 to serve as a fall-zone port. His son, William Byrd III, tried to add to the family trade monopoly by erecting a warehouse on land above the falls. Unfortunately for him, most farmers simply landed their crops and did not use the warehouse. So in 1745 Byrd asked the Assembly to officially recognize his building as "a public storehouse," requiring farmers to use the facility.[70] His scheme did not work and farmers continued to bypass the building. Ten years later, Byrd returned to the Assembly for a new law requiring payment from anyone who left cargo on his property more than twenty-four hours.[71] Randolph's new town created competition not only for Byrd's warehouse across the river but possibly even Richmond, which lay just seven miles downstream.

In order to attract investors, Randolph employed the services of Anglican clergyman and surveyor Robert Rose, who in 1750 began riding through the backcountry signing subscribers.[72] Rose proved to be an excellent promoter, interesting a number of influential people in the enterprise. But before events proceeded further, Beverley Randolph died suddenly. He left Westham Plantation to his younger brother Peter. Peter Randolph proceeded with the Westham project, and thanks to Rose's salesmanship, there was such interest in the town that he decided to expand it. He took out an advertisement in *The Virginia Gazette*, June 6, 1751, calling for the subscribers to assemble at the site to draw their lots.[73] In the meantime, Rose and William Cabell began laying out one hundred half-acre lots on fifty acres on one bank of the creek and fifty-five more on the land between the creek and the river. Rose died before the work could be completed, but there were enough lots to meet the original subscriptions. Randolph hired Peter Jefferson to finish the work in 1756.[74]

68. Anne Skinner, "The Attempt to Build a Town at Westham," Maude Howlett Papers, Virginia Historical Society, Richmond, VA, 1945, 3.

69. J. F. D. Smyth, *A Tour in the United States of America*, 2 vols. (London: G. Robinson and J. Sewell, 1784), 1:32; and Isaac Weld, *Travels Through the States of North America, and the Provinces of Upper and Lower Canada During the Years 1795, 1796, and 1797*, 2 vols. (London: John Stockdale, 1807), 1:153.

70. Hening, *Statutes* 5:377–80.

71. Ibid., 6:500–501; and Louis Manarin and Clifford Dowdey, *The History of Henrico County* (Charlottesville: Univ. Press of Virginia, 1984), 115.

72. Robert Rose, *The Diary of Robert Rose: A View of Virginia by a Colonial Parson, 1746–1751*, ed. Robert Emmett Fall (Verona, VA: McClung, 1977), 79.

73. *Virginia Gazette* (Hunter), June 6, 1751.

74. Rose, *Diary*, 298n769; and Hughes, *Surveyors*, 135.

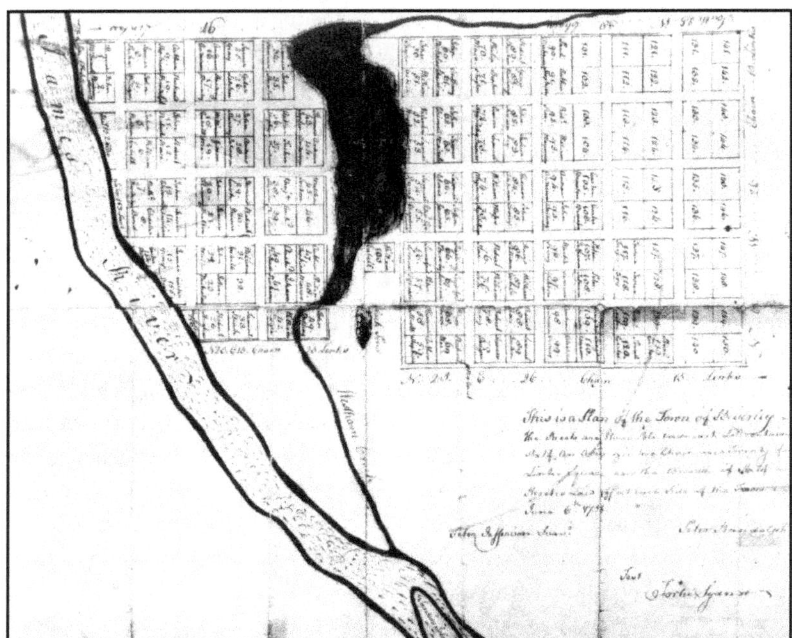

"This is a Plan of the Town of Beverley" 1756. Ambler Family Papers, 1638–1809, MMC-2527, Library of Congress, Washington, DC.

As it was finally laid out, Westham straddled the creek. The lots were divided into a regular grid pattern of blocks containing four lots each. The street width was narrow. For some reason, Peter Jefferson chose to use a width of three poles, or forty-nine and a half feet, instead of the more typical one Gunter's chain, or sixty-six feet.[75] Seventy-eight people purchased lots in the original offerings, and they included a number of important Virginians, such as surveyor and William and Mary professor Joshua Fry, William and Mary president William Stith, signer of the Declaration of Independence Carter Braxton, *The Virginia Gazette* publisher John Hunter, Peter Jefferson, and Robert Rose. Many people bought multiple lots, indicating that they were more interested in land speculation than living in the new town, and over the course of the next few years, several owners sold lots. By 1756 buyers had taken up 105 lots.[76] Those lots that did not sell were the ones located farthest from the river.

During the planning stages, Beverley Randolph called the town Westham, and Peter used that name when he deeded the first round of lots 1751. In the deeds he granted the next year, he started referring to the town as Beverley, in memory of his elder brother. Beverley was the official name used when the Assembly charted the town in 1752, though the name Westham remained in

75. Rose, *Diary*, 298n769; and Hughes, *Surveyors*, 135. Edmund Gunter introduced his chain in 1620. For surveying measurements see Hughes, *Surveyors*, 32.

76. Skinner, "Attempt," 3–4; and Rose, *Diary*, 298n769.

common usage. Ironically, the law creating Beverley was entitled "An Act for establishing the town of Westham, in the county of Henrico."[77]

Westham seems to have enjoyed a period of prosperity during its early years, and even the burgesses predicted that the town was "likely to become the chief place of trade for all the upper inhabitants" along the James and its tributaries.[78] A number of individuals erected private warehouses during the first year of the town's existence, though an attempt to build a public warehouse was beaten back, probably through the machinations of William Byrd III.[79] Still, Byrd recognized Westham's potential and took advantage of an opportunity that arose in 1753. After the Assembly chartered the town, Peter Randolph turned his attention to his primary plantation, Chatsworth, and his political offices. He sold Westham Plantation to his younger brother William, who then sold it to William Byrd III.[80]

The town of Westham developed into an important trading center. In addition to the warehouse facilities, the town had taverns, a smith, and a tailor shop and generated business for other craftsmen.[81] In an attempt to help increase trade, in 1765 the Assembly authorized a number of individuals, including Peter Randolph, William Byrd, and Peter Jefferson's son, Thomas, to form a company to build a canal around the falls—though preliminary survey work for the project did not get underway for almost a decade, and the canal was not completed until 1789.[82]

Because storage facilities dominated Westham's economy, the river became the town's lifeline. But occasionally it also brought disaster. Heavy rains in the summer of 1771 caused major flooding along the James, destroying the storage facilities. *The Virginia Gazette* reported that the "warehouses at Westham are entirely gone, with three Hundred Hogsheads of Tobacco."[83] It was a major setback for the town.

Life continued at Westham, and the town experienced a revival during the American Revolution. Westham became such an important center for arms production that in 1779 Thomas Jefferson once again tried to spur on the canal project, though after two years the forty-foot-wide canal extended only one mile. But there was "an elegant grist-mill with four pair of stones," a storage facility for gunpowder and small arms, and a cannon-boring mill.[84] Westham

77. Hening, *Statutes* 6:278–79.

78. Ibid., 6:278.

79. Ibid., 6:279; and Rose, *Diary*, 298n769.

80. Skinner, "Attempt," 5.

81. *Virginia Gazette* (Rind), Nov. 15, 1770, Oct. 31, 1771; and *Virginia Gazette* (Purdie and Dixon), Dec. 10, 1772.

82. Hening, *Statutes* 8:448–50; Kennedy and McIlwaine, *Journals of the House* 6:295; and "From William B. Giles," Dec. 13, 1789, in Thomas Jefferson, *The Papers of Thomas Jefferson*, ed. Julian P. Boyd et al., 29 vols. (Princeton, NJ: Princeton Univ. Press, 1950–2002), 16:26.

83. *Virginia Gazette* (Purdie and Dixon), July 18, 1771.

84. William Feltman, *The Journal of William Feltman of the First Pennsylvania Regiment, 1781–82* (Philadelphia: Historical Society of Pennsylvania, 1853), 8; "Bill for Establishing a Manufactory of Arms and Extending Navigation through the Falls of James River," Oct. 30, 1779, in Jefferson, *Papers* 3:142; and Skinner, "Attempt," 7.

became such a strategic arms center that the British made its destruction a priority during the southern campaign. January 5, 1781, several British companies under the command of General Benedict Arnold attacked. Arnold reported that his troops destroyed "Cartridge boxes and bayonets, 1800; barrels of powder, 330; hogsheads of brimstone, 19; chests of musket cartridges, 19; chests of flints, 3; chests of 6-pounder cartridges, 11; a foundry for casting iron cannon, a magazine mill, etc.," along with twenty-four cannon.[85] Lieutenant Colonel John Simcoe, an officer under Arnold's command, described the extent of the destruction:

> Upon consultation with the artillery officer, it was thought better to destroy the magazine than to blow it up, this fatiguing business was effected by carrying the powder down the clifts, and pouring it into the water; the warehouses and mills were then set on fire, and many explosions happened in different parts of the buildings, which might have been hazardous had it been relied on, that all the powder was regularly deposited in one magazine; and the foundery, which was a very complete one, was totally destroyed.[86]

Westham lay in ruins. The only thing that remained was a brewery, which "was saved by the intercession of the widow who owned part of it."[87]

After the war, Westham never really recovered. People held onto their lots, and a man named Mayo operated a ferry across to the Southside. Jefferson, who had inherited land in the town from his father, owned his four lots as late as 1810. However, there is no evidence of an attempt to rebuild anything after 1790 except references in connection to building the canal. Still, as late as 1796, lot owners got permission from the state for a five-year extension on the time to build on their lots.[88] The chance of Westham developing into any semblance of a town was long gone. The competition from William Byrd II's town downstream was simply too fierce. In 1779 Richmond became the capital of Virginia and grew rapidly. As Richmond grew, Westham faded into obscurity until the twentieth century, when the area became a city suburb.

Trade played an integral role in the success or failure of any backcountry town, but it was only one component. As Westham had shown, trade alone could not guarantee a town's success. Another factor that could help a fledgling town prosper was government patronage, specifically being named the seat of a county court. In the Piedmont, Brent Town could have been reinvigorated had the discussions of moving the court there continued. Alexander Spotswood used the court to try to stave off the demise of Germanna. In both

85. Benedict Arnold, "Arnold's Expedition to Richmond, Virginia, 1781," *William and Mary Quarterly*, 2nd series, vol. 12 (July 1932): 189.

86. John Graves Simcoe, *Journal of the Operations of the Queen's Rangers* (New York: New York Times and Arno Press, 1968), 163. See also Hening, *Statutes* 10:573–74.

87. Feltman, *Journal*, 8.

88. "To William Hay," [Jan. 9, 1790], in Jefferson, *Papers* 16:92; Shepherd, *Statutes* 2:52; and Skinner, "Attempt," 9.

cases, the revivals were fleeting because the courts ultimately moved to other locations. That was not the case of Leesburg, a town founded in the Piedmont section of the Northern Neck at midcentury.

Leesburg

Tavern keeper Nicholas Minor was well aware how the status as a county seat could affect the fortunes of a backcountry town. In fact, he operated a tavern at an important crossroads for several years before attempting to lay out a town on his property. The land was part of a four-thousand-acre grant Lord Fairfax made to Francis Awbrey in 1730. Awbrey and successive owners divided and sold the land over the next several years. By 1755 Minor had purchased 345 acres of the original grant, where he opened his tavern. He chose that parcel because two important roads met there—the Carolina Road, which ran from confluence of the Monacacy and Potomac rivers southwest into North Carolina, and the mountain road, which ran northwest from Alexandria through Waterford, Vestal's Gap, and on to Winchester. He was operating his ordinary, a private residence that had at least one public room, by April 1755, just in time to serve a division of troops on its way to fight the French at Fort Duquesne.[89]

Minor did not lay out a town for another three years. In 1745 he had proposed establishing a town named Cameron at the site of a tavern on Hunting Creek, though nothing came of this proposal. But in 1757 the legislature divided Fairfax County, creating Loudoun. It took a year to decide to locate a court site for the new county, but finally the justices settled on Minor's land, probably because of the convenient access of the roads and its proximity to the population centers. Once his land officially became the court site in 1758, any hesitation Minor had about founding a town vanished. That same year John Moss, James Hamilton, and Thomas Sorrell laid out streets and seventy lots. Initially, Minor called his community George Town in honor of the king, but very quickly, he changed the name to Leesburg in honor of the very wealthy and influential Lee family.[90]

The plan of Leesburg, surveyed and mapped by John Hough in 1759, was unusual in a number respects. It contained the usual half-acre rectangular lots divided by a rectilinear road system, but the number of lots in a block was inconsistent, as was the lot orientation. The town was divided by three streets running east-west (Back, King, and an unnamed street) and four streets running north-south (Royal, Loudoun, Market, and Cornwell), creating fifteen blocks,

89. Harrison, *Landmarks*, 327–28; and Eugene M. Scheel, "Leesburg Originally A Grant from Lord Fairfax," *Leesburg Times-Mirror*, Feb. 23, 1978, 1. There are suggestions that there may have been a fort named Fort George on the site during the French and Indian War, but only in secondary materials. See Charles P. Poland Jr., *From Frontier to Suburbia* (Marceline, MO: Walsworth, 1976), 10n26.

90. Hening, *Statutes* 7:419–23; Poland, *From Frontier*, 10–12; Scheel, "Archaeological Plan," 1; and Melvin Lee Steadman, *A Walking Tour of Leesburg* (Leesburg, VA: Potomac, 1967), 1.

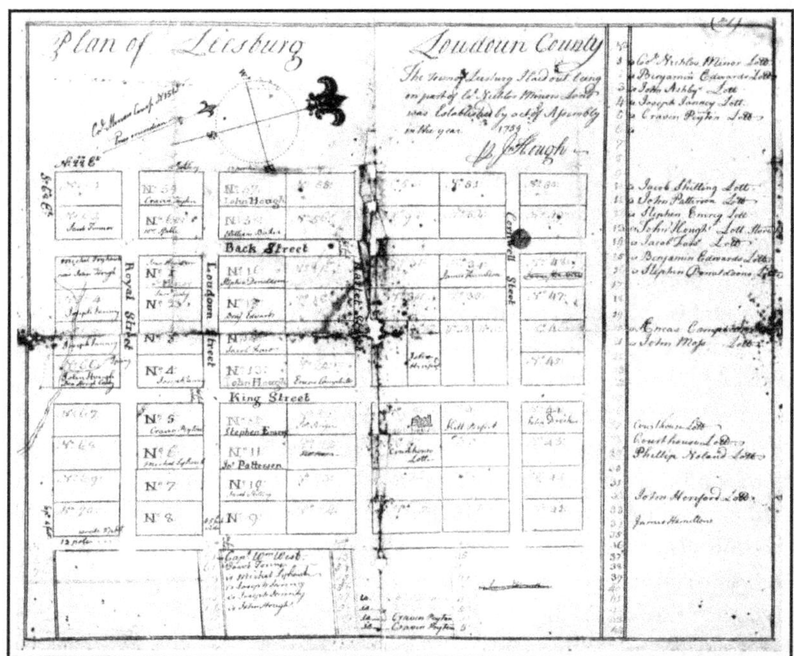

John Hough, "Plan of Leesburg," 1759. Loudoun Museum, Leesburg, Virginia. Courtesy of Gary M. Clemens, Clerk of the Circuit Court, Loudoun County, Virginia. This map and other documents are being preserved thanks to the Loudoun County Clerk of Court's archival preservation program.

which contained as few as two or as many as eight lots each. Most of the lots were oriented east-west, though four lots were turned north-south so that their short ends faced King Street. Another unusual feature of Leesburg's plan was the narrow streets, which varied in width from thirty-five to forty-five feet. Minor deeded the county two lots on the southeast corner of King and Market streets, though not until 1761. For himself he kept lot 1, a plot bounded by Royal, Back, and Loudoun streets. The way the lots are numbered suggests that Minor originally may have intended to lay out only forty-eight lots but then expanded the plan. When the Assembly chartered the town in 1758, it noted that Minor had laid off a total of sixty acres, suggesting that lots shown at the bottom of Hough's plat may have been left as outlots, large lots outside of the town that would provide their owners with wood, pasturage, or farmland. Alternately, the land may have been earmarked for future expansion.[91]

There was a good deal of interest in Leesburg, and the town grew steadily. When Hough made his plat just a year after the town was founded, Minor had granted twenty-nine of the seventy lots. A number of craftsmen, including a silversmith, blacksmith, shoemaker, and saddler, established operations in the town. There were a number of stores and taverns as well. In 1766 construc-

91. Hening, *Statutes* 7:284–85; Reps, *Tidewater*, 225; and Williams, *Legends of Loudoun*, 109–10.

tion began on a stone church, which was completed in 1770. Other buildings, including residences, were built of a variety of materials including logs, clapboards, stone, and brick. At the end of the colonial period Leesburg had a population of about five hundred residents.[92]

Despite the success of the town, travelers who left descriptions of Leesburg were not particularly impressed, probably because the young town paled in comparison to its larger and more established neighbors—Alexandria, Virginia, and Frederick, Maryland. Nicholas Cresswell spent a great deal of time in Leesburg. He was impressed with the fertile farmland in the area and noted it was excellent for wheat production, though he did not think much of the roads. In 1774 he described the town as "regularly laid off in squares, but very indifferently built and few habitants and little trade, tho' very advantageously situated, for it is at the conjunction of the great Roads from the North part of the Continent to the South and the East and West." Cresswell's criticism was not limited to the town itself; he was also concerned about the growing numbers of Methodists who lived nearby, a trend he blamed on "the great negligence of the Church Parsons."[93] A decade later, German physician Johann David Schoepf had a similar impression of Leesburg, calling it a "place of few and insignificant wooden houses," though he did comment on the town's "high, pleasant, and healthful situation," and applauded an effort to establish a Latin school there.[94] Cresswell and Schoepf may not have been particularly impressed by Leesburg, but thanks to a number of factors, including its location and the presence of the county court, Leesburg continued to prosper and grow. In spite its size, the town was politically active. In 1774, the same year as Cresswell's description, several leading citizens of the county signed a resolution banning the importation of "any tea or other East India commodity whatever," until Parliament dropped the Tea Act.[95]

Charlottesville

The last town created in Piedmont Virginia before the Revolutionary War stood southwest of Leesburg in Albemarle County. The colonial government originally created Albemarle in 1744 in response to the increase of population. In 1761 that population growth necessitated reorganizing Piedmont counties, and the Assembly adjusted various borders and divided Albemarle and Louisa counties to create Buckingham and Amherst. The resulting changes meant that Ablemarle's courthouse, located near Scott's Ferry on the James

92. *Virginia Gazette* (Rind), Oct. 15, 1772; Steadman, *Walking Tour*, passim; Melvin Lee Steadman Jr., *Leesburg's Old Stone Church, 1766* (Manassas, VA: Virginia-Craft Print, 1964), 1–7; and Scheel, "Archaeological Plan," 2.

93. Cresswell, *Journal*, 47–48.

94. Johann David Schoepf, *Travels in the Confederation*, trans. and ed. Alfred J. Morrison, 2 vols. (New York: Bergman Publishers, 1968), 2:30.

95. "Public Meeting in Loudoun in 1774," *William and Mary Quarterly*, 1st series, vol. 12 (Apr. 1904): 233.

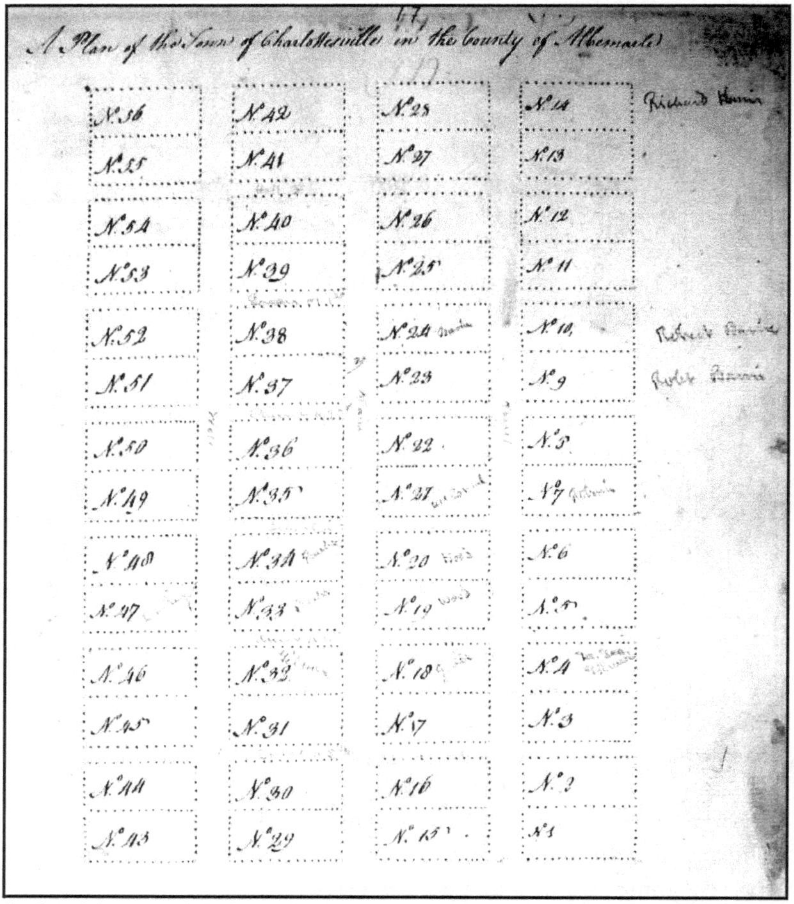

"A Plan of the Town of Charlottesville in the County of Albemarle," c. 1765. In "Albemarle County Surveyors Book, 1756–1790," vol. 1, pt. 2:77, Albemarle County Courthouse, Charlottesville, VA. Photo courtesy of Robert Vernon.

(modern Scottsville), was left on the southern edge of the reorganized county. To make the court more accessible to all of Albemarle's residents, the county purchased one thousand acres of land belonging to Henrico resident Richard Randolph and named Doctor Thomas Walker as trustee of the property. The tract sat in the geographical center of Albemarle, had fertile land and fresh water, and advantageously bordered the Three Chopt Road (so named for the blaze used to mark its route) to Richmond. It was an ideal spot to build a court town, and in 1762, the county magistrates did just that. They named the new town Charlottesville in honor of Charlotte Sophia of Mecklenburg-Strelitz, the new wife of King George III.[96]

96. Hening, *Statutes* 7:419–23, 597–98; Edgar Woods, *Albemarle County in Virginia* (Charlottesville, VA: Michie, 1901), 26–27; and *Charlottesville, 1762–1962* (Charlottesville, VA: Charlottesville 200th Anniversary Commission, 1962), 9.

Although it appears deceptively simple, Charlottesville's initial design is unusual in a number of respects. The position of the two-acre courthouse complex suggests that it was located on the edge of the thousand-acre tract to take advantage of the region's primary east-west road. Later, "fifty acres of land, contiguous to the courthouse," were laid out into streets and lots, leaving the courthouse on the northeast corner of Charlottesville instead of in the center of the town.[97] The design of the town proper is based on three parallel streets (Market, Main, and Water), each sixty-six feet wide, running mostly east-west. The surveyors diverted the main road east away from the courthouse to run down the central avenue, Main Street. The primary streets in turn were crossed by six narrower streets thirty-three feet wide. This grid divided the town into blocks of only two half-acre lots each, with the result that most of the lots bordered two main streets and one cross street. The courthouse property simply bordered the edge of the first row of lots (adjacent to lots 2 and 3), without any consideration being given for future expansion. When the town did expand to the north, one new street simply ended at the square, the courthouse property jutted into the middle of a second new street, and two lots and an odd remnant of land between lots 1 and a new lot, numbered 57, remained orphaned in order to fit them into the original grid pattern.

Once it was established, Charlottesville grew slowly. The county hired William Cabell to erect a frame porticoed courthouse, a replica of the courthouse in Henrico County. A jail, pillory, stocks, and a whipping post also stood on the square. The first sale of town lots took place in September 1763, and the results were not particularly encouraging. Fourteen lots sold, but only seven people bought them. Ten more lots sold in 1764. At a special sale in October 1765, the county sold thirty-three additional lots. But of those, two men, Benjamen Brown and David Ross, bought fourteen. The county divided the land it did not use for the town into fifteen outlots of differing sizes. The last of these sold in 1791.[98]

Despite the lackluster sales, some important people did establish themselves in Charlottesville. Before the Revolution, Albemarle's county town could boast a saddler, a blacksmith, and a physician. Tavern keeper John Jouett opened the Swan Tavern east of the courthouse. Charlottesville had a regular market where local goods, including tobacco, wheat, corn, barley, and oats were sold. The courthouse not only served government functions but was used for church services and social gatherings as well.[99] Charlottesville remained a bucolic backcountry county town until the Revolution. Unlike other towns that became the sites of forts or served as supply depots, the boost to Charlottesville's economy came when it became home to thousands of prisoners of war.

97. Hening, *Statutes* 7:597.

98. James Alexander, *Early Charlottesville Recollections*, ed. Mary Rawlings (Charlottesville, VA: Albemarle County Historical Society, 1942), 9; and Woods, *Albemarle County*, 27–28.

99. Woods, *Albemarle County*, 28–29; and *Charlottesville, 1762–1962*, 9.

Following British General John Burgoyne's surrender after the Battle of Saratoga in 1777, the American army took four thousand British and Hessian prisoners and sent them to Virginia. Overnight, Charlottesville's population exploded. The army erected special barracks for the prisoners. In a letter to Governor Patrick Henry, Thomas Jefferson boasted of the healthfulness of the barracks, remarking, "The officers tell me the troops were never so healthy since they were embodied."[100] Nearby residents entertained the officers in their homes and hired a number of the Hessians, who proved to be skilled craftsmen. But while common soldiers were faring well, the housing situation for officers was fairly desperate. British Colonel Thomas Anbury arrived in January of 1779 and explained in a letter that "no pen can describe the scene of misery and confusion that ensued." He found that "the officers of the first and second brigade were in the town and our arrival added to their distress; this famous place we had heard so much talk of, consisted only of a Court-house, one tavern, and about a dozen houses."[101]

To ameliorate their situation, the British and Hessian officers began to rent houses for themselves and their dependents. Jefferson explained they offered the local residents "such exorbitant rents as were sufficient to tempt independent owners to go out of them, and shift as they could." Often, simply procuring a house was not enough. Many of the structures stood in bad repair, and the officers had to lay out a great deal of money. Jefferson wrote, "One of the general officers has taken a place for two years, advanced the rent for the whole time, and been obliged moreover to erect additional buildings. . . . Independent of the brick work, for the carpentry of these additional buildings I know he is to pay fifteen hundred dollars. The same gentleman to my knowledge has paid to one person thirty-six hundred and seventy-dollars for different articles to fix himself commodiously."[102] The officers bought food, livestock, and seed to feed themselves and their men.

The Revolution meant an enlarged population and economic prosperity for Charlottesville, but it also brought danger. When the British moved into Virginia in 1781, the state government fled Richmond and, probably because then-governor Thomas Jefferson's plantation Monticello stood nearby, relocated in Charlottesville. A few days later, British Colonel Banastre Tarleton, commanding 250 cavalrymen, attempted to seize Jefferson and the members of the legislature. However, Charlottesville tavern keeper John Jouett spotted the British at Louisa Courthouse and rode to Charolttesville, sounding the alarm. Jefferson and the legislators moved once again—this time to Staunton. Disappointed, Tarleton spent two days in Charlottesville destroying weapons, powder, clothing, and tobacco but did not burn the town.[103]

100. As quoted in Woods, *Albemarle County*, 32.

101. Thomas Anbury, *Travels through the Interior Parts of America* (1789; Boston: Houghton Mifflin, 1923), 183–84; and Virginia Writers' Project, *Jefferson's Albemarle: A Guide to Albemarle County, Virginia* (Virginia Conservation Commission, 1941), 45.

102. Woods, *Albemarle County*, 32–33.

After the excitement of the war, Charlottesville slipped back into its prewar torpor. But slowly the town began to grow, and finally, in 1801, was large enough to incorporate. It remained small, however, until 1819 when then former President Jefferson convinced the Virginia General Assembly that the Piedmont town would make an ideal home for the University of Virginia.

The narratives of the six colonial towns founded in Piedmont Virginia demonstrate a wide range of urban experiences. Of the six, five were planned communities founded either by entrepreneurs or by county officials; the sixth, Waterford, was a rarity in colonial America—a community that developed organically without advanced planning. The two oldest towns, Brent Town and Germanna, failed very soon after their inception, and while Westham grew and prospered for a time, it did not revive after its destruction at the end of the American Revolution. The three towns that survived the colonial period, Waterford, Leesburg, and Charlottesville, did so through widely divergent circumstances.

Brent Town and Germanna are comparable in a number of respects. The fact that they were the two earliest attempts to establish towns in the Piedmont is significant and played an important role in their demise. Both towns were founded in areas that at the time were still very much part of the frontier and quite exposed to the dangers (both real and perceived) of Indian assault. Both communities constructed fortifications for their defense, and both George Brent and Alexander Spotswood used the defense of Tidewater settlements as an argument in their attempts to gain government support for the fledgling communities. Spotswood even went so far as to have the Assembly classify his miners as rangers to patrol the frontier. Needless to say, newly arrived European immigrants who were completely unfamiliar with life in Virginia were none too pleased to find themselves serving as a buffer between Tidewater planters and people they considered warlike savages.

The fact that their leaders looked abroad for large groups of settlers also links Brent Town and Germanna. George Brent and Alexander Spotswood were just two of the many people competing to draw large numbers of continental Europeans to their land. Other landowners, throughout the colonies, worked diligently to attract settlers through tax incentives, offers of citizenship, and religious tolerance. For European emigrants it was a buyer's market, and they could afford to shop for the best offers. The limited pool of continental settlers at the turn of the eighteenth century also helped trap destitute newcomers into servitude, as landowners attempted to keep them on their lands. Spotswood, through his refusal to grant land ownership and his manipulation of contracts, was particularly ruthless at this paternalistic game. In time, however, his actions backfired. As soon as they were able, the German residents abandoned Spotswood's lands altogether, leaving behind a ghost town.

103. Ibid., 44–45.

Religion also binds Brent Town and Germanna. One of the qualities that attracted landowners to this type of European settler was the fact that they were Protestants, many of them seeking refuge from persecution. While entrepreneurs worked to secure legal recognition for the colonists and pushed the Assembly to create parishes for them where they could worship freely, they failed to recognize the full importance of religious leadership to the solidarity of a community, especially one on the edge of civilization. The problems of attracting ministers or even building adequate spaces for worship helped spell the end of these early colonies. Brent Town was unique in the Virginia backcountry in that it was the only town to be considered a haven for Catholics. This singular distinction is all the more unusual considering it originally was intended for Huguenots.

Religion was also a key factor in the history of Waterford but in that instance largely responsible for its success. No one large group of people arrived to build a town, but individual families moved first into the neighborhood and later into Waterford itself, largely because they shared dissenting religious beliefs in a colony with a state religion. The institutional benefits of the Quaker Meeting provided Waterford with a system of social standards and a surrogate government, which were very successful in providing stability and building a sense of community. The Meeting also linked Waterford with other Quaker communities throughout the colonies and Great Britain.

Another advantage the four later towns (Charlottesville, Leesburg, Waterford, and Westham) had over Brent Town and Germanna was trade. All four were alive and well in 1776, though Westham's Revolutionary War experience literally left it in ashes, and no phoenix arose until the site became part of Richmond. In the Piedmont, two different organizational patterns came into play. Waterford is a wonderful example of a town developing to meet the needs of the agricultural community. Beginning as a mill site, it attracted a population to meet the needs of the surrounding agricultural community. Leesburg also began life as a service center, only in this instance as an inn, gathering a small population before being laid out as Loudoun County's court town. The two towns sat very close to one another, but Leesburg developed a larger population and a more diverse economy. What differentiated the two (apart from Waterford's unique religious and social character) were two factors: the court and proximity to the coast. In many ways, what happened in the development of these two towns is reminiscent of the model laid out in central place theory. The towns grew to meet local needs and the two worked together in a hierarchical arrangement, albeit a primitive one. A greater number of craftsmen lived and worked in Leesburg, providing some of the same basic services as Waterford craftsmen and many that were more specialized. Furthermore, Waterford residents depended on Leesburg as a place to obtain justice and other legal services related to daily life and government. In terms of trade, the hierarchical system took another step with agricultural products that were collected in Leesburg and then transported to the larger port city of Alexandria.

Other Piedmont towns suggest that the predominant agricultural product, tobacco, played a major role in shaping the region's urban experience. Tobacco was a primary staple requiring little processing (which took place on Piedmont farms and plantations) and could be shipped directly to collection points on the fall zone. That was the reason for Westham's existence. Sitting at the falls of the James River, Westham was the gateway to the Tidewater for the southern Piedmont and a portion of the Southside. People shipping products on the James literally had to stop and unload their products there, but as a trans-shipping community, Westham's success did not require the presence of many craftsmen. Except in wartime it did not grow very large and only maintained a few craftsmen in addition to its large number of warehouse facilities. While that might be considered an advantage for the town in that Westham did not need many craftsmen to help it survive, it was also a curse. After Westham burned, few people with business or emotional ties to the town remained; shipping could take place without streets, shops, and homes just as easily as it could with them. A number of prominent Virginians had purchased lots in Westham, but as an investment; none of them actually lived there or had any personal commitment to the town itself. Thus, it fits very nicely into staple theory. Staple theory also helps explain why, aside from the small government center of Charlottesville, no other Piedmont towns emerged during the colonial period. Fall-zone towns such as Westham, Richmond, Fredericksburg, and Alexandria dominated the region, helping to prevent the development of other central places. The tobacco economy helped stymie Piedmont towns until the fourth quarter of the eighteenth century, when population increases and the growth of a more diversified economic system overcame its influence.[104]

As trade was a common theme in both economic models, not surprisingly, the importance of roads and waterways was a common factor in the location of most of the Piedmont towns. Brent Town stood on an old Indian trail, Waterford and Charlottesville along important roads, and Westham on the banks of the James. Of the Piedmont towns, Leesburg was probably the most advantageously situated, because it stood at the crossroads of two major land routes, one linking Virginia to North Carolina and the other connecting the backcountry with the Tidewater. Germanna's position off an Indian path surrounded by a river was purely defensive and, by limiting people's access, may have played a part in its demise.

The experience of Piedmont towns also introduces the vital role that the county court played in the success or failure of towns in the Virginia backcountry, and it is a theme that was repeated in each of the geographical

104. Robert D. Mitchell, "The Southern Backcountry: A Geographical House Divided," in Crass et al., *Southern*, 20.

regions. In the backcountry, court towns were the most common local urban centers. The site of the county court did not assure the development of a town. In fact, such a venture was risky because with the creation of a new county, the court often moved once again. An important test of the strength of a backcountry town was whether it could survive the removal of the court. Most towns could not.

Three of the six colonial Piedmont towns served as county towns, and a fourth was considered as a potential locale. Brent Town could have been reborn had the Governor's Council chosen it as the seat of Prince William County. With his influence, Alexander Spotswood was able to choose the site of Spotsylvania County's county town and used the court to breathe life back into Germanna briefly. Once the Assembly shifted the court to Fredericksburg, Germanna simply collapsed.

Leesburg and Charlottesville were both founded as county towns, though by different routes. Nicholas Minor could have chosen simply to allow the courthouse to stand on his property, but he knew an opportunity when he saw it and laid out Leesburg. He was only one of many individuals who tried to capitalize on the court's location. The founding of Charlottesville, on the other hand, was similar to many other backcountry county seats in that it benefited from its location near the center of Albemarle County, but it was distinct in that the court and not an individual laid out the town. The stories of the Leesburg and Charlottesville differ in other ways. While Leesburg gained status from its court, it also developed a much more diverse economy than Charlottesville, attracting a larger number of craftsmen and merchants and serving as a collection point for neighboring agricultural products. Because of the craftsmen and trade, Leesburg probably could have survived the removal of the country court if it had ever occurred. For Charlottesville, the court meant life until it attracted a large enough population and sufficiently diverse economy to grow during the years following the Revolution.

The Revolution introduces one final theme that was important in the life of backcountry Virginia towns—the role of war, which brought both prosperity and danger to two Piedmont towns—Westham and Charlottesville. Westham's importance in producing and storing war materiel was not unusual for a backcountry town except perhaps in the amount of heavy weaponry it produced. Charlottesville was unique in the backcountry as a center for British prisoners of war. But the prosperity these positions brought to Westham and Charlottesville also left them vulnerable. The British looted Charlottesville, and Westham has the dubious distinction of being the only backcountry town burned in time of war.

Names are an important feature of towns and were used in a variety of ways, most typically for streets and for the towns themselves. In the Piedmont, Brent Town and Westham's official name Beverley commemorated people who founded the communities. Charlottesville and Leesburg's original name,

George Town, honored the royal family. The fact that Nicholas Minor changed George Town to Leesburg opens up interesting avenues of speculation as to what Minor may have intended: whether he was hoping to persuade the Lee family to invest in the town, needed their support with government recognition, thought it would be beneficial to link his town to the Lee name, or simply wanted to honor an important family residing in the neighborhood. Certainly that was why Charlottesville gave the new Jefferson Street that name when the town expanded.

Aside from its name, a town is best represented by the way it was laid out, its plan revealing the amount of time and thought involved, the personality or experience of the person creating the design, as well as the prospects for future expansion and the overall success of the community.[105] For the two earliest Piedmont towns, it is not possible to look at the streetscape because there is no record of what Brent Town looked like, and Germanna never developed beyond a line of small houses. Waterford, as mentioned above, was an anomaly in colonial America since its roads simply evolved, shaped by natural features and the needs and desires of the citizenry. While more typical of towns in the other parts of the Virginia backcountry, Westham, Leesburg, and Charlottesville share little in common other than the use of half-acre lots, the common grid road system, and narrow streets. Charlottesville was the only town with the typical street widths of sixty-six feet for its main streets, though the side streets were half that width. Westham's streets were much more narrow at forty-nine and a half, and Leesburg's streets varied in width from thirty-five to forty-five feet. Variety seems to have been a hallmark in Leesburg's lot plan as well, both in terms of the number of lots per block and their orientation. Charlottesville and Westham had regular numbers of lots in their blocks, but they were very low—two and four respectively. Charlottesville was also the only Piedmont town with a square, and it was put in seemingly as an afterthought on the edge of town. The hilly nature of Leesburg's terrain may account for the variety of its block sizes. But the town grid that was most influenced by geography was Westham, whose creek and marshy land effectively divided the town into two parts.

In many respects, the Piedmont serves as a microcosm of town development in the backcountry of colonial Virginia. Many of the elements that shaped the history of the six Piedmont towns came into play in other backcountry regions. The timing of town founders was vital to the success or failure of a community. As many entrepreneurs learned, towns could not survive in a vacuum; in order to succeed they had to have the support of a surrounding population. Founders who counted on recruiting large immigrant populations discovered that such ventures were fraught with difficulties. After all of the hard work of negotiating and convincing groups of refugees to settle their

105. Town design in Virginia is discussed in more detail in chapter 6.

lands, landowners and their colonists had very different notions of how their communities would function, and the citizenry resented paternalistic policy. Factors such as religion, trade, location, and war played important roles in the life of a town. The presence of a county court could make or break a town. Leesburg, the most successful colonial Piedmont town, demonstrates how a combination of factors (its situation at a crossroads, its role as a country seat, its trade with the surrounding community, and its connections with other towns) were necessary for a town to flourish and develop. The Piedmont experience also demonstrates how a colonial town that flourished for a couple of decades could fail quickly because of a change in circumstance, while another could exist for decades as merely a name and a few streets and houses, only to develop later. Most importantly, the six towns of the Piedmont show that the people of colonial Virginia held that whether they succeeded or failed, founding towns was a natural and vital part of settling the backcountry.

Chapter 3

The Southside

Colonial Virginia's Southside presents something of a paradox. At first glance, because of its proximity to the Tidewater and its rich agricultural lands, the Southside seems to be a prime area for early development, but that was not the case. Transportation difficulties, potential conflicts with Indians, the border dispute with North Carolina, and government policy all combined to hamper its development until long after the American Revolution. That does not mean there was no interest in settling the land. Indeed, Tidewater planters were keen on spreading their influence in the Southside as they had in the Piedmont. But the vast wilderness that was the Southside proved to be a formidable region to conquer, and at the end of the colonial period, the territory bore only a slight resemblance to the social, economic, and political character of the rest of Virginia. The region remained sparsely populated, and although there were impressive stands of crops, plantations were still separated by vast stretches of forest. Building a townscape in the Southside also proved hard and frustrating. People made six attempts to establish Southside towns during the colonial period. Three towns failed, and one town struggled through the centuries as a small county seat. While two communities prospered during the eighteenth century, in the twenty-first century they are little more than place names. At the turn of the eighteenth century, however, settlers and entrepreneurs looked over the Southside and saw a land rich with promise.[1] They attempted to establish six towns there.

King William's Town (Manakin Town)

Not surprisingly, town development in Southside Virginia began with the entrepreneurial efforts of William Byrd I, a member of the Tidewater aristocracy. As part of one of Virginia's wealthiest families, Byrd had acquired vast land holdings in the west and was anxious to develop them. Byrd and other Virginia landowners wanted to find large groups of settlers to take up and develop their lands, rather than to have to work with individuals or small families. With this goal in mind, a number of landholders competed to attract groups of religious refugees who were fleeing Europe, primarily French Huguenots. Indeed, a number of Huguenots settled in Tidewater Virginia even before Louis XIV revoked the Edict of Nantes in 1685. Baron de Sancé led a colony to Virginia as early as 1630, and other Huguenots followed, assisted by the London-based Huguenot Relief Committee. In 1686/87 George Brent made the first attempt to establish a town in the backcountry, using Huguenots as colonists. But large-scale government support for such schemes did not exist until William III assumed the English throne in 1688 and gave his full support to efforts to settle Huguenot émigrés in Virginia.[2]

Though Byrd was ultimately the leading force in settling the largest group of Huguenots in Virginia, it was English court physician Daniel Coxe who initiated the contacts. Coxe dabbled in colonial ventures primarily in New Jersey, though he also had claims to land in Tidewater Virginia and along the Gulf of Mexico. He approached two Huguenot leaders: Oliver, Marquis de la Muce, and Charles de Sailly. In 1698 they agreed to lead two hundred Huguenots to America to settle on 500,000 acres of Coxe's land on the Gulf. De la Muce petitioned the king for assistance. William provided three thousand pounds to assist the colonists and persuaded the Protestant Relief Fund to donate an additional twelve thousand. He turned the project proposal over to the Board of Trade. While the Board supported the idea of the colony, its members rejected the Gulf property as indefensible and recommended that the Huguenots settle on Coxe's land in Norfolk County, Virginia, instead.[3]

1. Beeman, *Evolution*, 14–16; and Farmer, *In the Absence*, 5–8.

2. Richard L. Maury, introduction to "The Vestry Book of King William Parish, VA, 1707–1750," trans. and ed. R. H. Fife, *Virginia Magazine of History and Biography* 11 (1903–4):289; Richard L. Scribner, "Manakinetowne in Virginia," *Virginia Cavalcade* 3 (Winter 1953): 38; and Leslie Tobias, "Manakin Town: The Development and Demise of a French Protestant Refugee Colony in Colonial Virginia, 1700–1750," M.A. thesis, College of William and Mary in Virginia, 1982, 9.

3. "[Council Meeting] At the City of Williamsburgh, Dec. 9th, 1700," in R. A. Brock, ed., *Documents, Chiefly Unpublished, Relating to the Huguenot Emigration to Virginia* (Richmond: Virginia Historical Society, 1886), 52–53; James L. Bugg Jr., "The French Huguenot Frontier Settlement of Manakin Town," *Virginia Magazine of History and Biography* 61 (1953): 360–61; Maury, introduction to "Vestry Book," 290; and Scribner, "Manakinetowne," 38.

At this point in the proceedings, Byrd learned the details of the proposed colony and intervened. He sent a letter to the Board of Trade in 1698 outlining six potential problems with Coxe's Norfolk property, which he described as "low Swampy ground, unfit for planting and Improvement," with "very moist and unhealthy" air.[4] His chief arguments dealt with the fact that the land was claimed by both Virginia and the younger proprietary colony of North Carolina, which he declared would soon become a haven for escaped criminals and runaway servants. Were the Huguenots to settle in North Carolina, they would probably become a burden to the crown and end up dispersing. On the other hand, he assured the Board that the colonists would have greater support and opportunity in Virginia, and he promised that Lieutenant Governor Francis Nicholson, with whom he had probably consulted, would "be exceedingly active in an undertaking of so great Charity, and will place them in such a part of ye Country as may be most happy for them."[5]

The land that Byrd had in mind was the site of an abandoned Monocan Indian village, known as Manakin Town. The property lay twenty miles west of the falls on the James, along a boundary line the General Assembly designated in 1691 demarcating the extent of European settlement and the beginning of Indian lands. Byrd did not hold title to the tract, but he did own adjacent acreage and knew he would have greater success attracting settlers to his own property with a buffer zone protecting the frontier. Furthermore, as the Huguenots' nearest contact, he would become their chief trade source. Even without owning the land, Byrd stood to benefit from a colony there. But the Board rejected Byrd's arguments, and King William instructed Lieutenant Governor Nicholson to assist the Huguenots in settling Norfolk County.[6]

On July 23, 1700, Nicholson personally greeted 207 Huguenots as they arrived at Hampton aboard the ship *Mary Ann*. He informed the startled colonists that they would be settling at Manakin Town and not Norfolk County. It is unclear exactly what transpired between Nicholson and Byrd that led to the governor's defying the king's instructions, but it is clear that the two had conspired to relocate the colony. When Nicholson explained his actions in a report to the Board of Trade in August, he used arguments identical to Byrd's, and the move received the unanimous approval of the Governor's Council, of which Byrd was a member. Certainly the change was a testament to Byrd's power and influence in Virginia politics.[7]

To be fair to Nicholson and the Virginia government, they were very generous in their assistance. The colonists received ten thousand acres as an outright gift from the colony, and in December 1700, the Assembly created King

4. William Byrd I, "Proposals Humbly Submitted to the L'ds of Ye Councill of Trade and Plantations for Sending Ye French Protestants to Virginia," [1698], in Brock, *Documents*, 6.

5. Ibid.

6. Manarin and Dowdey, *History*, 72; and Bugg, "French Huguenot," 362.

7. "Communication from Governor Francis Nicholson of Virginia," [Aug. 12, 1700], in Brock, *Documents*, 251–53; and Bugg, "French Huguenot," 359, 363.

William Parish, allowing the Huguenots to have their own ministers and exempting them from parish levies. The same act granted the refugees an exemption from colonial and county taxes for seven years. Additionally, they received full citizenship. To help alleviate any fears of Indian attack, the Council ordered regular military patrols.[8]

After the initial surprise of the change in their colony's location wore off, the Huguenots faced more serious challenges. They had paid for passage only as far as Hampton and were forced to dip into their common fund, which they had planned to use to sustain them until their first harvest, in order to travel to the site. As if that were not bad enough, one of the boats they hired to transport their goods sank in the James River en route. By the time they arrived at the first falls on the river, the last bastion of European civilization, they were mentally and physically exhausted. Byrd and fellow planter and council member Benjamin Harrison escorted the settlers to the falls, but only 120 were well enough to continue on to Manakin Town, escorted by a company of soldiers for protection against Indian attack. De la Muce remained at the falls and ultimately left Virginia, while de Sailly led the vanguard into the wilderness. The first months were not encouraging. More than half of the colonists lay sick at the falls, while at the settlement six people died and twenty others deserted, "some for libertinage and lazinesse and some for want of bread, being not able to suffer hunger and take patientence when we meet with dissappointments."[9]

In 1705, when Nicholson's successor Robert Beverley wrote his *History and Present State of Virginia*, he painted William Byrd's role during the initial settlement period of Manakin Town in glowing terms:

> I must not here omit doing Justice to the Goodness and Generosity of Colonel Byrd, towards these distressed Hugonots. Upon their first Arrival in that Country, he receiv'd them with all the tenderness of a Father; and ever since has constantly given them the utmost Assistance. He not only relieves them, but with a Charity very uncommon, is fond of doing it. He makes them the object of his particular care, employing all his Skill, and all his Friends, to advance their Interest, both publickly and privately. He spares no Expense, and what is more than that, he refuses no trouble for their Incouragement.[10]

While this acclaim is certainly exaggerated, Byrd's patronage was essential to the Huguenots' survival in the backcountry. When the settlers had exhausted their supplies, even selling their weapons and clothing to buy food, Byrd collected supplies from his neighbors to relieve their plight and allowed them the

8. Hening, *Statutes* 3:201, 478; Maury, ,introduction to "Vestry Book," 290; and Bugg, "French Huguenot," 365.

9. "At a Council Meeting held at the Hon'ble Mr. Auditor Byrd's, 14th day of November, 1700," in Brock, *Documents*, 49–50; and Bugg, "French Huguenot," 364–66.

10. Robert Beverley, *The History and Present State of Virginia* (Chapel Hill: Univ. of North Carolina Press, 1947), 282–83.

free use of his mill and storehouse. He was also instrumental in gaining political concessions for the colony. When Byrd died in 1704, his son, William Byrd II, served as the colonists' personal liaison to the government.[11]

Byrd's generosity toward the Huguenots was not limitless, nor were his motives as selfless as Beverley painted them in his report. When he visited the colony in the spring of 1701, Byrd was disappointed by the paltry amount of land the Huguenots had cleared and planted and told them that "they must not expect to enjoy ye land unless they would endeavour to improve it, and if they make no corne for their subsistance next yeare they could not expect any further relief from the Country."[12] The people of the Manakin Town tract grew to resent Byrd's patronizing position and were convinced that he meant to profit by them. Indeed, when he laid out their property at the direction of the colonial government, he set aside 344 acres of the land for himself, along with an additional 3,664 acres straddling the road to the community, land where a colonist had discovered a coal deposit.[13]

In addition to his other assistance in establishing the Huguenots' settlement, Byrd may have designed their central town. The name Manakin Town referred to the entire 10,033-acre tract, but most of that was wilderness. The design for the colony called for a nucleated village surrounded by farms. Residents would live in town, traveling to their farms to work during the day.[14] On the frontier, with the threat of Indian attack, this type of settlement pattern had defensive advantages. The name of the village was King William's Town.

The only existing plan for King William's Town shows a village designed around a central square named in honor of Lieutenant Governor Nicholson. Three streets ran north-south: two provided the town's borders, and the center street ran north to the James River. These three streets were crossed by Byrd Street, the only east-west avenue, which served as the main entrance to the community and became the road to the falls. There is no scale to the plan, but assuming the "very mean" huts Byrd described in 1701 were around twelve feet square and the plan is to scale, then Byrd Street would be about 50 feet wide, and Nicholson Square would be 150 by 250 feet.[15] The design incorporated garden plots on the north and south border and in the town itself between rows of houses running north to south. Larger plots for cash crops stretched east and west along the river. The plan also called for public buildings—a church, a hospital, a combination townhouse and school, and a parish house—to stand in each corner of the square.

Under the leadership of Charles de Sailly, the settlers laid out King William's Town, but when a second group of colonists arrived from England

11. William Byrd II, *The Secret Diary of William Byrd of Westover, 1709–1772*, ed. Louis B. Wright and Marion Tinling (Richmond, VA: Dietz, 1941), 258; and Bugg, "French Huguenot," 367.

12. William Byrd I, "The State of the Ffrench Refugees," [May 10–11, 1701], in Brock, *Documents*, 43.

13. Ibid., 43–44; Scribner, "Manakinetowne," 38–39; and Manarin and Dowdey, *History*, 72, 75.

14. Reps, *Tidewater*, 195–96.

15. Ibid., 196; and Byrd, "State of the Ffrench,", 42.

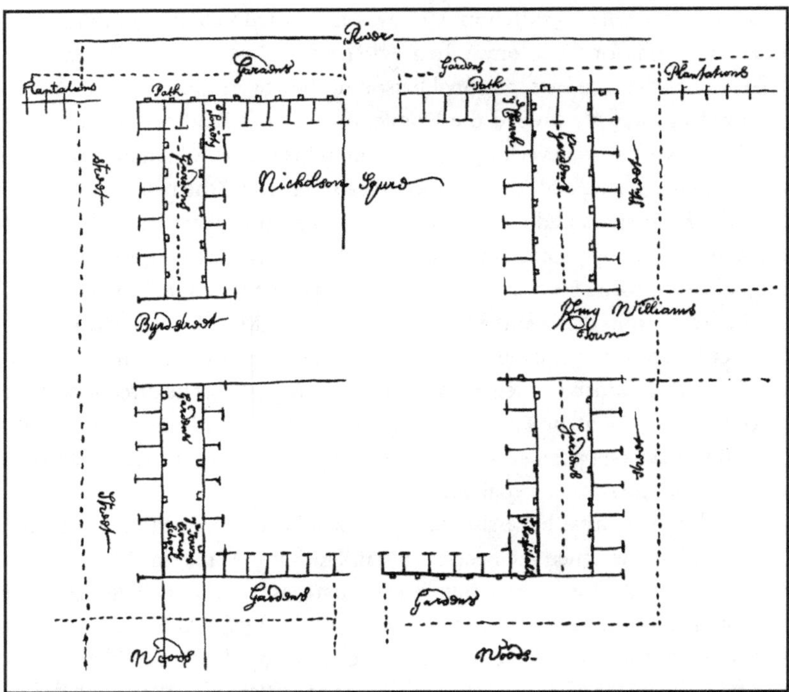

Drawing of King William's Town by William Byrd I [?], c. 1700. From R. A. Brock, ed., *Documents, Chiefly Unpublished, Relating to the Huguenot Emigration to Virginia* (Richmond: Virginia Historical Society, 1886). The original map has disappeared. See H. R. McIlwaine, "The Huguenot Settlement at Manakin Towne," *Huguenot* 6 (1933): 75.

in October 1700, their presence strained already tenuous conditions. De Sailly informed the newcomers that "he had no bread nor sustenance for 'em" and that "he opposed those who desired to take up such tracts of land as were adjacent to the Lands he had marked out for those of his first party, unless they would swear an oath of fidelity to such particular persons as he had made Justices of the Peace, which oaths those of the second party refused to take."[16] The new group, under the leadership of Benjamin de Joux, whom the bishop of London had commissioned as the colony's minister, ultimately created a separate "lower settlement" four or five miles east of King William's Town. A third ship arrived late in October, and the Virginia government decided to have those colonists disperse among the general population instead of creating even more problems for Manakin Town. The passengers of a ship that arrived in May 1701 were headed to settle along the York River, though about fifty of them ended up on the Manakin Town tract. Lieutenant Governor Nicholson was so concerned about the financial and political problems the Huguenots

16. "[Petition] to His Excellency Francis Nicholson, Esquire, His Maj'ties Lieutenant and Governor-General of Virginia," in Brock, *Documents*, 56.

were creating in the colony that he requested that the British government not send any more of the refugees to Virginia.[17]

Another problem that plagued Manakin Town was the fact that many of the colonists were craftsmen with urban backgrounds. They were simply ill prepared to survive in the wilderness, and many of them ended up choosing to leave. Nevertheless, reports to London suggested that, frontiersmen or no, the Huguenots were making valiant efforts to develop their land. Lieutenant Governor Beverley reported that in their first four years the Huguenots had built up herds of cattle that gave "abundantly more Milk, than any other in the Country," and they had plans to develop a breeding program involving buffalo. According to Beverley, they were manufacturing much of their own clothing, and had begun "an Essay of Wine, which they made of the wild Grapes gather'd in the Woods; the effect of which, was a Noble strong-bodied Claret, of curious flavor."[18]

Despite these early efforts, over time tobacco became the Huguenots' chief crop, and the settlers were very interested in gaining possession of their own farmland. They sent a series of petitions to the Virginia government, but only half of the acreage had been distributed by 1706. Four years later, Justice of the Peace Abraham Sallé met with William Byrd II to ask him to serve as intermediary with the Governor's Council to petition to have the rest of the land distributed. With agriculture dominating the economy of Manakin Town, and as the frontier became safer with the passage of time, fewer and fewer residents chose to reside in King William's Town.[19]

The discontent of the Huguenot residents continued even after all of the land was distributed in 1710. Soon after George I's accession to the throne four years later, Abraham Sallé petitioned the new king after seeing "in public prints that Your Majesty has approved a project which has been presented to you to settle French protestants in Ireland." Sallé explained that the Huguenots' minister had died and they were having great difficulties finding a replacement. He also pointed out that "our families which are pretty numerous and the place which we occupy quite limited, we find ourselves in the impossibility of procuring any situation for our children or even to have them instructed or give them any education." In short, Sallé begged the king "to withdraw us from a place where we suffer. For a long time we would have been out of it, if we had been in the state to leave it of ourselves—and to pay our passage, but we are wanting in means for that purpose."[20] The petition went unanswered. Sallé died in Manakin Town in 1719, while other Huguenots sold their lands to outsiders and moved away.[21]

17. Bugg, "French Huguenot," 368–71, 373.
18. Beverley, *History*, 282; and Reps, *Tidewater*, 196.
19. Byrd, *Secret Diary*, 258; "At a Council Held at the Capitol the 18th Day of Novem'r, 1710," in Brock, *Documents*, 71–73; and Bugg, "French Huguenot," 378–79.
20. Abraham Sallé, "Abraham Salle to George I," *Virginia Historical Magazine* 34 (1926): 159–60.
21. Ibid., 159; and Reps, *Tidewater*, 196.

Although it is difficult to date the precise year the village ceased being a viable community, it is possible to get some idea from the stories of Manakin Town's church buildings. Benjamin de Joux oversaw construction of the first church soon after his arrival in the fall of 1700. It was an octagonal frame building located in King William's Town, constructed with funds provided by the king. By 1710, the population of the parish had outgrown the original building, and they replaced it with a larger one. Within two decades this second structure needed major repairs, but by that point, most of the congregation members had moved away from the village, so instead of repairing that structure, the parishioners tore it down and built a third structure away from King William's Town. By 1750, although settlers were living throughout the Manakin Town tract, King William's Town had ceased to exist and the entire had been site sold.[22]

Eden

Despite the ultimate failure of Manakin Town/King William's Town, William Byrd II continued his father's efforts to develop land through a variety of settlement schemes and town creations. He met with success in the Tidewater, establishing towns at the falls of the James and Appomattox rivers in 1733. Richmond and Petersburg both developed into important collection points for goods coming from the west, which were then transported by ship to the coast. Flush with these successes, in 1737 Byrd wrote English naturalist Mark Catesby about the Richmond project as well as a new plan to develop land on the Southside, where he intended to "plant a colony of Switzers on my land upon Roanoke. For this good purpose, I expect to make a beginning with one hundred families at the fall."[23] A number of Swiss immigrants seemed to be interested in settling in Virginia largely because of the work of François Louis Michel and his partners, and Byrd believed he could attract them to his land in southwest Virginia.

The tract Byrd intended to colonize was part of 105,000 acres south of the Roanoke (modern Dan) River that he had accumulated through purchase and a large land grant. His concept of urban design was unique, calling for not a single town but a series of nucleated villages stretching along the river connected by a system of roads. Each village was a complete unit, consisting of a village square surrounded by individual homes. Larger lots around the square were to be reserved for a church and other important buildings. Land in between each village undoubtedly was to be used for agriculture. He called his community Eden.[24]

22. Scribner, "Manakinetowne," 39–41.

23. William Byrd II to Mark Catesby, June 27, 1723, in William Byrd I, William Byrd II, and William Byrd III, *The Correspondence of the Three William Byrds of Westover, Virginia, 1684–1776*, ed. Marion Tinling, 2 vols. (Charlottesville: Published for the Virginia Historical Society by Univ. Press of Virginia, 1977), 2:519.

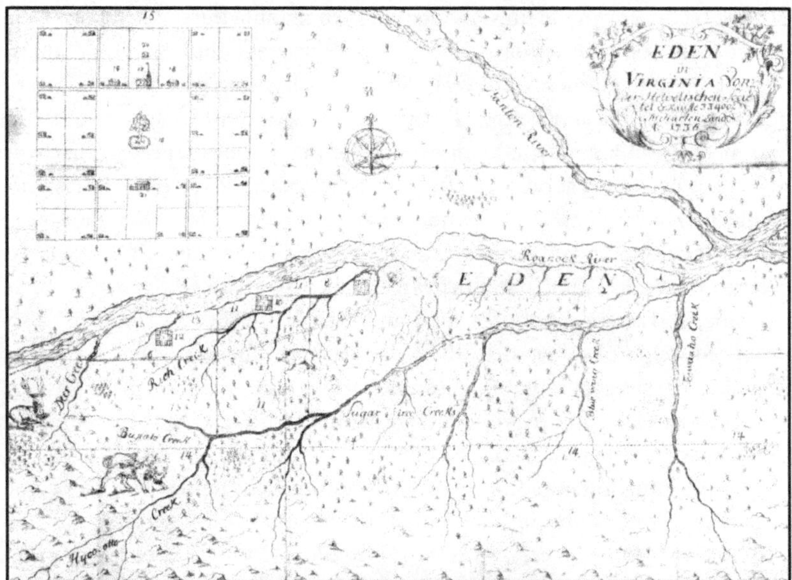

"Eden in Virginia von der Helvetischen Societet er kaufte 33400 Jucharten Land A: 1736." In *Neugefundenes Eden. Oder: Ausführlicher Bericht von Sud- und Nord-Carolina, Pensilphania, Mary-Land, & Virginia* (Bern, Switzerland: In Truck verfertiget durch Befelch der Helvetischen Societät, 1737).

Despite the elaborate nature of the design and his high expectations for the project, Byrd's plans for Eden ran into difficulties almost immediately. From the outset, he was determined to find Swiss colonists to settle his land along the Roanoke "because they have commonly more vertue and industry than other people. Besides the clymate is intirely suitable to what they have been us'd to both for heat and cold, and consequently will agre with their constitutions."[25] Byrd began negotiations with Johann Rudolph Ochs, a Swiss engraver working at the English mint. Between 1731 and 1735 Ochs made several petitions to the Commissioners of Trade for land in the Virginia backcountry on behalf of a group of Swiss living in England. When the petitions failed, he started contacting wealthy Virginia landowners directly.[26]

Byrd and Ochs began exchanging correspondence in 1735. Byrd wasted no time in trying to persuade Ochs that Eden was a perfect place where settlers could "exercise their industry upon everything that genius leads them to." The land was bountiful, and Byrd explained that colonists would be able to grow a number of crops, including grapes, mulberry trees for silk production,

24. (Previous page) William Byrd II to Johann Rudolph Ochs, 1735?, in Byrd, Byrd, and Byrd, *Correspondence* 2:451. The Roanoke tract should not be confused with the land in North Carolina that Byrd explored while running the Virginia–North Carolina border and later described in his work "A Journey to the Land of Eden Anno 1733." See Byrd, *Prose Works*, 381–415; and Byrd, *Histories of the Dividing Line*, 268–72.

25. William Byrd II to John Perceval, Earl of Egmont, July 2, 1737, in Byrd, Byrd, and Byrd, *Correspondence* 2:521.

26. Byrd, Byrd, and Byrd, *Correspondence* 2:452n1.

"as fine flax as any in the universe, for a linnen manufacture;" "hemp as good as any from Riga, for cordage of all kinds," silk-grass, nuts, grain, potatoes, peas, "fruit in great plenty of every sort, and everything that grows in a garden as good as the world affords." Byrd continued, "And what may surprise you most, I can assure you from experience many times repeated, that you may make exceeding good sugar, from a tree we call a sugar tree, which is very plentiful in these parts." As for animals, Byrd assured Ochs that Eden was perfect for "cattle and hoggs, for sheep and goats, and particularly there is a large creature of the beef kind, but much larger, called a buffalo, which may be bred up tame, and is good both for food and for labour." Eden's landscape also promised riches of other sorts. Byrd claimed that "there is water as clear as crystal and as sweet as milk, and pleasant streams for any kind of mills. Besides all these advantages above ground, there are many promiseing shews of mines [and] quarrys of marble upon the hills."[27]

Despite this glowing account, the Swiss group Ochs represented chose not to take Byrd's offer and instead settled further south. Byrd wrote merchant and horticulturalist Peter Collinson in July 1736, "I was so unlucky as to be disappointed of my Swiss colony last fall. It seems they were deluded into South Carolina, which has proved the same grave to them it had to several of their country folks before."[28] But despite the loss of this first colony, Byrd continued to negotiate. In later correspondence, he assured Ochs that Eden had no swampland full of "foul exhalations" but "the air is cool and reviving, perfectly gratefull to the lungs, and refreshing to the animal spirits." Ochs seemed to be considering North Carolina as an alternative location for a colony, so Byrd tried to dissuade him, pointing out that all of the good land in the region was already patented, there would be no roads, the quitrents would be double those in Virginia, and "the government of that province is quite unsettled and full of confusion. I might add to that all the officers there are as hungry as hawks, and like them make a prey of every poor creature that falls into their pounces." Virginia's government, on the other hand, was "much better constituted than any of His Majesties colonys and the libertys of the people more intirely securd." There were already public roads to Eden "made fit for every sort of carriage."[29]

Byrd was so intent on having Ochs's colonists settle in Eden that he offered to give them ten thousand acres of land rent free and promised to try to win them tax incentives from the Governor's Council. He also assured Ochs that the settlers would be able to choose their own ministers and politicians. The catch was that Byrd wanted the colonists there by May 1737, though he argued that the short period of time would not be a problem. Byrd assured Ochs that

27. William Byrd II to Johann Rudolph Ochs, 1735?, in Byrd, Byrd, and Byrd, *Correspondence* 2:450–51.

28. William Byrd II to Peter Collison, July 18, 1737, in Byrd, Byrd, and Byrd, *Correspondence* 2:493.

29. William Byrd II to Johann Rudolph Ochs, July 15, 1736, in Byrd, Byrd, and Byrd, *Correspondence* 2:490–91.

"Any of our merchants will be glad to send away a ship in September or October, for the benefit of a good number of passengers. Particularly my freind Capt. Norwood, who waits upon you with this letter, will be glad to bring over your colony in the fall."[30]

Quite simply, the reason Byrd was in such a generous mood was the fact that he was running out of time. In 1735 Byrd had jumped the gun on his plans and petitioned the Council for 100,000 acres of land. The Council had granted his request and given him the land, provided he settle one family per hundred acres. He needed one hundred families on the land within two years, and he was getting worried.[31] In his letter to Ochs on July 15, 1736, Byrd casually mentioned, "If I should fail in my intention of planting a Swiss colony in this delightfull part of the world, (which are the people of the earth I woud choose to have) I must then seat my land with Scots-Irish, who crowd over to Pensylvania in such numbers, that there is no more room for them." It was not an idle threat. In his letter to Peter Collinson, Byrd mentioned the alternative plan as well, though in that version he revealed his distaste for Ulster Scots, saying, "They swarm like the Goths and Vandals of old, & will overspread our continent soon." But still no Swiss came, so Byrd extended his deadline from May to October.[32]

Finally, Byrd got his colony of Swiss settlers but not through the assistance of Johann Ochs. Instead, in 1736 he struck an agreement with Samuel Jenner of Bern, Switzerland, an agent of the Helvetian Society. Byrd made arrangements to sell the society 33,400 acres of land on the Roanoke, though the sale never went through. He provided Jenner with information about Eden that was as extremely favorable (if not outright fictitious) as the accounts he had sent Ochs. Jenner took Byrd's descriptions and added factual information from a variety of other sources. The next year, the society published a tract entitled *Neu-gefundenes Eden*, complete with the map of the proposed colony and a purported copy of a deed between Byrd and the society's Virginia agent, Samuel Tschiffely.[33] The pamphlet was tremendously successful and garnered a lot of interest in the settlement. In August 1738, about three hundred Swiss settlers boarded a small ship bound for Virginia.

The news of the Swiss colonists delighted Byrd. He wrote Irish politician and longtime family friend John Perceval, Earl of Egmont, "After the first are happyly fixt, I make no question but many more will be tempted to follow

30. Ibid., 2:491–92.

31. McIlwaine, Hall, and Hillman, *Executive Journals* 4:355–56.

32. William Byrd II to Johann Rudolph Ochs, July 15, 1736 in Byrd, Byrd and Byrd, *Correspondence* 2:492; William Byrd II to Peter Collison, July 18, 1736, in Byrd, Byrd, and Byrd, *Correspondence* 2:492–93; and William Byrd II to Johann Rudolph Ochs, Apr. 30, 1737, in Byrd, Byrd, and Byrd, *Correspondence* 2:506.

33. William Byrd II, *The London Diary (1717–1721) and Other Writings*, ed. Louis B. Wright and Marion Tinling (New York: Oxford Univ. Press, 1958), 41–42; Wust, *Virginia Germans*, 25–26; and Percy G. Adams, "The Real Author of William Byrd's Natural History of Virginia," *American Literature* 28 (1956): 211–20. The tract was translated back into English and published as William Byrd II, *William Byrd's Natural History*.

them by the charming landskape they will receive of the place."[34] The Helvetian Society also felt encouraged about the prospects of the Eden colony. Both Byrd and the society petitioned the Governor's Council to assure the future success of the endeavor. At its October 26, 1738, meeting, Byrd informed the Council of the colonists' eminent arrival, and it granted him a year's extension on his grant. At the November 23 meeting, the Council granted Tschiffely a 30,000-acre tract adjacent to Byrd's land.[35] The press got wind of the project, and the next day *The Virginia Gazette* announced the news that a ship was coming "with a considerable Number of Switzers on board, who are bound for this Colony, to settle here, on the back Lands."[36] Finally, everything seemed to be falling into place.

The settlers seemed cursed from the start. The small, overcrowded ship of colonists took four months to cross the Atlantic. It encountered several other ships en route, whose crews reported accounts of a devastating voyage. Disease and hunger were the biggest problems. During the trip, the captain, the first mate, and almost sixty passengers, mostly children, died. Finally, the boat arrived off of the coast of Virginia on January 3, 1739, and dropped anchor in Lynnhaven Bay in Princess Anne County (modern Virginia Beach). Even though they were only two hours out of Hampton, their port of destination, the passengers had not eaten in several days and insisted on "going ashore to get Provisions."[37] Several people landed but found no food and no sign of civilization. Meanwhile, a storm blew in. The force of the wind snapped the anchor line, and a second anchor could not keep the ship from being driven aground. The ship flooded and sank so quickly that "between 40 and 50 drowned between decks" before they had a chance to escape, and several others drowned trying to swim to shore.[38] Two ships that were anchored nearby lowered their boats and rowed survivors to shore, but "receiving no Shelter, from the Inclemency of the Weather, about 70 of them were frozen to Death, some on the Beach, and others in the Marshes, as they were scattered about, in Search of Houses."[39] When the tempest passed, county residents did what they could for the survivors, and Lieutenant Governor William Gooch provided government assistance, but only ninety lived. The Swiss lost most of what they brought with them.[40]

In the days following the accident, the survivors said they planned to continue to Eden, but most of them later changed their minds and settled elsewhere.[41] In a letter Byrd wrote naturalist John Bartram in March, he blamed

34. William Byrd II to John Perceval, Earl of Egmont, July 2, 1737, in Byrd, Byrd, and Byrd, *Correspondence*, 2:521.

35. McIlwaine, Hall, and Hillman, *Executive Journals*, 4:426, 432.

36. *Virginia Gazette* (Parks), Nov. 24, 1738.

37. *Virginia Gazette* (Parks), Jan. 19, 1738 (Old Style); and Lloyd Haynes Williams, "The Tragic Shipwreck of the Protestant Switzers," *William and Mary Quarterly*, 3rd series, vol. 9 (1952): 541–42.

38. *Virginia Gazette* (Parks), Jan. 19, 1738.

39. Ibid.

40. Ibid.; *Virginia Gazette* (Parks), Jan. 12, 1738; and Williams, "Tragic Shipwreck," 542.

the accident on "the villany or stupidity of the master," but he also revealed a kind of pragmatic optimism about the project. "Some few of these unhappy wretches," Byrd wrote, "are gone upon my land to make a beginning, and will soon be followd by more." He sent Samuel Tschiffely off "to Philadelphia to try if he can prevail with any of his countrymen to come and settle on my land."[42] Some Germans traveled down to Virginia and settled in Richmond, but it was not the large group Byrd was hoping to settle in Eden. He reminded Tschiffely, "[M]y land was not to be parcelled out in small tracts to men that came singly and were not able to pay for them."[43] But the Helvetian Society was not able to provide another colony.

Still, Byrd did not give up but tried to find other sources for his colonists. Apparently he struck a land deal with Johann Ochs involving 31,000 acres. But by the fall of 1740 there were problems, and Ochs tried to back out of the deal. "Now you must be a very [poor] lawyer, or at least must imagin me so, when you say this [agreement] will not bind you in any court or country upon earth," Byrd wrote in September. "Your intent of parting with the land thus purchased to other persons, makes no difference in the case, so long as you judge fit to transact the matter in your own name, and for your own use only."[44] Despite the threatening tone of the letter, Byrd let Ochs out of the project. He then offered the land to a variety of candidates, including some Ulster Scots living in Pennsylvania and Scottish settlers who had landed in Norfolk, but again he had no success. When Byrd died in 1744, Eden remained a community only on paper.[45]

The demise of King William's Town and Eden marked an end to the first phase of urban development on the Southside, and it was another twenty years before someone else attempted to establish towns in the region. Byrd's success in Richmond and Petersburg had played a role in the failure of his two backcountry projects. Farmers living in the Southside had no access to navigable rivers and were forced to rely on the two fall-zone ports, to the detriment of the development of any towns in the interior. The colonial government contributed to the monopoly Richmond and Petersburg had on Southside trade by passing additions to the Tobacco Inspection Act of 1730, which required all tobacco be sent to the nearest fall zone town for inspection and export. The nature of tobacco production and the reliance on slave labor simply meant that there was little need for backcountry towns to provide goods and services.[46] Until the region's economy diversified and its population grew large enough to support an economic center, a Southside town

41. *Virginia Gazette* (Parks), Jan. 12, 1738, and Jan. 19, 1738.

42. William Byrd II to John Bartram, Mar. 23, 1738/39, in Byrd, Byrd, and Byrd, *Correspondence* 2:531.

43. William Byrd II to Samuel Tschiffely, Nov. 15, 1740, in Byrd, Byrd, and Byrd, *Correspondence* 2:572.

44. William Byrd II to Johann Rudolph Ochs, Nov. 5, 1740, in Byrd, Byrd, and Byrd, *Correspondence* 2:555.

45. Reps, *Tidewater*, 198.

46. Farmer, *In the Absence*, 7–8.

could only flourish if it could fill another niche. The obvious answer for future town promoters was to develop a town around a county court.

Dalstonburg/Marysville/Charlotte Court House

When the Virginia Assembly created Lunenburg County in 1745, Clement Read became clerk of court. He later served the county as a burgess and surveyor.[47] A wealthy Southside planter, Read invested heavily in lands along the Roanoke River, building a home in the 1730s known as Bushy Forest.[48] During the French and Indian War, Lieutenant Governor Robert Dinwiddie ordered that a powder magazine be established in the area, and he placed Read in charge of its construction and maintenance.[49] The structure attracted people who were interested in settling nearby, possibly drawn by a sense of security. Recognizing the economic potential of the site, Read laid out a town at the magazine in 1757. In August of that same year, the county court appointed him to oversee the construction of a road from the Lunenburg courthouse and a nearby church to the road "that leads through the new Town over the county Bridge just above his Plantation."[50]

In 1759, through his connections in Williamsburg, Read was able to have his town chartered only two years after it was established, despite its limited population. Possibly a wartime measure, the act chartering the town, which sought to enable frontier inhabitants "better to defend their lives and properties on any sudden incursion of the enemy," pointed out only that lots had been laid out and that "many persons had subscribed" for them.[51] Essentially, the act chartered one hundred acres of woodland that belonged to Read and John Pleasant, who later sold Read his holdings. The town was named Dalstonburg after Catherine Dalston, the wife of Lieutenant Governor Francis Fauquier.[52] It had no industry, no trade, and when the war ended in 1763, the town's population melted away. No lot sales had been recorded.

47. Hening, *Statutes* 5:383–85; "Order Book," Lunenburg County Courthouse, Lunenburg, VA, 1:2, 3:177; Alice Read Rouse, *Clement and Madame Read of Bushy Forest, Lunenburg County, Virginia, Their Eight Children, Their Descendants and Allied Families* (Cincinnati: Johnson & Hardin, 1930), 20; and Landon C. Bell, *The Old Free State: A Contribution to the History of Lunenburg County and Southside Virginia* (Baltimore: Genealogical Publishing, 1974), 345.

48. "Land Office Patents," Library of Virginia, Richmond, 29:112, 36:563; and Bell, *Old Free State*, 88, 102, 104. Read's holdings appear on early editions of the Fry and Jefferson map. See Fry and Jefferson, "Map of the most Inhabited" in Stephenson and McKee, *Virginia in Maps*, Map II-21 C.

49. "Governor Dinwiddie to Colonel Clement Read, Aug'st 23rd, 1756," in Robert Dinwiddie, *The Official Records of Robert Dinwiddie, Lieutenant-Governor of the Colony of Virginia, 1751–1758*, ed. R. A. Brock, 2 vols. (Richmond: Virginia Historical Society, 1884) 2:485–86; and "Governor Dinwiddie to Colonel Read, Decemb'r 15th, 1756," in Dinwiddie, *Official Records* 2:564.

50. "Order Book," Lunenburg County, 4:369; and Timothy S. Aailsworth et al., *Charlotte County: Rich Indeed* (Richmond: Whittet & Shepperson, 1979), 303. See also "Order Book," Lunenburg County, 5:23, 44, 6:18.

51. Hening, *Statutes* 7:305–7.

52. Aailsworth et al., *Charlotte County*, 303–4.

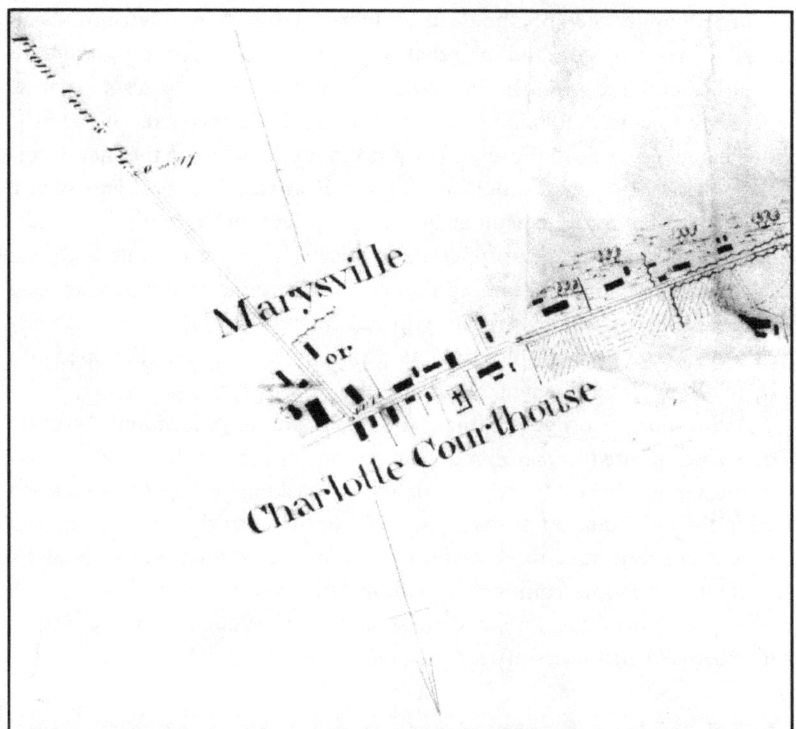

"Map of a Section of Territory Adjacent to Marysville or Charlotte Court House," c. 1840. Archives and Records Division, Map Collection, Library of Virginia, Richmond. Courtesy of the Library of Virginia.

Read died the same year. All of his land holdings were divided between his sons Thomas and Clement.[53] Clement, who received the Dalstonburg tract, realized that the town was doomed to failure unless he could attract settlers. When the Assembly divided Lunenburg County to create Charlotte County in 1765, Clement quickly proposed that the "place called the Magazien" become the county seat, agreeing to sweeten the deal by building a thirty-by-twenty-two-foot courthouse and a two-room prison.[54] John Tankersley ran a tavern nearby until his death in 1782, mostly to serve people when court was in session.[55] This small assemblage of buildings, located at a T-shaped intersection, became the nucleus for the newly reborn Dalstonburg. The town grew organically, the elder Read's original plan having been forsaken because of the lack of inhabitants.

53. "Will Book," Lunenburg County Courthouse, Lunenburg, VA, 2:278–84; "Order Book," Lunenburg County, 9:86; and "Deed Book," Lunenburg County, 9:6–8.

54. "Order Book, Charlotte County," Charlotte County Clerk's Office, Charlotte Court House, VA, 1:4, 27; and Hening *Statutes* 8:41–42.

55. "Deed Book, Charlotte County," Charlotte County Clerk's Office, Charlotte Court House, VA, 1:27.

In September of 1765, the Read brothers arranged with their mother to transfer three tracts of land in exchange for the widow's portion granted to her in her husband's will. In the agreement she acquired 724 acres of farmland, sixty-four acres surrounding a grist mill, and "Seventy acres of Land situated lying and being in the town of Dalstonburgh," including the "new Ordinary House, Courthouse, and Prison."[56] Mary Read was an impressive woman, who through her business acumen became proprietor of Dalstonburg in addition to managing her farm property and raising seven young children.[57] But her town, increasingly becoming known as Marysville (modern Charlotte Court House), grew slowly. Even with the court, it simply failed to attract many businesses or a sizeable population and as a result never developed into a large urban center during the colonial period.

Dalstonburg's slow development was due in part to its location. Charlotte County was located too far east to reap the benefits of the dramatic increase in settlers migrating into Virginia from the north along the Great Wagon Road during the third quarter of the eighteenth century. But despite this setback, Dalstonburg continued to exist as a small village until the area finally had a sufficient population from which to draw citizens and attract trade. Playing host to the county court assured Dalstonburg's continued existence until it had other elements necessary for growth.

New London

Another Southside court town further west experienced a fate quite the opposite of Dalstonburg. When the Assembly created Bedford County in 1753, William Calloway proposed building a county town on his land. Calloway was a member of one of the elite families that had monopolized power and land in the area for a generation. He served as an officer in the French and Indian War and was elected as Bedford County's first representative to the House of Burgesses. He was involved in a number of financial enterprises, including a mercantile business and an important ironworks. He also had acquired over seventeen thousand acres of land.[58]

Initially Calloway faced a rival in one Matthew Talbot, who successfully petitioned to have the prison bounds laid out on his land.[59] But in August 1754, Calloway offered to donate one hundred acres of land to the court at a fork in the road near his mill on Buffalo Run. Even though he would not own the town itself, Calloway envisioned a rise in property value of the surrounding land, as well as increased business at the mill from future town residents. The

56. Ibid., 1:24, 26, 27; and "Order Book," Charlotte County, 1:83–84.

57. Aailsworth et al., *Charlotte County*, 304; and Rouse, *Clement and Madame Read*, 33.

58. Ann Smart Martin, "Buying into the World of Goods: Eighteenth-Century Consumerism and the Retail Trade from London to the Virginia Frontier" (Ph.D. diss., College of William and Mary in Virginia, 1993), 222.

59. Hening, *Statutes* 6:381–83; and "Bedford County Order Book," Bedford County Courthouse, Bedford, VA, 1A:8, 25, 1B:3, 4, 12, 17.

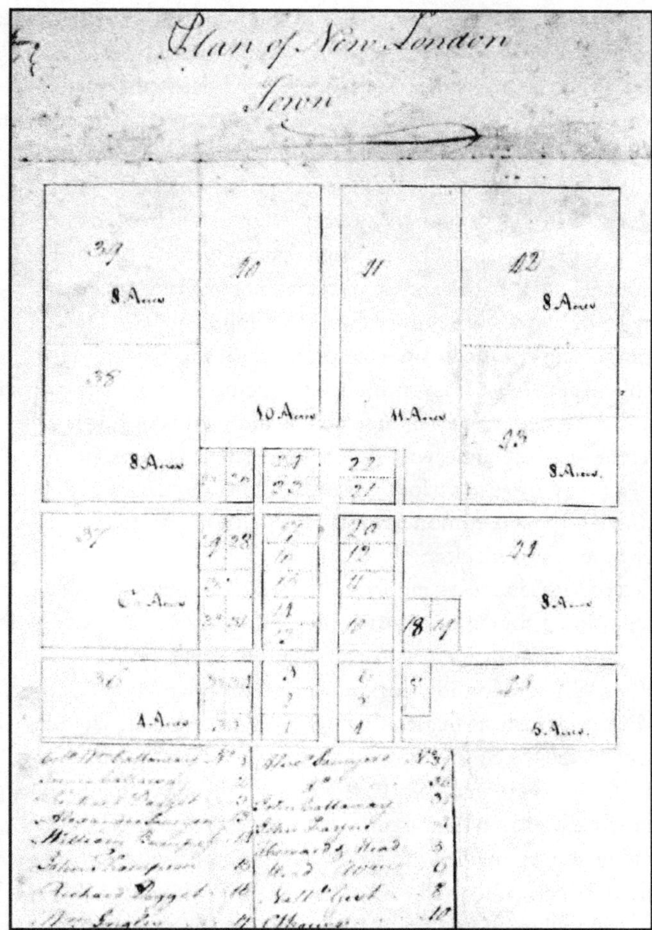

"Plan of New London Town," n.d. In "Deed Book," A:434, Bedford County Courthouse, Bedford, Virginia.

court agreed to the plan and commissioned Calloway to build a timber prison and a rough building to serve as a courthouse. The court met in the new building in November. The next year, the justices appointed trustees for the new town and authorized them to lay out and sell lots.[60] Calloway did not transfer title to the land for three years, and when the deed finally was drawn in 1757, the court ordered trustees Richard Calloway, Zachary Isbel, and Benjamin Howard to lay out the town in half-acre lots. To encourage the town's success, the court stipulated that a sixteen-by-twenty-foot frame house had to be built on each lot within a year of its sale, and a brick chimney be added to each house within four years. People bought the lots through blind subscription so that purchasers did not know the location of their lots until they were drawn

60. "Bedford County Order Book," 1A:34–35, 175, 222, 1B:50–51; and Daisy I. Read, *New London: Today and Yesterday* (Lynchburg, VA: J. P. Bell, 1950), 28.

at the court May 1758. As a testament to the founders' vision and the hope they had for the future of the new town, they named it New London.[61]

The plan of the new town was a regular grid pattern created by two parallel avenues crossed by a main street. Smaller cross streets, parallel to the main street, cut the grid into blocks five lots wide and one lot deep. The courthouse was located on a one-acre tract on the corner of the main street and the southern avenue (lot 10). The lots on the two central blocks all fronted the main street. The block consisting of lots twenty-eight through thirty-one had four of the tracts fronting the avenues and an interior tract fronting the cross street. Unfortunately the plat does not reveal future development plans for New London. The arrangements of the lots north and south of the avenue suggest that the five-lot block pattern would continue—lots facing the main street or arranged to front the avenues. However, the spacing and widths of future cross streets and avenues are left undrawn. Twenty-one different subscribers originally purchased thirty-three town lots in New London. Then, instead of holding the remaining land as a common for future expansion, the trustees sold the remainder in ten large blocks.[62]

An act of the General Assembly formally established New London in 1761. It also appointed four more trustees and established a fair held twice each year.[63] A powder magazine was constructed in New London to help protect the frontier. With the confidence bestowed on the town by colony officials, the Bedford County justices made attempts to improve public facilities. In 1766 the court ordered the construction of a new courthouse, "to-wit twenty four by thirty six feet 12 feet Pitch, two 12 feet Square Rooms with a Brick Chimney a fire place in each Room Wainscoted 4 feet High & Plaistered above the Wainscoting to be well Wrought, with six Glass Windows," underpinned with brick piers one and one-half feet tall.[64] Two years later the whole structure was moved fourteen feet to the east and raised three feet to accommodate a fourteen-foot addition to the west end to house two jury rooms.[65] In addition to the new courthouse, the town was also the home of an academy, which began operating as early as 1765. An Anglican church was built on the academy lands. It was originally a log building but later was replaced with a frame structure. The Anglicans, who were eventually outnumbered, shared their church with Ulster Scots Presbyterians.[66]

61. "Deed Book," Bedford County Courthouse, Bedford, VA, A:113–14, 434; "Bedford County Order Book," 1B:73–74; and Martin, "Buying," 223.

62. "Deed Book," Bedford County, A:434. Willard Pierson Jr. credits the plan to R. Calloway, Howard, and Wm. Mead. See Willard Pierson Jr., "John Hook: 'A Merchant of Colonial Virginia,'" Honors thesis, Duke Univ., 1962, 27.

63. Hening, *Statutes* 7:473–76.

64. "Bedford County Order Book," 3:270–71.

65. Ibid., 3:440.

66. F. B. Kegley, *Kegley's Virginia Frontier: The Beginning of the Southwest, The Roanoke of Colonial Days, 1740–1783* (Roanoke: Southwest Virginia Historical Society, 1938), 322; and Read, *New London*, 37–38.

Unlike Lunenburg and Charlotte, Bedford County stood in a propitious location that enabled it to profit from the burgeoning population of the backcountry. The county was located at a juncture where settlers from the North could either turn east into the Southside or continue on into North Carolina. Throughout the third quarter of the eighteenth century there was no shortage of traffic through Bedford County. In 1756 James Maury, a minister from Louisa County, noted three hundred people moving through in one week.[67] Bedford's county town stood on a main thoroughfare from Richmond into the Roanoke Valley, making it very attractive as a distribution center for merchants. Sitting 150 miles west of Richmond, it was far enough away to build its own clientele from the surrounding countryside without direct competition from the Tidewater town.

William Calloway and his son James operated the first store in New London (lot 1), providing goods for county planters and buying their tobacco and hemp crops. Their store was in business by 1750 even before New London was founded.[68] After 1768, the Calloways were supplied by the Scottish mercantile firm of James and Robert Donald and Company, which later opened a branch of its own in New London. But the Calloways' chief competition came from James Hook, who established a store in 1766. Hook worked as the representative of another Scottish firm, William Donald and Company. In 1772 he struck out on his own in partnership with David Ross, who operated a firm in Petersburg. In addition to tobacco and hemp, Hook occasionally supplemented the trade by buying local ginseng crops and deerskins. By the time of the Revolution there were at least four merchants sending backcountry products overland from New London to Richmond and Petersburg in exchange for manufactured goods.[69]

New London prospered during the Revolution. When he traveled through the town in 1781, Jean Marquis de Chastellux, a major general in the French army, described it as "an infant town, but already pretty considerable, for there are at least seventy or eighty houses."[70] The town was home to some three hundred residents. New London was becoming an important supply center. People established gun repair shops near the arsenal, and war industries flourished. Gunpowder was manufactured there, and there was a prison for captured British soldiers.[71] Just as the last war had brought a measure of prosperity to

67. James Maury, "Letter of Rev. James Maury to Philip Ludwell on the Defense of the Frontiers of Virginia, 1756," *Virginia Magazine of History and Biography* 19 (1911): 293.

68. Read, *New London*, 30.

69. "Advertisement," *Virginia Gazette* (Rind), July 18, 1766; Pierson, "John Hook," 27–30, 32, 59–61; Read, *New London*, 133; and Martin, "Buying," 223. For information on the layout of Hook's store specifically and retail space in Virginia generally, see Ann Smart Martin, "Commercial Space as Consumption Arena: Retail Stores in Early Virginia," in Sally McMurry and Annmarie Adams, eds., *People, Power, Places*, Perspectives in Vernacular Architecture, VIII (Knoxville: Univ. of Tennessee Press, 2000), 201–18.

70. François Jean Marquis de Chastellux, *Travels in North-America in the Years 1780, 1781, and 1782*, 2 vols. (London: G. G. J. and J. Robinson, 1787), 2:117.

71. Martin, "Buying," 223.

Dalstonburg, the Revolution was a boon to New London. But with the coming of peace, the town's economy suffered. The repair facilities closed, and the magazine was removed to another location. With the loss of the war industries, New London relied more heavily on its role as the Bedford County seat. Even so, a number of businesses left. New London was suffering from its proximity to a new vibrant town that was flourishing just a dozen miles away at a ferry site on the James River—Lynchburg.

Then in 1781 the Assembly divided Bedford County, and New London was left standing on the edge of newly created Campbell County, an undesirable location for a county seat. The old Bedford County courthouse reverted to Calloway and for a time served as the meeting site for a district court, but soon it too ceased to meet there. An academy still operated in New London, but it could not continue long without the sustained business brought by the court.[72] For a time, the road to Richmond continued to bring travelers passing through New London who stayed at local taverns. One such traveler, John Howell Briggs, who was on his way to visit Sweet Springs in 1804, found New London "to be in a declining state, a number of handsome & comfortable houses are tenantless and there seems to be but few inhabitants. It was some years ago a very thriving place, and owes its decline to the removal of the district Court from it." Briggs also noted another problem that haunted other urban endeavors in the backcountry: "The whole of the Town almost is the property of Colo. Calloway and this has also I have no doubt, had a tendency to reduce it to its present state."[73] Although it showed occasional signs of revival, New London never regained its former glory and instead became a rural farming community.

Peytonsburg

Two Southside county towns that failed to develop were the projects of the same individual. James Roberts Jr. began his career as a town founder in Halifax County. In 1753 the county courthouse was located at a place called Punchy Spring near the center of the county. For several years the brick structure stood alone, but Roberts saw an opportunity to make some money and laid out 104 acres next to the courthouse into a town. In 1759 the Assembly, noting that "several persons are now settled there, and many more would soon settle if the same was by law erected into a town," officially created the town of Peytonsburg.[74] It was part of the same act passed during the French and Indian War that established Dalstonburg, noting the need for security in the backcountry.

72. Ibid., 223–34.

73. John Howell Briggs, "Journal of a Trip to the Sweet Springs, commencing July 23d and ending September 29th 1804," in *First Resorts: A Visit to Virginia's Springs* (Richmond: Virginia Historical Society, 1987), 27.

74. Hening, *Statutes* 7:305–7; "Book of Pleas," Halifax County Courthouse, Halifax, VA, 1:5, 11, 21, 35, 94; and Frances Hallam Hurt, *Eighteenth-Century Landmarks of Pittsylvania County, Virginia* (Lynchburg, VA: Blue Ridge Lithographic, 1967), 2.

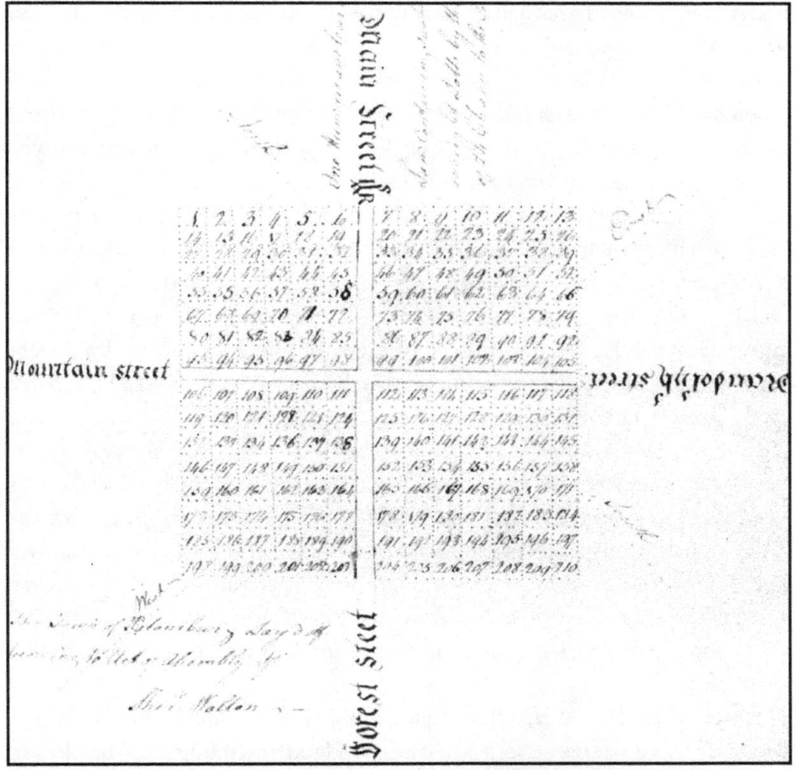

“The Town of Patonsburg Layed off According to Act of Assembly by Sherd. Walton,” 1761. In “Deed Book, Halifax County,” 3:149, Halifax County Courthouse, Halifax, Virginia.

Roberts took a chance in the timing of Peytonsburg. He did not gain title to the land his town occupied until 1760.[75]

The plan for Peytonsburg is one of the strangest town designs in Virginia. Sherwood Walton, an assistant surveyor for Halifax County, laid out the town, though Roberts himself may have drawn up the plan.[76] The town was oriented forty-five degrees off the usual compass points, probably to follow the lines of an existing road or trail.[77] It had 208 half-acre lots, but only two streets, leaving 154 lots without any access. The streets cut the town into four blocks, two with forty-eight lots and two with fifty-six lots. Both streets had two names, changing at the town’s only intersection. Main Street became Forest (or Royal Forest) and Mountain (or Montaine) became Randolph Street.[78] The oddness of the

75. “Deed Book, Halifax County,” Halifax County Courthouse, Halifax, VA, 2:174–75.

76. Hughes, *Surveyors*, 135.

77. Such was also the case with Salisbury, a town founded in the North Carolina backcountry in 1755. See Hendricks, “Town Development,” 87–90. Another possible, though unlikely, explanation may be found in book 1, chapter 6, of Roman architect and engineer Marcus Vitruvius Pollio’s *The Ten Books on Architecture*, in which he suggests orienting street plans according to “climatic conditions.” See Vitruvius, *The Ten Books on Architecture* (New York: Dover, 1960), 24–31.

78. See “Deed Book,” Halifax County, 2:177, 266.

design may reflect a gradually evolving street plan. The court ordered a new street to be surveyed and opened in 1761, for example. Or the plan may simply reveal a delay in actually laying out the lots and plotting them, as the court also ordered in 1761.[79] Whatever the case, the plan for Peytonsburg was anything but convenient. In a town of 210 lots, only fifty-four had direct access to a street, and any new street that was established robbed acreage from the adjoining lots.

Despite the peculiar plan, Roberts sold several lots during the first years of his town's existence.[80] Five individual mercantile concerns, four of which were based in fall-line towns, bought lots. A wheelwright and a carpenter set up shop in the town, and three ordinaries opened nearby.[81] During the waning years of the French and Indian War, Peytonsburg became an important supply center, attracting merchants, gunsmiths, blacksmiths, and farriers. Some tavern keepers opened shop to house an increasing number of travelers. After the war, warehouses opened and the town began to profit from the grain trade. But Peytonsburg's initial success was short lived. In 1766 Pittsylvania County was cut out of the western section of Halifax, and Peytonsburg, just inside the Pittsylvania County line, was ill placed to serve as a seat for the new county.[82] The Halifax court continued to meet there until that county could be surveyed and a site chosen near the center for its new courthouse. Peytonsburg's days were numbered; it was doomed to lose the court and all of the prestige that went with it.[83]

Roberts quickly realized that Peytonsburg faced a doubtful future. In desperate financial straits, he sold 1,570 acres of land, including sixty-one lots in Peytonsburg, to Roger Atkinson, a merchant in Dinwiddie County.[84] But the town did not fold immediately. During the Revolution it again became an important supply center, attracting tradesmen such as blacksmiths and wagon makers, as well as merchants. There was even a factory that produced canteens for the army. However, with the end of the war, Peytonsburg once more went into decline. In 1778 Roberts sold his remaining lots to another merchant, John Wimbish, who eventually consolidated the old Peytonsburg property as a homestead and a store.[85] As the town dwindled, even the name fell out of use. Traveling home from Philadelphia in 1791, South Carolina Congressman William Loughton Smith passed through what was left of Peytonsburg: "Breakfasted at Halifax Old Town; or Old Town, as it is called: it has no other pre-

79. "Book of Pleas," Halifax County, 3:188, 273.

80. "Deed Book," Halifax County, 2:176–81; 3:6–8, 238–44. See also "Book of Pleas," Halifax County, vol. 5, pt. 2:485.

81. Farmer, *In the Absence*, 57–58.

82. Maud Carter Clement, *The History of Pittsylvania County, Virginia* (Lynchburg, VA: J. P. Bell, 1929), 57; Pocahontas Wight Edmunds, *History of Halifax*, 2 vols. (N.p.: n.p., 1978?), 2:30–31; and Hening, *Statutes* 8:205.

83. "Book of Pleas," Halifax County, 6:157.

84. "Deed Book," Halifax County, 2:294–97.

85. Ibid., 5:203; Hurt, *Eighteenth-Century*, 2; Farmer, *In the Absence*, 58; Clement, *History of Pittsylvania*, 95; and Edmunds, *History of Halifax* 2:32.

tension to the name than by containing two or three old houses inhabited by some wretched old women: I, however, got a decent breakfast and went on."[86]

Chatham/Callands

The majority of Roberts's remaining landholdings stood in Pittsylvania County, and he was appointed to serve on the new county court. As a justice for the county he was privy to knowledge of court proceedings. Moving quickly, he located land near the center of Pittsylvania. When the court met at the Halifax courthouse in Peytonsburg in June 1767, the justices decided to meet next at Roberts's new plantation on Sandy River.[87] Possibly because of his haste, Roberts had obtained the land through questionable circumstances, buying it from John Morton, who either had yet to get a deed from Hannah Austin, or was working as her agent. The court stipulated that Roberts had to obtain a clear title to the property from Austin. He did not get a deed to the property until 1771.[88]

When the court met again, Roberts was hard at work securing the county seat. He converted the house he was building on the Sandy River property into the county prison. Then the court ordered county surveyor John Donelson to run a line twenty-seven miles west from the midpoint of the Halifax/Pittsylvania County line and find a site nearby for the courthouse. Roberts's new land just happened to be near that point, and he offered to build a courthouse "of the same Dimensions of Halifax old Courthouse" on the property and that it would be finished in eighteen months.[89] Anxious to make a profit from the venture, Roberts, with partner Thomas Tunstall, obtained a license to open an ordinary at the courthouse. He also received permission to build a gristmill.[90] Finally, well aware of the early success of Peytonsburg, Roberts laid out fifty acres of land for a town. In 1769 the Assembly chartered it, naming it Chatham in honor of William Pitt, Earl of Chatham, for whom the county had also been named.[91]

Roberts's preoccupation with money-making ventures kept him from his court responsibilities. He became sheriff in 1769 but was fined less than a year later for neglecting his duties. His makeshift prison continually had to be repaired, and he had yet to build a courthouse. In 1770 an impatient court issued an ultimatum: "unless the said James Roberts shall give Bond with sufficient security to build and Compleat the said Courthouse within two Months from this time that he be immediately after prosecuted in the General Court."[92] Apparently he completed the task, because he was not prosecuted and there was

86. William Loughton Smith, *Journal of William Loughton Smith*, ed. Albert Matthews (Cambridge, MA: The Univ. Press, 1917), 71.

87. "Pittsylvania County Court Records," Pittsylvania County Courthouse, Chatham, VA, 1:3.

88. Ibid.; and "Deed Book," Pittsylvania County, 2:70–71.

89. "Pittsylvania County Court Records," 1:5, 7, 19.

90. Ibid., 1:11, 85.

91. Hening, *Statutes* 8:417.

92. "Pittsylvania County Court Records," 1:93, 197–98, 209.

a courthouse standing in 1772.[93] Still the court had had enough. When the prison deteriorated beyond tolerance in 1771, Roberts did not get the contract to build a new one. Instead, the task fell to Michael Rowland.[94]

Chatham (not the modern county seat of the same name) shared some of the early success Peytonsburg experienced. By 1768, a Scotsman named Samuel Calland opened a store that flourished there. Later, the mercantile firm of James Smith, Murdock and Company started an operation in Chatham. Thomas Brune built a second tavern in town in 1771.[95] Nonetheless, James Roberts did not experience the same success as his town. Years of unsuccessful land speculation and the demise of Peytonsburg had ruined him. Always in bad financial straits, Roberts was never able to post the bonds required by the court for his building contracts. Apparently his fellow justices merely overlooked that fact. However, during his term as sheriff, Roberts failed to turn thousands of pounds of tobacco, collected as tax levies, over to the court. The county and several individuals who were held liable for the missing taxes sued him. In 1772 he was forced to mortgage all of his possessions, including Sandy River Plantation and his town.[96] Finally in January 1775, an unusual advertisement appeared in *The Virginia Gazette*:

> TO BE SOLD, On the fourth Thursday in March next, being Pittsylvania Court Day, by virtue of a Deed of Trust from James Roberts, A VALUABLE Tract of LAND lying in the said County, containing about 400 Acres, being the Land whereon the Court house stands, near 100 Acres of which are cleared, and in good Order for Cropping. It is well calculated for a Taverner, as there are sundry Houses built for that purpose, and is rented, this Year, for sixty Pounds. There are 50 Acres laid off in Lots for a Town, on several of which are Houses built that will suit Tradesmen.[97]

Chatham outlived the demise of its founder only a few years. In 1777 the Assembly divided Pittsylvania County, and the court moved the county seat east toward the new center of the county. Although it was known as Competition for a time, the new county seat later commandeered the name Chatham as well as the court.[98] Meanwhile, the original Chatham continued to exist because of the Smith and Calland stores. Eventually the two operations combined under Calland's leadership, and the buildings around the store became

93. "Deed Book," Pittsylvania County, 3:79; and Hurt, *Eighteenth-Century*, 4.

94. "Pittsylvania County Court Records," 1:290.

95. Ibid., 1:49; "Deed Book," Pittsylvania County, 5:345; and Clement, *History of Pittsylvania*, 100–101.

96. "Pittsylvania County Court Records," 2:105; "Deed Book," Pittsylvania County, 3:79; and Hurt, *Eighteenth-Century*, 4.

97. William Tunstall, "Advertisement," *Virginia Gazette* (Dixon and Hunter), Jan. 14, 1775. Apparently the sale was not successful because a similar advertisement appeared in April. See William Tunstall, "Advertisement," *Virginia Gazette* (Dixon and Hunter), Apr. 14, 1775.

98. Hening, *Statues* 9:241–43; and Farmer, *In the Absence*, 57. Farmer mistakenly thought the two towns were the same, but Callands is located eleven miles west of the current town of Chatham.

While there are no plats of the original Chatham, two buildings still stand there: the 1772 courthouse, which Samuel Callands later used for his store, and this building, the Clerk's Office, built in 1767. Photo courtesy of Lee Hendricks Turpin.

known as Callands.[99] Just as had happened with Roberts's first town, Chatham survived only as the location of a Scots store.

The failure of the original Chatham to continue functioning as a town once it lost its court is emblematic of the problems of the settlement of Southside Virginia. That only two Southside Virginia towns of the six founded in the colonial period (Dalstonburg—modern Charlotte Court House—and New London) still exist as anything more than place names is astounding given the size and resources of the region. Sparsely populated, the Southside did not have the critical mass needed to support many towns during the period, though its colonial urban experience was not very different from the wealthier and more heavily populated Piedmont.

99. Madalene Vaden Fitzgerald, *Pittsylvania: Homes and People of the Past* (Chatham, VA: Madalene Vaden Fitzgerald, 1974), 55.

The first two towns attempted in the Southside (King William's Town and Eden) were entrepreneurial efforts by wealthy individuals who intended their communities to be populated by religious refugees from the European continent. Much as George Brent and Alexander Spotswood attempted to attract Huguenots and Lutherans to towns in the Piedmont, the first two William Byrds also based the success of their backcountry towns on being able to attract religious groups and keep them in the Southside. But therein lay the problem. They were too anxious to establish King William's Town and Eden before a natural population had grown large enough to be able to support a town. Quite simply, both towns were too far west. When the Huguenots first made their way to the Manakin Town tract, there was not even a town at the falls of the James, only a fort. Almost four decades later, Eden was still situated much too far west, approximately one hundred miles from Petersburg, to have any real chance of becoming a viable town, no matter how idyllic the landscape. And when William Byrd II was peddling his ideas for Eden in 1738, Petersburg was only five years old and was far from a flourishing urban center itself.

Another thing that kept King William's Town and Eden from succeeding was the approach both Byrds employed in looking for colonists. They wanted town-size populations immediately and were either unwilling or unable to take the time or devote the finances necessary to find and maintain individuals or families who actually wanted to move that far into the backcountry. There were inherent risks in this kind of venture, as William Byrd II learned when his Eden colonists were shipwrecked. With the loss of its citizenry, the project never recovered. Trying for the big prize, Byrd had gambled and lost.

Even though William Byrd I succeeded in getting a large group of refugees to the site of his town, he faced problems. First, there was the lack of trust that existed from Byrd's first associations with the Huguenots, when he waylaid them with the assistance of Lieutenant Governor Nicholson. Being sent far from where they had expected to settle must have left the colonists feeling extremely vulnerable. Then, despite aid from the colonial government and Byrd's own financial assistance, the project was grossly underfunded, forcing the desperate colonists to almost literally sell the clothes off their backs. Many of the Huguenots were craftsmen who needed a surrounding population to support a craft economy based at King William's Town. They were not farmers, nor did they have any desire to be, so many of them left. And then there were problems with the community's leadership, not only the rivalries and petty jealousies of the Huguenot leaders themselves but also the patronizing attitude of Byrd, who often seemed to be more interested in profit than the actual needs of the citizenry.

The four towns established during the second phase of activity (Chatham, Dalstonburg, Peytonsburg, and New London) were alive at the end of the colonial period, though eventually Chatham and New London declined and Peytonsburg ceased to exist entirely. For the most part, the Southside remained a region dominated by separate plantations. At the close of the colonial period it had a population of only about two thousand inhabitants, almost half of whom were enslaved. Residents received most of their goods and services from country stores and itinerant tradesmen.[100] Central place theory does not come into play in the Southside because no places developed from internal factors causing populations to gather together. The only places that developed were towns with court responsibilities (although New London was founded at an isolated mill site and Dalstonburg at a powder magazine).

Another factor that came into play in the life of Southside towns was stores. Part of mercantile theory emphasizes the role of external trade forces aiding in the creation of central places. Chatham, Peytonsburg, and New London were all important trade outlets with stores that maintained ties to entrepôt towns on the fall zone, particularly Petersburg. Chatham was home to two stores, and five mercantile concerns (four based in fall zone towns) invested in the development of Peytonsburg.[101] The most successful of all the Southside towns during the colonial period, New London, benefited the most from its entrepôt connections not only because of its connections to the fall zone ports but also because of its proximity to a branch of the Great Wagon Road that turned into the Southside en route to North Carolina. It had at least four mercantile operations and had ties not only with Petersburg to the east but with stores in Staunton to the west. And New London could benefit from servicing its own hinterland as well as the traffic of people moving south. Another part of mercantile theory holds that, in exchange for finished goods, central places served as collection points for local frontier products. This was true at least in the case of New London, where members of the surrounding community collected ginseng and hunted for deerskins to bring into town to trade.

The most useful theory for a description of the Southside urban experience, however, is once again staple theory. The Southside was even more dependant on the tobacco trade than the Piedmont, and the export nature of the crop and the presence of a large enslaved population diminished the need for central places. One of the ironies in the history of urban development in Virginia is that the Southside was incredibly supportive of the fall-zone ports of Petersburg and Richmond, to the detriment of its own towns.[102]

Important government installations provided the impetus for establishing Southside towns. A public arsenal became the site of Dalstonburg, and the town later became home to the Charlotte County court. Courthouses also provided the basis for the other Southside towns: New London, Peytonsburg, and Chatham. But while a courthouse was enough to establish a town, it was

100. Robert D. Mitchell, "Metropolitan Chesapeake: Reflections on Town Formation in Colonial Virginia and Maryland," in Lois Green Carr, ed., *The Chesapeake and Beyond: A Celebration* (Crownsville: Maryland Historical and Cultural Publications, 1992), 111.

101. Farmer, *In the Absence*, 57, 186.

102. Ibid., 7, 8, 190.

not enough to help it flourish. Still, the court could mean continued existence. Until the demographic and/or economic factors shifted more favorably for Dalstonburg, it depended on the county court to sustain it.

It seems that in Southside Virginia, much more than in the Piedmont, it took a war to help a town prosper and grow. Indeed, the act that chartered both Dalstonburg and Peytonsburg mentioned security. Both towns benefited from serving as supply centers during the French and Indian War. Although New London was founded as a county town, it was also established in hopes of enticing settlers to live together, "which will enable them the better to defend themselves on any sudden incursions of an enemy."[103] That proved to be the case during both the French and Indian War and the Revolution, bringing the town new prosperity. But such life was fleeting, based on a temporary and unusual set of circumstances. When the theater of war shifted elsewhere, all three towns slipped back into their prewar existence. Large-scale economic demands simply did not yet exist for the long term.

Geographic location was a major factor shaping colonial Southside towns. The obsession with locating a county seat in the center of a county spelled the doom of New London, Peytonsburg, and Chatham. With the life support of the court removed, the towns had little reason to exist. Only New London, positioned on a major east-west road, had a chance to outlive its role of county seat and become an important center for trade, and it had the added advantage of being home to an academy. However, its location ultimately proved fatal, because one town's proximity to another posed a difficult balancing act. In northern Virginia, Waterford, Leesburg, and Alexandria functioned well together, funneling agricultural products to the coast. Leesburg stood thirty-five miles inland from Alexandria, far enough away to have a hinterland of its own. And while Waterford's situation near Leesburg, only some ten miles distant, would normally have been detrimental for a colonial Virginia town, its unique religious and cultural character helped to shield it.

New London flourished as an important trading center until a rival emerged at the end of the century just twelve miles away. During the colonial period, Lynchburg was merely the location of a ferry, a tobacco warehouse, and one or two houses. But when it was laid out as a town at the end of the century, Lynchburg became a rival too formidable for New London to continue in its role as a supply center. As a result, it devolved into an agricultural hamlet. That Dalstonburg, located some fifty miles away from New London, its nearest Southside neighbor, and eighty-odd miles from Petersburg, the closest fall-line town, did not prosper as a collection point or trading center until the nineteenth century may be attributable to the types of agricultural products produced in the region. Crops such as tobacco did not require towns for processing (though both New London and Dalstonburg were also established

103. Hening, *Statutes* 7:473.

near mills). Another factor could have been competition from rural stores (the fate of Peytonsburg and Chatham), which may have adequately filled the mercantile needs of the Southside.

The potential profits of a successful town may have been the primary motivation for individuals such Clement Read, William Calloway, and especially James Roberts, just as they were for the Byrds during the first phase of town development in the Virginia Southside. Certainly they went to great lengths to attract the court to their land. Calloway gave Bedford County officials almost the entire town land of New London. Read used his influence in the legislature to create, at least on paper, a town where none stood—a town not coincidently named in honor of the lieutenant governor's wife. Finally, Roberts received much support and tolerance from his fellow justices in his efforts to build both Peytonsburg and Chatham.

Dalstonburg was not the only example of the use of a name in an attempt to curry favor with powerful people. William Byrd I may have chosen King William's Town in an attempt to deflect government criticism over the questionable way his colony was founded. Certainly, he honored Francis Nicholson for his assistance when he named the town's square, and he was not beyond a little egotism in naming a street for himself. The name of Chatham simply followed the colonial government's lead in honoring the same prime minister for whom Pittsylvania County was named, William Pitt, Earl of Chatham.

Once they were laid out, the plans of the colonial Southside towns reflect a diverse range of road schemes. William Byrd I's plan for King William's Town is unique in its use of a square with public buildings in each of the corners. His son's design for Eden, with its line of nucleated villages, reveals a much more comprehensive plan of settlement than most colonial town schemes. As it developed, Dalstonburg grew organically along a T-shaped intersection, though it may have had a more organized design that was lost when it failed to develop initially. If it did, Dalstonburg, by then known as Charlotte Court House, was unique in that it eventually had three plans, since it was replatted in 1817.[104]

Grids dominate other Southside plans, though with varying degrees of success. At first glance, New London fits into a general grid pattern, though there were innovations in that its blocks contained only five lots each, one row deep, with the lots oriented to front main streets whenever possible. On the other hand, James Roberts's plan for Peytonsburg was naïve in its lack of streets and the complication of name changes on the two streets that did exist. One might hope that his design for Chatham, while almost certainly some type of grid, was more successful.

Though the track records of colonial towns in the Southside were not nearly as good as those of the other regions of the Virginia backcountry, they

104. Aailsworth et al., *Charlotte County*, 304.

reveal some important lessons. It is astounding that in a region facing as many settlement problems as the Southside there were just as many attempts to establish towns as there were in the Piedmont, an area with many more advantages in terms of wealth, population, power, and prestige during the colonial period. The towns in both regions were similar in their evolution, beginning with frontier refugee colonies followed later by court and trading towns. Many of the lessons of the successes and failures were repeated in both regions. Town plans and use of naming were similar. That a smaller proportion of the towns established in the Southside were successful has more to do with the larger factors in the region than anything else. When looking at colonial towns in the Southside, the question should not be why so many failed but rather why so many were attempted in the first place.

Chapter 4

The Great Valley

An important landscape feature included in the 1755 edition of Joshua Fry and Peter Jefferson's map of Virginia was the delineation of "The Great Wagon Road from the Yadkin River thro' Virginia to Philadelphia distant 435 miles."[1] This route, which developed out of a series of Indian trails, animal paths, and trading routes, not only served as the major corridor for the flood of immigrants pouring into the Virginia backcountry from Pennsylvania and Maryland but also became an important artery for trade and communication.[2] Gradually, a line of towns grew along the length of the road to meet the demands of the increasing population in the backcountry. Virginia's leaders were pleased when settlers, mostly foreigners, began moving into the area. They believed that just like the foreign colonists in the Piedmont, these people would help create a buffer with the Indians.[3] The influx of people into the Valley led to the establishment of nine towns.

Pennsylvania provided its emigrants to Virginia with a variety of models for town development. William Penn planned for his colony to be divided into

1. Fry and Jefferson, "Map of the most Inhabited," in Stephenson and McKee, *Virginia in Maps*, Map II-21 A–D. See details Map II-21 C and A.

2. Richard George Remer, "The Great Wagon Road," M.A. thesis, College of William and Mary in Virginia, 1974, 2, 104; and Wellenreuther, "Urbanization," 666.

3. Hofstra, *Planting*, 81–84.

townships, each with a village that allowed his settlers to live in close proximity to create a sense of neighborhood and support. Different village plans called for well-spaced homes, possibly a reaction to the outbreak of plague in London in 1665 and the Great Fire, which destroyed much of the city the following year. Another pattern developed in German Township with a series of small hamlets along the main route through the township, dominated by Germantown, a street village created by a single row of houses along the road with gardens and fields stretching out behind them. Several Pennsylvania court towns emulated Philadelphia's use of public squares and adopted them in their streetscapes.[4]

When the remarkable influx of settlers into the Great Valley began, the pattern of town development that had occurred in Pennsylvania continued with the creation and growth of Virginia's Valley towns. The steady flow of settlers strained existing administration and judicial systems, and to meet the needs of a growing population in the Valley, the General Assembly created new counties. These early court towns, although founded by English settlers, quickly became home to large numbers of Germans, Ulster Scots, and other non-English settlers.[5] The migratory movement remained important through the close of the colonial period, affecting the towns directly in their role as service centers. The same influx of people that was important to the development of the county towns also aided in the creation and growth of other towns along the Great Wagon Road.

Winchester

The first two towns established in the Great Valley were both court towns. The Virginia Assembly made provisions for the creation of Frederick County and Augusta County in the Shenandoah Valley in 1738. The area consisted of the portions of Orange County lying west of the Blue Ridge and was to be divided into new counties when there was sufficient population.[6] Orange County surveyor James Wood was in a unique position to profit from the creation of

4. John Stilgo, *Common Landscape of America, 1580–1845* (New Haven, CT: Yale Univ. Press, 1982), 78–79; Reps, *Making*, 158–74; Wolf, *Urban Village*, 27–31; and Lemon, "Urbanization," 510–11. For more references on Pennsylvania town development and German influences in American town planning see chapter 1 n. 45.

5. Ethnic influences in the Shenandoah Valley can be seen in a variety of ways, including architecture and other forms of material culture. See Fischer and Kelly, *Bound Away*, 111–19; Ann E. McCleary, "Ethnic Influences on the Vernacular Architecture of the Shenandoah Valley," in Michael J. Puglisi, ed., *Diversity and Accommodation: Essays on the Cultural Composition of the Virginia Frontier* (Knoxville: Univ. of Tennessee Press, 1997), 252–74; and Edward A. Chappell, "Acculturation in the Shenandoah Valley: Rhenish Houses of the Massanutten Settlement," *Proceedings of the American Philosophical Society* 124 (1980): 55–89. The Chappell article also appears in Dell Upton and Michael Vlach, eds., *Common Places: Readings in American Vernacular Architecture* (Athens: Univ. of Georgia Press, 1986), 27–57. For a breakdown of county population in the Shenandoah Valley by ethnic origin, see Mitchell, *Commercialism*, 43.

6. The legislature made provisions for both counties in the same act. Hening, *Statutes* 5:78–80.

Frederick County, the first new county in the northern part of the Valley. His experience in surveying, as well as his close ties with government officials, provided him with planning skills and information unavailable to many people. When the new government was formed in November of 1743, its members met at Wood's home near Shawnee Spring. He became the clerk of court. In 1744 Wood laid out the first town in the Valley on his 1,241-acre tract of land. Originally called Frederick Town, it was later chartered as Winchester.[7]

The new town stood in a valley on the eastern side of Wood's unpatented land. At first glance his choice gives the impression that Wood merely wanted to establish the county court somewhere on his property. Presbyterian clergyman Philip Fithian observed, "The situation is low & disagreeable."[8] French social reformer François Alexandre-Frédéric de La Rouchefoucauld-Liancourt noted when he visited the town near the end of the century, "It is difficult to conceive the motives that led to the construction of a town on this spot, where only as much water is found as is required for the use of the houses, and which is upwards of twenty miles distance from all navigation;" adding that a site along the Shenandoah River would have been more advantageous.[9] In reality Wood made a skillful and propitious choice. The town was located where the main artery through the Valley crossed one of the few streams in the area at the site of an old Indian village. Although the town was not near the geographic center of the new county, it did sit between two established population centers—the Hopewell settlement to the north and the Opequon settlement to the south. Wood's town was easily accessible and well situated to exploit an existing market and population base.[10]

The new town was modest, consisting of twenty-six numbered and four unnumbered half-acre lots arranged along two, thirty-three-foot-wide streets (Cameron and Loudon), and one cross street (Boscawen). The thirty-three-foot street width was narrow, half the width of the streets in most Virginia

7. "Order Book," Frederick and Winchester Judicial Center, Winchester, VA, 1:1; "Common Law Order Book," Frederick and Winchester Judicial Center, Winchester, VA, 34:166; Hofstra, *Planting*, 180–81; and Robert D. Mitchell, "'From the Ground Up': Space, Place, and Diversity in Frontier Studies," in Puglisi, *Diversity*, 40. The name may have been suggested by Thomas, Lord Fairfax, who served in the Royal Regiment of Horse Guards under the command of Charles, Marquis of Winchester. Hofstra, *Planting*, 194. Local tradition holds that Wood may have been a native of Winchester, England. See Greene, *Winchester, Virginia*, 16; Morton, *Story of Winchester*, 41; and William Couper, *History of the Shenandoah Valley*, 3 vols. (New York: Lewis Historical, 1952), 2:340.

8. Philip Vickers Fithian, *Philip Vickers Fithian: Journal, 1775–1776, Written on the Virginia-Pennsylvania Frontier and in the Army Around New York*, ed. Robert Greenhalgh Albion and Leonidas Dodson (Princeton, NJ: Princeton Univ. Press, 1934), 13.

9. La Rouchefoucault-Liancourt, *Travels through the United States of North America, the Country of the Iroquois, and Upper Canada, in the Years 1795, 1796, and 1797; With an Authentic Account of Lower Canada*, trans. H. Neuman, 2 vols. (London: R. Phillips, 1799), 2:210.

10. "Common Law Order Book," Frederick County, 34:168; Warren R. Hofstra and Robert D. Mitchell, "Town and Country in Backcountry Virginia: Winchester and the Shenandoah Valley, 1730–1800," *Journal of Southern History* 59 (Nov. 1993): 628–29; Hofstra, *Planting*, 181; Mitchell, "'Over the Hills,'" 75; and Morton, *Story of Winchester*, 40, 43.

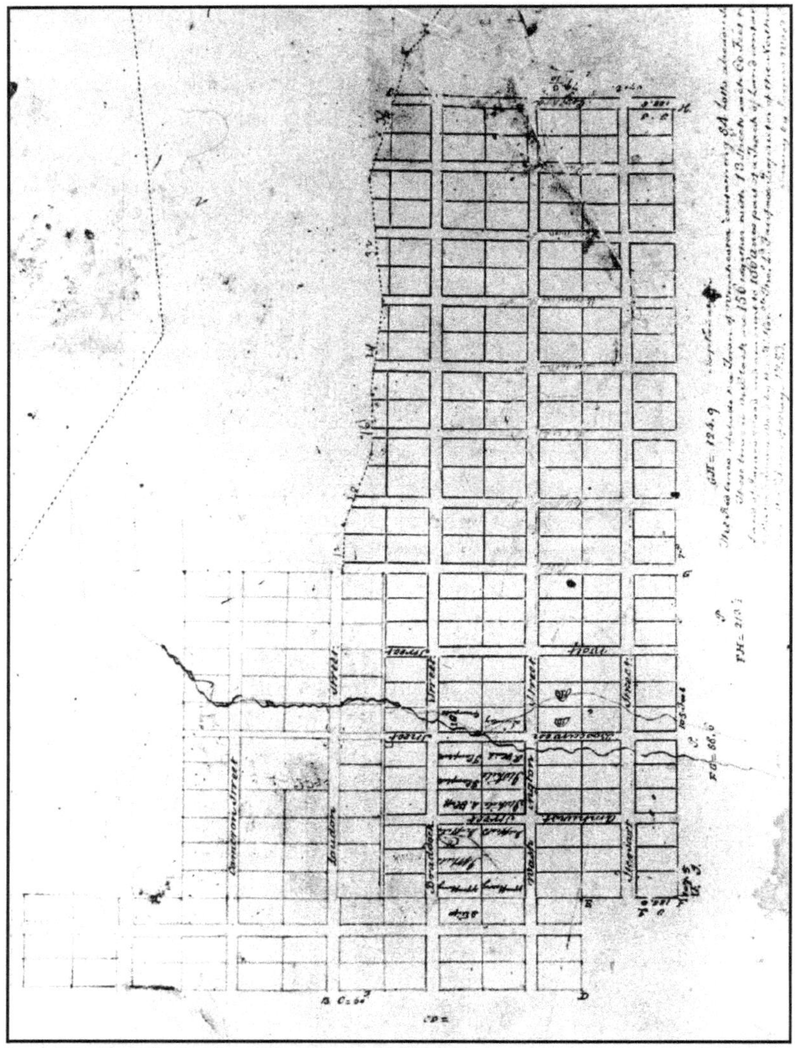

James Wood Jr., "The Rod lines include the Town of Winchester containing 84 Lotts already Tested by act of Assembly," 1758. In "Surveys," 66, Frederick and Winchester Judicial Center, Winchester, Virginia.

towns.[11] Wood retained four of the lots, but conveyed the rest to the county, designating the four unnumbered lots for public use. To assure Winchester's growth, lot purchasers had to construct log or frame buildings with dimensions of at least sixteen by twenty feet within a period of two years or forfeit their property. Realizing that county officials might be timid in accepting the arrangement until the resolution of the land dispute with Lord Fairfax (see chapter 1), Wood stipulated that the scheme was subject to Fairfax's approval and posted a security bond. Eventually, in order to secure the property, Wood

11. Hughes, *Surveyors*, 137.

agreed to pay Fairfax's composition fee and quitrents in arrears to 1745. To seal the success of the new town, Wood successfully lobbied to make it the county seat, purportedly for the cost of a bowl of toddy.[12]

Wood's care and planning paid off, and the original section of Winchester was a great success. By 1745 at least sixteen people had purchased lots in the new town. The investors were mostly local landowners, including Lewis Stephens, who established a town of his own to the south some years later. Wood built a shop on his property, while Robert Rutherford and a "Mr. Hunter" established larger stores.[13] The four public lots that made up the town center were located in the regular grid pattern of the plan, facing Water (Boscawen) Street. The court approved construction of the jail and courthouse on these lots in 1744 and contracted James Hardiner to do the work. Progress was slow, and seven years later the court was still making levies to pay for materials and furniture. In 1747 the official religion of the colony was represented when an Anglican chapel was added to the public lots. Later, clerks' offices and a market were also built. By the next year the town boasted at least one ordinary, two stores, and a number of residences.[14]

Constructed of squared logs, the public buildings set the tone for the frontier town. Traveling on his way to take up lands in North Carolina in 1753, Moravian minister Adam Grube recorded, "At noon we passed through Friedrichstown, which consists of sixty houses badly built."[15] The fledgling town supported between two and three hundred residents.[16] Although Winchester may have borne a shabby appearance in its early years, it had at least survived, and the prospects for its future seemed promising. Wood had surveyor John Baylis lay out fifty-four new lots in 1752. Instead of proving a hindrance, Lord Fairfax, who began to reside permanently in Frederick County in 1750, took an active part in Winchester's development by donating 490 acres to the town in 5-acre parcels to serve as outlots, thus providing citizens with a wood source, pasturage, and land for gardens. Wood and Fairfax struck a deal that recognized Fairfax's right to regrant all of the town lots under his proprietorship except those Wood owned himself. And in 1752 Lord Fairfax

12. "Deed Book," Frederick and Winchester Judicial Center, Winchester, VA, 1:72–73; "Common Law Order Book," Frederick County, 34:168; Morton, *Story of Winchester*, 44–45; Garland A. Quarles, *The Churches of Winchester, Virginia: A Brief History of Those Established Prior to 1825* (Winchester, VA: n.p., 1960), 3; Greene, *Winchester, Virginia*, 43; T. K. Cartmell, *Shenandoah Valley Pioneers and Their Descendants: A History of Frederick County, Virginia* (Winchester, VA: Eddy, 1909), 207; and Rebecca A. Ebert and Teresa Lazazzera, *Frederick County, Virginia: From Frontier to the Future* (Norfolk, VA: Donning, 1988), 25.

13. Hofstra and Mitchell, "Town and Country in Backcountry Virginia," 629; Kercheval, *History of the Valley*, 239; and John W. Wayland, "The Germans of the Valley," *Virginia Magazine of History and Biography* 10 (July 1902): 41.

14. "Order Book," Frederick County, 1:407; "Common Law Order Book," Frederick County, 34:168; Mitchell, "'Over the Hills,'" 75; Quarles, *Churches*, 15; and Greene, *Winchester, Virginia*, 43.

15. [Bernhard Adam Grube?], "Diary of a Journey of Moravians from Bethlehem, Pennsylvania, to Bethabara in Wachovia, North Carolina, 1753," trans. Adelaide L. Fries, in Mereness, *Travels*, 334.

16. Robert D. Mitchell, "'From the Ground Up,'" 39.

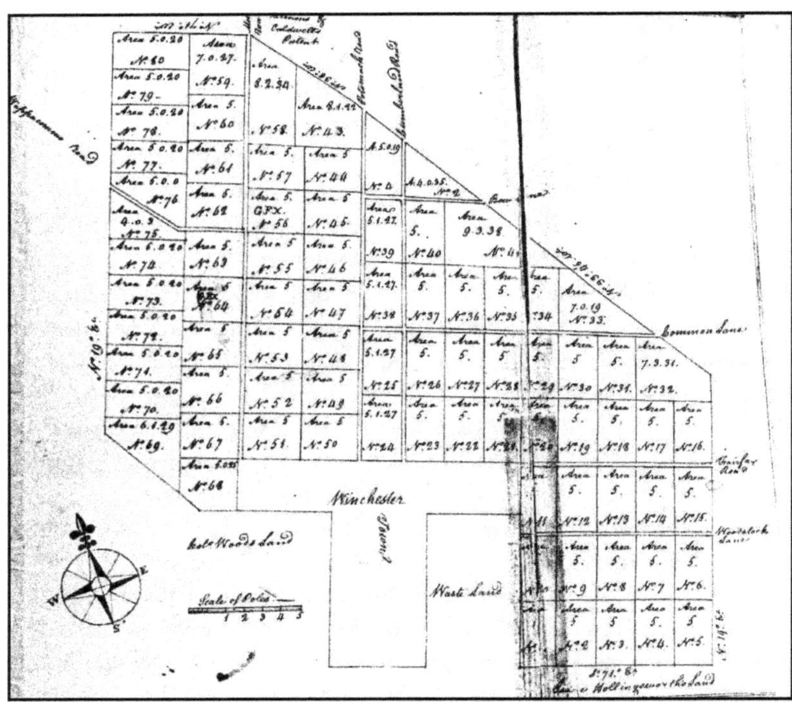

"This Original platt of the Town of Winchester, and of the Commons, which was deposited in Lord Fairfax's Office, was returned into Court by Robert Macky and on his motion is admitted to record," 1794. In "Deed Book," vol. 24B:91, Frederick and Winchester Judicial Center, Winchester, Virginia.

joined the other county justices in petitioning the Assembly for a town charter. The House of Burgesses granted the request that same year, giving governing officials the right to hold two annual fairs.[17] Added to the stores and two weekly markets, the fairs provided residents in the surrounding area with economic and trading opportunities. Forty or more lots were granted or sold from 1752 to 1757, and local landowners were quick to join in the profits of an active economy.[18]

Events of the French and Indian War also enhanced Winchester's growth. In 1755 British Major General Edward Braddock used Winchester as his staging area before launching his disastrous campaign against the French at Fort Duquesne. Braddock brought Winchester closer to the eastern part of the colony by cutting a military highway through the mountains. The same year Lieutenant Governor Robert Dinwiddie appointed George Washington colonel of a Virginia regiment and placed him in charge of the region's defenses. Washington was familiar with the region from survey work he had done for

17. Hening, *Statutes* 6:268–70; Hofstra, *Planting*, 193–95; Mitchell, "'Over the Hills,'" 75; Hofstra and Mitchell, "Town and Country in Backcountry Virginia," 629; and Hughes, *Surveyors*, 137.

18. "Northern Neck Grants and Surveys," Library of Virginia, Richmond, H:307–8, 318; and Greene, *Winchester, Virginia*, 36.

Lord Fairfax in 1748. When he arrived in September, Washington found the countryside in an uproar, with farmers in the region flocking to Winchester for safety and citizens of Winchester simultaneously abandoning their homes and fleeing eastward.[19] The Assembly ordered Washington to supervise construction of Fort Loudoun, which began in 1756 on one of the unoccupied outlots.[20] The threat of imminent attack gone, Winchester's citizens settled down to reap the benefits the war would bring.

The arrival of troops, as well as the influx of refugees attracted by the security of the fort, was a boon to Winchester's economy, creating demands for food, services, and lodging. Along Cameron and Loudoun Streets, seven taverns or ordinaries and at least five merchants were operating by 1757. Cameron Street was also home to a number of craftsmen: two blacksmiths, a gunsmith, two tailors, a shoemaker, a cooper, a stonemason, and a joiner. The merchants actively consolidated trade connections to Alexandria, seventy-five miles east in the Tidewater, and Philadelphia, two hundred miles to the north. For the duration of the war cattle drovers in the backcountry chose to divert their herds to Winchester rather than risking the long journey to Philadelphia. With the rerouting of the Great Wagon Road, Winchester increasingly became an important stopping point for settlers moving into the Great Valley and on into North Carolina.[21] The population of Winchester doubled by 1756, and the town prospered as local farmers, merchants, and tavern keepers supplied their customers with hay, grains, oats, and liquor.[22] Writing in 1760, English clergyman Andrew Burnaby described a very different place from the one Adam Grube passed through just seven years previously. Burnaby described a booming town having "about two hundred houses," clearly noting that "It is the place of general rendez vous of the Virginia troops, which is the reason of its late rapid increase and present flourishing condition."[23]

Encouraged by the new prosperity, Wood added 106 acres to the west side of the town in 1756 and sold the new lots through various schemes, including land auctions and a lottery.[24] Not to be outdone, later that year Lord Fairfax hired Wood's son to mark off 173 lots to the east, essentially demarcating Winchester's borders until the twentieth century.[25] Reflecting the new regard both

19. Mitchell, "'Over the Hills,'" 71; and Warren R. Hofstra, "'A Parcel of Barbarian's and an Uncooth Set of People': Settlers and Settlements in the Shenandoah Valley," in Warren R. Hofstra, ed., *George Washington and the Virginia Backcountry* (Madison, WI: Madison House, 1998), 90.

20. Hening, *Statutes* 7:33; Greene, *Winchester, Virginia*, 80–81; and Walter C. Kidney, *Winchester: Limestone, Sycamores, and Architecture* (Winchester, VA: Preservation of Historic Winchester, 1977), 13–14.

21. Mitchell, "'From the Ground Up,'" 40; Hofstra and Mitchell, "Town and Country in Backcountry Virginia," 631; and Hofstra, *Planting*, 243, 263–64.

22. Mitchell, "'Over the Hills,'" 77; and Hofstra, *Planting*, 245–56.

23. Burnaby, *Travels*, 45; and Hofstra, *Planting*, 258–59.

24. Hening, *Statutes* 7:285; James Wood, "A List of Ticketts in the Winchester Lottery. Signed and Sold by James Wood, 1760," Handley Library, Winchester, VA; and Greene, *Winchester, Virginia*, 105.

25. Hening, *Statutes* 7:314–17; Hughes, *Surveyors*, 137; and Morton, *Story of Winchester*, 49.

had for what had been a frontier village, the streets in the new additions were widened to sixty feet.[26] When naming streets as Winchester expanded, Wood chose names of heroes of the French and Indian War, including Washington, Loudoun, Boscawen, and Wolfe. Fairfax tended to name streets after famous locations in the British isles, such as Pall Mall, Bond, Leicester, Piccadilly, and Cork, maybe in an attempt to lend Winchester a more cosmopolitan flare.[27] The rapid growth was not without its disadvantages. The General Assembly was forced to act to curb damage done by hogs that ran free through the town, digging up springs and generally creating a nuisance.[28]

James Wood died in 1759, but the sale of his Winchester landholdings continued under the direction of his wife, Mary. Lots in the new additions continued to sell, and previously purchased lots changed hands. Speculators and businessmen tried to benefit from Winchester's growth and regularly placed advertisements in *The Virginia Gazette*.[29] Several people built new structures and replaced old ones. In 1762 Anglican Church leaders hired Charles Smith to construct a new sanctuary out of stone.[30] Meanwhile, other church congregations acquired land from Lord Fairfax. Members of the Reformed Calvinist Church built a meetinghouse while Lutherans opened a log school.[31] In 1762 the county began construction on a new stone jail. Limestone, frame, and clapboard-covered log houses appeared throughout the city but especially on Loudoun and Cameron streets, the newer Piccadilly Street, and Fairfax Lane.[32]

After the cessation of hostilities, Winchester and its environs began to take an active role in the emerging regional economy. Winchester became a local market center for dairy products. Other items produced in the surrounding countryside, such as cattle, wheat, and flour, passed through Winchester en route to Baltimore, Philadelphia, Alexandria, Fredericksburg, and Falmouth. These items were not processed in Winchester, but local merchants such as Bryan Bruin and brothers Philip and Daniel Bush played a vital role in financing this commodity trade. An increasing demand and legislative encouragements gave rise to large-scale hemp production. Winchester not only served as a collection point for the new crop but also grew into a rope manufacturing center. Finally, the familiar Virginia standby, tobacco, slowly became a significant part of the region's agricultural production. The town, however, did not serve solely as a collection and marketing center for the export of these agricultural products to eastern markets; it also functioned as a regional distribution center for imported necessities such as sugar, salt, and glass, as well

26. Greene, *Winchester, Virginia*, 118.

27. Hofstra, *Planting*, 259–61.

28. Hening, *Statutes* 7:411–12.

29. "Advertisement," *Virginia Gazette* (Rind), Jan. 5, 1769, Mar. 21, 1771, Sept. 26, 1771; "Advertisement," *Virginia Gazette* (Purdie and Dixon), Oct. 17, 1771; and Hofstra and Mitchell, "Town and Country in Backcountry Virginia," 632.

30. "Common Law Order Book," Frederick County, 34:169; and Quarles, *Churches*, 18.

31. Wust, *Virginia Germans*, 66; and Quarles, *Churches*, 27.

32. Cresswell, *Journal*, 49; Hofstra and Mitchell, "Town and Country in Backcountry Virginia," 632; and Kidney, *Winchester*, 5.

as British luxury goods. Winchester also became known as a manufacturing center for a variety of craft items in its own right. The spectacular development of Winchester secured its place as leader in an emerging hierarchy of smaller communities in the Valley.[33] In 1779 the General Assembly recognized the town's importance to the region by incorporating Winchester, granting its citizens the right to elect a mayor and other city officials, raise taxes, and pass ordinances without petitioning Virginia's government. It was the first incorporated town west of the Blue Ridge.[34]

Nicholas Cresswell wrote of Winchester at the close of the colonial era, "It is one of the largest towns I have seen in the colony."[35] The remarkable growth of Winchester was unique in the backcountry and was partly due to the advantage the town had of being the first established in the region. However, careful planning by founder James Wood is also evident through the town's location along a major north-south corridor and its proximity to populated areas. The town was able to function as a regional market center and serve migrating settlers. The healthy competition of two land proprietors as well as the active participation of local landowners assured the active sale of town lots. Chance also played a role in Winchester's growth with the coming of war and its accompanying increase in population and demand for goods. Beginning as a small court town in the Shenandoah Valley, by the end of the colonial period, Winchester, with its population of around fifteen hundred people, had grown to be the largest town west of the Blue Ridge Mountains. And at the end of the eighteenth century, Winchester was home to somewhere between one-quarter and one-third of the Lower Shenandoah Valley's entire population of 53,000 people.[36]

Staunton

Almost one hundred miles to the south of Winchester, Augusta County was organized in 1745, just two years after Frederick County.[37] Anticipating the county's new status, William Beverley, at his own expense, had a courthouse

33. Mitchell, "'From the Ground Up,'" 40; Mitchell, "'Over the Hills,'" 77; Hofstra and Mitchell, "Town and Country in Backcountry Virginia," 632, 634–43; Mitchell, "Southern Backcountry," 24–25; Hofstra, *Planting*, 8, 285–88; and Earle and Hoffman, "Staple Crops," 68–78. For more on production and trade, see Mitchell, *Commercialism*, 162–87; and Hofstra, *Planting*, 187–97, 204–35. For period discussions of Winchester's products and economic role, see La Rouchefoucault-Liancourt, *Travels* 2:103; Harry Toulmin, *The Western Country in 1793*, ed. Marion Tingling and Godfrey Davies (San Marino, CA: Henry E. Huntington Library and Art Gallery, 1948), 55–59; and Howard R. Marraro, "Count Luigi Casiglioni: An Early Italian Traveler to Virginia (1785–1786)," *Virginia Magazine of History and Biography* 58 (Oct. 1950): 489. For more on the relationship between town and country in the Valley, see Hofstra, *Planting*, 288–94.

34. Hening, *Statutes* 10:172–76; and Hofstra and Mitchell, "Town and Country in Backcountry Virginia," 644.

35. Cresswell, *Journal*, 49.

36. Hofstra and Mitchell, "Town and Country in Backcountry Virginia," 632; and Hofstra, *Planting*, 287. The elevation of the Shenandoah Valley declines as one travels north, so the northern half of the Valley is referred to as "Lower" and the southern half as "Upper."

37. Hening, *Statutes* 5:78–80.

built near his mill on Beverley Manor, and presented it to the county court along with two acres of land. He later increased the gift to include twenty-five acres.[38] The mill settlement, already a considerable hamlet, was located at the crossing of the Rockfish Gap Indian road and the north-south Valley Indian road.[39] Philip Fithian found that the site for the court had an "improper situation," and was not easily accessible because, as he noted, "It is built in a Valley, into which you must descend, & very much too, from every Part."[40] Later in the century, La Rouchefoucauld-Liancourt agreed with Fithian's assessment, adding, "It would be difficult to account for this spot having been chosen for the site of a town in preference to others, but for the numerous springs of excellent water, and a rivulet, which bursting from a hill near the town, turns two mills, and might turn many more."[41]

In August 1746, a court-appointed committee reviewed the portion of the tract offered to the county and found it "intirely Inconvenient and useless being most part of it on a Barron hill or Mountain where the County Cannot Pretend to Sell one Lot if the sd Land be received nor Fall into any way of method for to raise the Quitrents of the Land it afording neither firewood nor Water no Spring being Included in the Whole Twenty five Acres tho several are Nigh and Adjacent to the sd Land."[42] Undaunted, Beverley, who was in Williamsburg sitting in the House of Burgesses at the time, presented his proposal to the Assembly, and the site became Augusta Courthouse.[43]

The courthouse that Beverley gave the county was primitive. When the court met there in December 1745, the justices immediately ordered the courthouse repaired and set about building a prison and stocks.[44] Three years later there were still problems. In 1748 grand jury foreman William Christian described the courthouse as a log structure with "some of the cracks between the logs quite open, four or five inches wide and four or five feet long, and some stopped with chunks and clay, but not quite close, two small holes cut for the windows, but no glass or shutters to them; the inside is not furnished nor fitting for his Majesty's Judicatory to sit."[45] The jail proved to be a suitable companion to the courthouse, "built with squared logs near one foot thick,

38. "Order Book, Augusta County," Augusta County Courthouse, Staunton, VA, 1:69; Kennedy and McIlwaine, *Journals of the House* 6:10; "Deed Book," Augusta County, 2:246; Edward Aull, *Early History of Staunton and Beverley Manor in Augusta County, Virginia* (Staunton, VA: McClure Printing, 1963), 19; and Joseph A. Waddell, *Annals of Augusta County, Virginia, From 1726 to 1871* (Staunton, VA: C. Russell Caldwell, 1902), 52.

39. J. Lewis Peyton, *History of Augusta County, Virginia* (Bridgewater, VA: C. J. Carrier, 1953), 255; and Armstrong, "Urban Vision," 45.

40. Fithian, *Philip Vickers Fithian*, 138.

41. La Rouchefoucault Liancourt, *Travels* 2:90.

42. "Order Book, Augusta County," 1:102–3.

43. McIlwaine, Hall, and Hillman, *Executive Journals* 5:200; and Lyon Gardiner Tyler, ed., *Encyclopedia of Virginia Biography*, 5 vols. (New York: Lewis Historical, 1915), 1:186.

44. "Order Book, Augusta County," 1:3.

45. Ibid., 2:34.

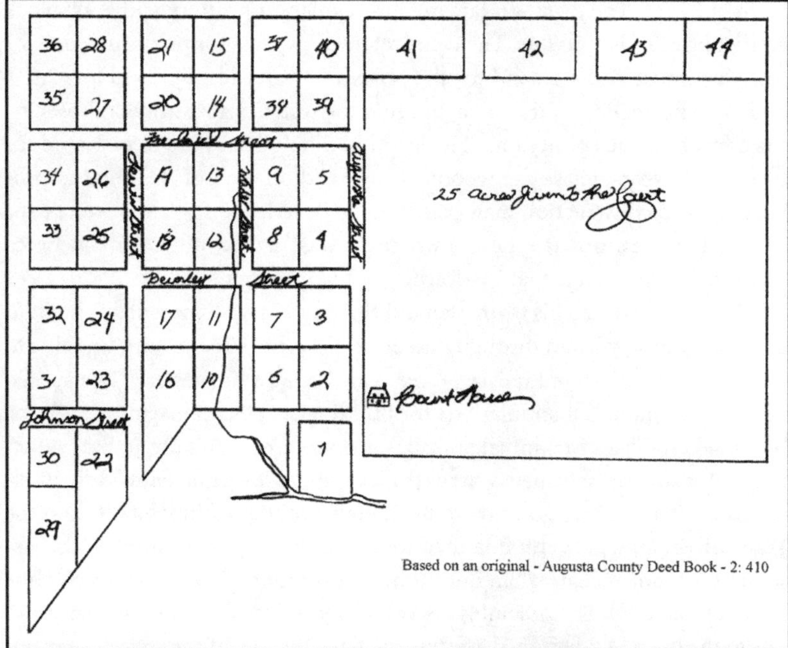

Staunton, 1750. William Beverley marked out the lots appearing here. When Thomas Lewis laid out the county's portion of the town, he again began with lot number one. Map based on "A Plan of the Town of Staunton Augusta County," 1749/50, in "Deed Book," vol. 2: 410, Augusta County Courthouse, Staunton, Virginia. Map by the author.

holes at ye corners and elsewhere two or three inches wide, and so poorly dovetailed at the corners that it would be a very easy matter to pull it all down."[46]

After capturing the court, Beverley set about building a town. In 1747 he hired county surveyor Thomas Lewis to lay out thirteen half-acre lots. A year later, he added thirty-one lots, and Beverley presented his plan to the court February 27, 1749/50.[47] Four of the lots along the edge of the court's land each contained one acre (lots 41–44). Three lots were irregularly shaped and contained three-quarters to nine-tenths of an acre (lots 16, 22, and 29). No geographical feature is responsible for the lots' unusual shape. Beverley may have granted the adjacent land previously.

After the court accepted the plan, Beverley formally deeded the twenty-five promised acres east of his lots to the justices. The division between Beverley's lots and the county's became Augusta Street. The court ordered county surveyor Thomas Lewis to divide the county acreage into lots on March 3, 1749/50. The county began selling the lots in the eastern half of the

46. Ibid.

47. Ibid., 2:313–14; "Deed Book," Augusta County Courthouse, Staunton, VA, 2:410; and Hughes, *Surveyors*, 135.

town in 1752.[48] The town was laid out in a regular grid pattern with each block consisting of only four lots. The court retained two lots for public use, one for the courthouse and a second for the prison. Beverley himself held lots 2, 10, and 11 in his section of the town, but sold the rest. Commissioners chosen by the court sold the county lots. The lots that did not sell were to be leased for twenty-one years. Fifty-acre woodlots were laid off west of the town to provide fuel and construction materials.[49] Both "Beverley" and "Lewis" were used as street names, but the new town itself was named after Lady Rebecca Staunton, wife of Lieutenant Governor William Gooch.[50]

Beverley recorded his town plan in February 1749/50, presented his gift to the county in April, and through his connections in Williamsburg was able to have Staunton chartered in May, three years before Winchester.[51] The act did not include the usual stipulations for building specifications and deadlines, but it did establish two annual fairs. It was quite a coup, but the act was short-lived. Not surprisingly, newly arrived Lieutenant Governor Dinwiddie disallowed the act in 1752, pointing to the "small Number of Inhabitants and the Want of Persons properly qualified to constitute a Corporation."[52] The Assembly did not recharter Staunton until November of 1761, by which time Beverley had died. The Assembly also officially added the county's twenty-five lots to the town. Aside from forfeiting the fairs, the loss of the charter may not have had any practical impact, but the presence of a charter would have lent the new town status and possibly hastened its development.[53]

Despite the setback, Staunton prospered, and Adam Grube was able to record in 1753, "[W]e came to Augusti Court House, a little village of twenty houses, surrounded by hills."[54] In 1755 the county sold the courthouse as a dwelling, had it moved, and had a new log structure built in its place. Staunton's inhabitants began constructing a church in 1760. Built by Francis Smith, a Hanover County resident, the building was made out of brick laid in lime mortar and stood twenty-five by forty feet. Although the building was not completed until 1763, the church vestry was active with projects such as providing Staunton with a home for orphans and illegitimate children.[55]

48. Hughes, *Surveyors*, 135; and "Deed Book," Augusta County, 4:315. Actually, Beverley sold the lots to the county for six pence. See "Deed Book," Augusta County, 2:246.

49. Hughes, *Surveyors*, 135; Waddell, *Annals*, 65, 72; and Mitchell, "Upper Shenandoah," 174. The lots in the two town sections had separate numbering systems. Probably surveyor Thomas Lewis began numbering the county lots with a system that did not mirror Beverley's.

50. Waddell, *Annals*, 64.

51. Waverley K. Winfree and Randolph Church, eds., *The Laws of Virginia: Being a Supplement to Hening's The Statutes at Large* (Richmond: Virginia State Library, 1971), 431–32; Kennedy and McIlwaine, *Journals of the House* 7:362, 374.

52. H. R. McIlwaine, ed., *Legislative Journals of the Council of Colonial Virginia*, 3 vols. (Richmond, VA: Colonial Press, Everett Waddey, 1918–19), 2:1084.

53. McIlwaine, Hall, and Hillman, *Executive Journals* 5:212; Kennedy and McIlwaine, *Journals of the House* 6:10.

54. Grube, "Diary," 338.

Like Winchester, Staunton depended on overland trade to transport its goods, because as Johann David Schoepf noted, "Staunton has no navigable stream near it."[56] County officials diligently worked to have roadways cleared, sometimes enlisting the aid of the colonial legislature.[57] With the development of a road network to the county seat, inns and taverns prospered, and stores quickly followed. Felix Gilbert established a store in town by 1748, and soon faced competition from Israel Christian. Alexander Wright, a merchant operating in Fredericksburg, purchased two lots in Staunton and opened operations there, signaling growing interest in the new town from Tidewater merchants. By 1764 there were five mercantile concerns, each bringing new connections in the east, and other merchants had connections to the north.[58] William Crow, for example, drove cattle to Winchester and Philadelphia on a regular basis. George and Sampson Mathews demonstrate how diversified mercantile operations were in Staunton. In addition to their store, they operated an ordinary, speculated in land both in town and in the surrounding countryside, and brought servants and slaves to sell. But despite the number of merchants and the diversity of their mercantile concerns, because Staunton was the only town in the Upper Shenandoah Valley, traveling peddlers and rural storekeepers often handled Augusta County's merchant trade.[59] Still, Scottish physician J. F. D. Smyth observed that "Staunton is a pretty large town, considering it lies beyond the mountains, and carries on a brisk inland trade."[60]

Not surprisingly, Staunton and Winchester marketed many of the same agricultural products and played similar roles as trading and service centers. After the French and Indian War, Augusta's county town developed into a processing, collection, and distribution center, "carrying on much trade with the farther mountain-country."[61] On the eve of the Revolution there were thirteen gristmills operating within a five-mile radius of the town. Hemp, wheat, and cattle were leading exports, but Staunton also was a market for corn, rye, linseed wax, honey, and skins. Much of the trade went north to Winchester and then on to Baltimore and Philadelphia, but merchants also shipped products east to Tidewater trading towns such as Fredericksburg and Richmond. Staunton was an important center of an import trade as well, distributing high-quality items such as fabrics, pottery, spirits, and iron.[62] Staunton's position at a crossroads

55. "Order Book, Augusta County," 1:319; and Aull, *Early History*, 23–24. Aull incorrectly identifies the church as being Presbyterian. It was actually Anglican. See "Augusta Parish Registry" [photostat], Alderman Library Special Collections, Univ. of Virginia, Charlottesville, 323–24.

56. Schoepf, *Travels* 2:69.

57. Hening, *Statutes* 8:546–48; and Armstrong, "Urban Vision," 60, 189.

58. Mitchell, "Upper Shenandoah," 174, 325–57.

59. Albert H. Tillson Jr., *Gentry and Commonfolk: Political Culture on a Virginia Frontier, 1740–1789* (Lexington: Univ. Press of Kentucky, 1991), 10–11.

60. Smyth, *Tour* 2:156.

61. Schoef, *Travels* 2:69.

62. Fithian, *Philip Vickers Fithian*, 138; La Rouchefoucault Liancourt, *Travels* 2:41, 91; and Tillson, *Gentry*, 10; Hart, *Valley*, 12–13; Mitchell, "Upper Shenandoah," 439–40; and Mitchell, *Commercialism*, 159.

proved beneficial. The town benefited not only from the traffic of settlers moving south but also from people traveling to the mineral and thermal springs that were developing as resort areas in the mountains to the west. Indeed, the connection with western towns such as Warm Springs was key to Staunton's dominance in the commercial market. Before the Revolutionary War, Staunton merchants routinely provided western settlers with manufactured goods, ammunition, and whiskey. After the war, western communities became even more important to Staunton's success as merchants such as William Bowyer and Staunton mercantile firms White, Kirk, and Company and Mustoe and Chambers expanded into the western market.[63]

Wanting to settle his vast lands, William Beverley used the county court to attract settlers. Through the enticements of land and a courthouse, as well as his position in the colonial government, Beverley was able to establish a county town with minimal financial investment. He chose a location near a mill, guaranteeing himself at least a modest return from the monthly court day trade. The site also lay on a crossroads along the main road through the Shenandoah Valley, giving it an excellent chance of developing into a local and regional trade and service center. Beverley's skillful political maneuvering and his careful choice of geography were successful. By the close of the colonial era, Staunton had grown from a small frontier settlement into "a place by no means inconsiderable," and by the end of the century the town could boast of close to two hundred houses and eight inns, three quite substantial.[64]

It should be no surprise that the two earliest towns in the Great Valley were its largest and most successful. Both Winchester and Staunton flourished in part because of their positions as county seats but also because for the first decade of their existence, there was no other competition. Even though other towns would be established nearby, Winchester was able to dominate the Lower Shenandoah Valley, and because the Upper Valley was less densely populated and farmland was still readily available, Staunton had no rivals.[65] But over time, Winchester and Staunton saw increasing competition as other towns were established during the colonial period.

Mecklenburg/Shepherdstown

One of the northernmost towns in the Shenandoah Valley was Mecklenburg (modern Shepherdstown, West Virginia). Lord Fairfax granted a 457-acre tract along the south shore of the Potomac River to Thomas Shepherd in 1751.[66] By 1754 Shepherd had constructed a stone home, which he could easily fortify in case of Indian or French attack from the west. The house stood

63. Briggs, "Journey," 12; Armstrong, "Urban Vision," 60, 159; Mitchell, "Upper Shenandoah," 440, 442, 444; and Mitchell, *Commercialism*, 219–20.

64. Schoepf, *Travels* 2:69; and Tillson, *Gentry*, 11.

65. Mitchell, "Upper Shenandoah," 233, 236.

66. "Northern Neck Grants and Surveys," G:545.

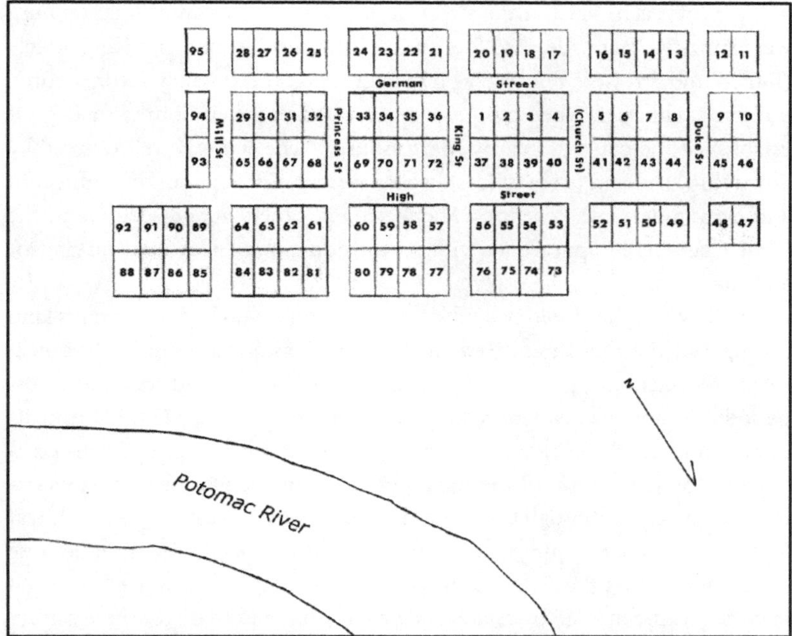

Mecklenburg, 1758. Map by the author.

on a ridge above the river at a crossing known as Pack Horse Ford.[67] When the French and Indian War broke out, settlers in the region began flocking to Shepherd's "fort" for protection. Faced with a sudden overflow of people, Shepherd recognized an economic opportunity and laid out twenty half-acre lots around his house and promised to allow subscribers to hold the land rent free for the duration of the hostilities.[68] The response was tremendous, and by 1762 Shepherd had laid off a total of fifty acres into lots. That year, acting on petition from the inhabitants, the Virginia Assembly granted Shepherd's town a charter, naming it in honor of the Queen, Charlotte of Mecklenburg.[69]

Shepherd laid out the original portion of his town in blocks of four lots each along the road passing in front of his house (lot 1). He later extended both lines of lots two blocks west (lots 21–36). Gradually, with later additions, the plan of Mecklenburg evolved into a traditional grid pattern. The town was based on two main avenues, German and High streets, which ran roughly parallel to the banks of the Potomac as it bent to the southwest. Ninety-five half-acre lots were laid out on either side of these two avenues, with cross streets (Mill, Princess, King, Church, and Duke) cutting the town into square blocks

67. Millard Kessler Bushong, *A History of Jefferson County, West Virginia* (Charles Town, WV: Jefferson, 1941), 16; Danske Dandridge, *Historic Shepherdstown* (Charlottesville, VA: Michie, 1910), 36; and Cartmell, *Shenandoah Valley*, 231.

68. Dandridge, *Historic Shepherdstown*, 36–37; and A. D. Kenamond, *Prominent Men of Shepherdstown during Its First 200 Years* (Charles Town, WV: Jefferson County Historical Society, 1963), 12.

69. Hening, *Statutes* 7:600.

of eight lots each. Most of the streets in the original section of Mecklenburg were sixty-five feet wide. Two lots on the corner of German and King Streets (lots 35 and 36) were reserved as public grounds and possibly future county buildings, although when the Assembly created Berkeley County in 1772, it established the court at nearby Martinsburg.[70] The site was well watered by Town Run, a stream fed by at least twenty springs. Throughout the eighteenth and early nineteenth centuries, Shepherd and others added sections to the town, changing its appearance with the introduction of alleys and varying lot and road widths.[71]

In 1764 Shepherd sold several lots to the people who had lived on his land throughout the French and Indian War. He transferred more lots the next year.[72] Mecklenburg grew steadily, and Shepherd continued to transfer lots periodically and held two more large land sales in 1767 and 1774.[73] During its early years, Mecklenburg was settled predominately by people of English origin, but the population of the town gradually took on an increasingly German character.[74] Although the community did not stand directly on the Great Wagon Road, a large number of settlers were drawn to the location because of the ford across the Potomac below the town. Shepherd moved to profit from the traffic in 1765 by establishing a ferry but had to discontinue service a few months later because Thomas Swearington had already been licensed to operate a ferry a few miles upstream.[75]

Shepherd's other business ventures were more successful. In the 1760s, he built a stone gristmill (lot 63) and a sawmill just out of town, down the slope of the hill. He built a third mill even closer to the river in 1772. These three mills did much to elevate Mecklenburg into a regional trading center. In 1766 the Assembly gave the town a boost by establishing two annual fairs.[76] However, the most important factor in the town's success was the large number of "German mechanics" who opened shops, mostly along German Street.[77] By the end of the colonial period, Mecklenburg supported a coppersmith, clockmaker, gunsmith, potter, brewer, butcher, tanner, whitesmiths, blacksmiths,

70. Clifford S. Musser, *Two Hundred Years' History of Shepherdstown, 1730–1931* (Shepherdstown, WV: The Independent, 1931), 7–11.

71. Some of the additions were unsuccessful. See "Deed Book," Jefferson County Courthouse, Charles Town, WV, 3:381–82; and Dandridge, *Historic Shepherdstown*, facing 262.

72. "Deed Book," Frederick County, 9:374–522, 10:619–34 passim.

73. See for example, ibid., 11:144, 243, 465–73 passim; and "Deed Book, Berkeley County," Berkeley County Courthouse, Martinsburg, WV, 3:160–203 passim.

74. Shepherd's own background is open to debate. John Wayland claims that Shepherd's family name was originally the German form Schaefer, though most historians believe he was English. See Wayland, "Germans," 34; and A. D. Kenamond, "Early Shepherdstown and Its Churches," *Magazine of the Jefferson County Historical Society* 11 (Dec. 1945): 35.

75. Hening, *Statutes* 7:146–47, 263–64; and Musser, *Two Hundred*, 12.

76. "Will Book, Berkeley County," Berkeley County Courthouse, Martinsburg, WV, 1:61–62; "Berkeley County Minute Book," Berkeley County Courthouse, Martinsburg, WV, 1:35; and Hening, *Statutes* 8:255–56.

77. Kercheval, *History of the Valley*, 241.

and carpenters.[78] During the Revolution, the migration up the Valley diminished greatly, but the town still flourished as tradesmen supplied the American army with food, clothes, shoes, hats, guns, saddles, wagons, and other supplies. With peace the economy grew even stronger as the tide of migration returned. Mecklenburg entered its greatest period of prosperity.[79]

As Mecklenburg grew, a number of institutions were established to meet the needs of its ethnically diverse population. A Lutheran congregation organized in 1765. Its members built a log church, which they may have shared with members of a Reformed Church, although they had no permanent minister until 1776.[80] By that year, an "English Church" had also been constructed (lot 40). Philip Fithian described it as "the most elegant Building, for a Place of Worship, that I have seen yet in this Colony."[81] Mecklenburg was also home to a school begun by Robert Cockburn in 1762. Cockburn ran an English school for elementary and higher education. There was also a second school by 1762 that taught in German (lot 72). A third school, located near the gristmill, was in operation by 1773 (lot 82).[82]

In 1760 the population of Thomas Shepherd's town was about three hundred people. By 1770 its population had grown to seven hundred, and by 1776 it was over a thousand.[83] When Shepherd died in 1776, Mecklenburg was one of the largest and most successful towns in the backcountry. The key to its success was its location at an entrance into the Great Valley. The passage of settlers moving south brought an endless source of trade as well as a supply of new inhabitants for the town. Mecklenburg had begun life during the French and Indian War as a refugee camp; by 1790 promoters in the community, largely known by this time simply as Shepherdstown, were making a bid to become the new capital of the United States, hoping to attract President George Washington's attention as he chose a site along the Potomac.[84]

Stephensburg/Stephens City

After crossing into Virginia, people moving south traveled up the Shenandoah Valley to Winchester. While Frederick's county town was the largest and most productive town in the backcountry by the close of the colonial period, it did

78. Gladys Hartzell, *On This Rock: The Story of St. Peter's Church Shepherdstown, 1765–1965* (Shepherdstown, WV: Shepherdstown Register, 1970), 10–11; and A. D. Kenamond, "The Sheetz Gunsmiths," *Magazine of the Jefferson County Historical Society* 24 (Dec. 1958): 18–19.

79. Dandridge, *Historic Shepherdstown*, 262–63, 279.

80. "History of Jefferson County," in *Historical Hand-Atlas Illustrated* (Chicago: H. H. Hardesty, 1883), 29; Musser, *Two Hundred*, 13; and Kenamond, "Early Shepherdstown," 36.

81. Fithian, *Philip Vickers Fithian*,182; and "Will Book, Berkeley County," 64.

82. "Deed Book, Berkeley County," 2:95–99; A. D. Kenamond, "Shepherdstown's Schools, 1762–1782," *Magazine of the Jefferson County Historical Society* 5 (Dec. 1939): 28; and Dandridge, *Historic Shepherdstown*, 52–53.

83. Mabel Henshaw Gardiner and Ann Henshaw Gardiner, *Chronicles of Old Berkeley* (Durham, NC: Seeman, 1938), 59.

84. Dandridge, *Historic Shepherdstown*, 278–82.

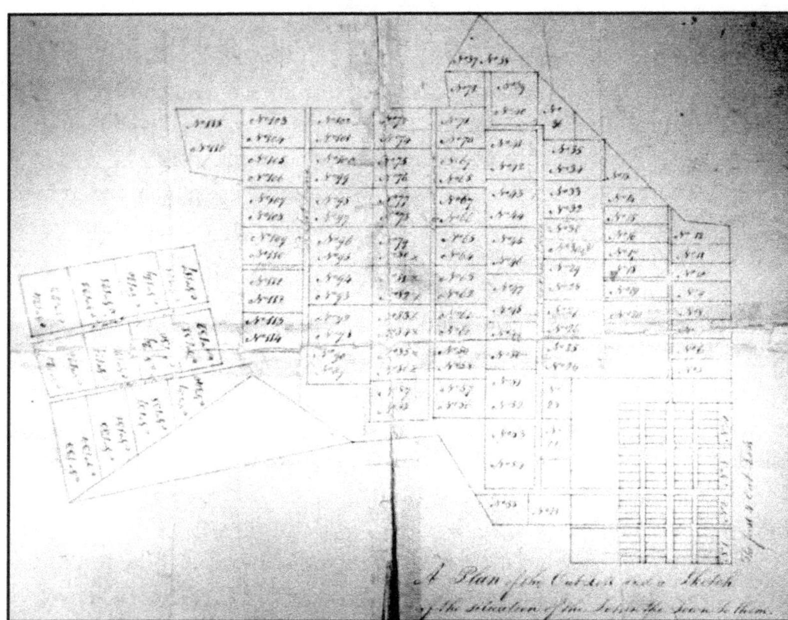

"Plan of the Out Lots and a Sketch of the situation of the Lots in the Town and to them." In "Stephens City, Virginia Records," n.d., Handley Regional Library, Winchester, Virginia. Courtesy of the Handley Regional Library.

have competition. Lewis Stephens, an investor in Winchester, settled in the Valley with his father in the 1730s. In 1752 he patented several tracts of land in the Northern Neck.[85] Other settlers in the region, mostly German, moved onto Stephens's land near the relative security of his hexagonal private fort with the increase of Indian hostilities. They felt secure in part because of the structure's ingenious design. It was three stories, mostly underground, and was supplied with water fed inside by an underground pipe.[86] But the mounting numbers of refugees created a problem, and like Thomas Shepherd, Stephens decided to lay out a town and apply to the colonial government for a charter. In 1758 the Assembly officially created the town of Stephensburg.[87]

The plan of Stephensburg (modern Stephens City) was a design utilizing a system of inlots and outlots. The town proper, standing in one corner of the tract, contained eighty half-acre lots, which were divided into quadrants by a main avenue and a narrower cross street. In turn, each quadrant was again divided by smaller streets, creating linear blocks of five lots each. Stephens stipulated that a twenty-by-fifteen-foot house had to be constructed on each lot within eighteen months of its purchase.[88] On two sides of the town,

85. "Northern Neck Grants and Surveys," H:80–81, 130, 187. Stephens also purchased land from his father in 1755. See "Deed Book," Frederick County, 4:31–32. See also "Land Office Patents," 15:336; and "Will Book," Frederick and Winchester Judicial Center, Winchester, VA, 2:226, 8:198. For a description of the Northern Neck, see chapter 1.

86. Ebert and Lazazzera, *Frederick County*, 24.

87. Hening, *Statutes* 7:234–36.

Stephens left common land for public use and future expansion. The outlots lay beyond the town proper. Twenty outlots contained five acres each. Sixty others held ten acres each In all, the Virginia Assembly actually chartered nine hundred acres of land.

Despite the grand scale of its design, Stephensburg did not immediately attract many settlers. At least seven lots were sold in 1759, and twenty-three more sold over the next two years, mostly to German settlers from the Opequon community. The original townspeople included a minister, a lawyer, and two storekeepers, but Stephensburg simply could not compete with its neighbor just eight miles to the north.[89] One problem was that Stephens charged an annual ground rent three times higher than that in Winchester. However, a smallpox epidemic, which broke out in Winchester in 1759, brought an infusion of investors into Stephensburg despite the higher fees. When the Frederick County court relocated to the town, lot sales skyrocketed. During the next two years almost half of the lots in town were transferred. But the boom was short lived. When the court returned to Winchester, the number of lot sales fell to an average of five or six per year.[90]

The economy of Stephensburg stagnated without the court. Winchester held a virtual monopoly on craft production and professional services in Frederick County. Eventually, Stephensburg came to depend on the migratory trade to survive. A majority of people purchasing lots in town were German settlers. At least two merchants invested in the community, and tavern keepers established inns to profit from the town's location on the road. In 1775 Philip Fithian described the town as "A small Village—Well situated—4 Taverns kept in this Town—One large store by Mr. Holmes."[91] Later in the century, La Rouchefoucauld-Liancourt estimated Stephensburg's population at about five hundred people, mostly German.[92] Though Stephensburg could not seriously compete with its neighbor to the north, it was able to survive and slowly develop as one of the line of towns up the Shenandoah Valley.

Strasburg

After Stephensburg, the next town along the Great Wagon Road was established on the north fork of the Shenandoah River near a mill built by Jacob Funk around 1743. During the 1740s, Funk's mill became a regular stopping

88. Robert D. Mitchell and Warren R. Hofstra, "Town and Country in the Colonial South: Winchester and Frederick County, Virginia, 1738–1783," paper presented to the Eastern Historical Geography Association, Oct. 24, 1986, 15. A copy of this paper may be found on file at the Handley Library, Winchester, VA.

89. Mitchell, "Metropolitan," 114.

90. Mitchell and Hofstra, "Town and Country in the Colonial South," 15; and James V. Hutton Jr., "Local History Articles," 1971, Handley Library, Winchester, VA, 39. See also "Advertisement," *Virginia Gazette* (Rind), Sept. 26, 1771, 3.

91. Fithian, *Philip Vickers Fithian*, 14; and Mitchell and Hofstra, "Town and Country in the Colonial South," 15.

92. La Rouchefoucault Liancourt, *Travels* 2:101.

point along the road through the Valley where travelers could purchase supplies and camp for the night.[93] In 1749 Peter Stover, son of the early settler Jacob Stover, purchased the mill and 439 acres of land. Gradually, people began to congregate and establish homes around the mill settlement. Funk's mill began to develop into a small craft center known as Staufferstadt, Stover's Town, and Funk's Town.[94]

The number of inhabitants increased with the advent of Indian hostilities. Stover laid out a town and petitioned the Virginia Assembly for a charter. The legislature moved slowly, though Frederick County Burgess George Washington assured Stover that passage of the bill was only a matter of time.[95] Finally, in 1761 the charter passed into law. Stover suggested the community be named Strasburg, presumably after Strasbourg in Alsace.[96]

According to Philip Fithian, who passed through the town in 1775, Strasburg was "built on a rich fine Spot of Land" along a small rise.[97] The plan was based on three parallel avenues: King, Queen, and Holliday streets. The main route through town followed the Great Wagon Road as it entered a cross street from the north and then turned west along Queen Street.[98] Strasburg's rectilinear plan was similar to others in the Valley. Where the two main streets would normally intersect, Stover had the streets pass around the square then continue on their original course. But people interested in developing the town viewed the square as a waste of space; the streets were cut through the middle of the square, and the land sold off.

People established religious and educational institutions in Strasburg very early. A Lutheran church stood in the mill community by 1747, before the town was even laid out. A larger hewn-log structure replaced it in 1769.[99] Similarly, there were efforts to open a school as early as 1752. Henry Sangmeister, a monk from the Ephrata Cloister, a communitarian religious community in Pennsylvania, arrived in Strasburg intending to establish a book bindery and open a school, but local inhabitants were suspicious of his motives.[100] Eventually, the Lutherans hired Simon Harr as a salaried teacher. Peter Stover provided the financial support to open a school on Queen Street.[101]

93. Grube, "Diary," 335; and Wust, "Story of Colonial Strasburg," 9.

94. Wust, "Story of Colonial Strasburg," 13.

95. George Washington, "To Peter Stover," Nov. 9, 1761, in *The Papers of George Washington, Colonial Series*, eds. W. W. Abbot et al. 10 vols. (Charlottesville: Univ. Press of Virginia, 1983–95), 7:97–98.

96. Hening, *Statutes* 7:473–76. Albion and Dodson state that Stover was a native of Strasbourg. See Fithian, *Philip Vickers Fithian*, 136n3.

97. Fithian, *Philip Vickers Fithian*, 136.

98. Virginia Hinkins Cadden, *The Story of Strasburg* (Strasburg, VA: n.p., 1961), 4.

99. John W. Wayland, *A History of Shenandoah County, Virginia* (Strasburg, VA: Shenandoah, 1927), 125; and Cadden, *Story of Strasburg*, 5.

100. For more on the Ephrata Cloister see E. G. Alderfer, *The Ephrata Commune: An Early American Counterculture* (Pittsburgh: Univ. of Pittsburgh Press, 1985).

101. "Will Book, Shenandoah County," Shenandoah County Courthouse, Woodstock, VA, E: 209; Wust, "Story of Colonial Strasburg," 10, 14; and Cadden, *Story of Strasburg*, 5.

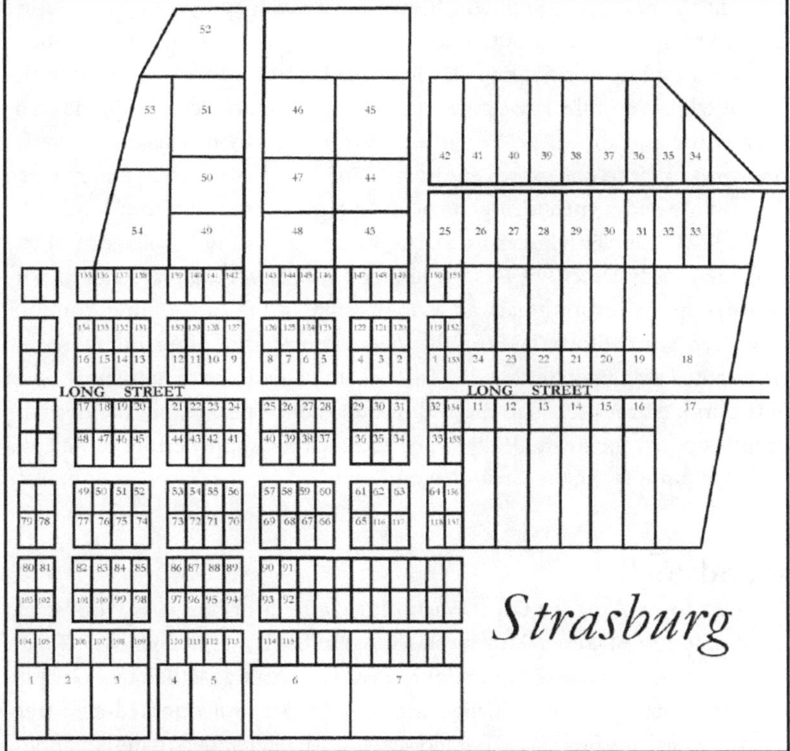

Based on Alexander Hite, "A Plat for the Town of Strasburg or Stover Made by Alexander Hite," 1783. Strasburg Town Hall, Strasburg, Virginia. Map by the author.

Industry and trade developed in Strasburg quickly as well. A majority of the town's inhabitants were farmers, but the miller, a blacksmith, a cooper, and a carpenter all attracted business from the surrounding neighborhood. The French and Indian War not only brought the town new inhabitants, it also gave a boost to the town's economy as the community developed into a regional collection point to supply British troops with livestock and produce. The livestock trade in cattle, pigs, and sheep continued into the next century, though La Rouchefoucauld-Liancourt noted that only the smaller farmers tended to trade with Strasburg merchants. The wealthier landholders drove their livestock directly to Philadelphia via Winchester.[102]

A few disaffected members of the Ephrata Cloister located in Strasburg in the 1750s and quickly left their mark on the town's economy. Samuel Eckerlin was a leading force in these efforts. Although a trained physician, one of two working in Strasburg, he also was involved in establishing a trade in skins and pelts. In 1761 Eckerlin spearheaded an effort to begin a potting industry. He

102. La Rouchefoucault Liancourt, *Travels* 2:100; and Wust, "Story of Colonial Strasburg," 8, 14.

brought the required equipment from Pennsylvania and persuaded another Ephrata monk, Brother Sirone, to serve as a master potter and train apprentices. Strasburg rapidly became known for its earthenware, and as other potteries were established in the late eighteenth and early nineteen centuries, the community became known as "Pot Town." Encouraged by this success, Eckerlin branched out into one more venture. In 1763 he initiated a systematic search for iron ore and helped formulate plans to erect an iron furnace.[103]

In 1775 Philip Fithian recorded that Strasburg was a small village of "thirty families, mostly Dutch."[104] Despite its small size, Strasburg played an important role in the institutional and economic life of the surrounding community. Even before Stover laid out the town, a number of different crafts were represented at the mill settlement. Farming remained a leading occupation of Strasburg's citizens through the end of the colonial period, but the diversity of industry left the town ideally suited as a regional supply center as well as a stopping point along the Great Wagon Road.

Woodstock

The next town along the Great Wagon Road after Strasburg was Woodstock, the southernmost colonial town established in the Lower Shenandoah Valley. Woodstock started life as a migratory town. The area was settled by a German immigrant named Jacob Mueller, who obtained a four-hundred-acre tract from Lord Fairfax in 1752.[105] For ten years, as Mueller added to his land holdings, relatives and friends settled on his land along the road through the Valley. Mueller may have built a fortification attracting even more settlers during the French and Indian War.[106] Gradually a village developed known as Muellerstadt or Millerstown. Mueller had laid out the village into a town by 1761, using the log church as the town center. That year, in a bill sponsored by George Washington, the Assembly chartered the town, giving it the name Woodstock.[107]

Mueller's vision for Woodstock was impressive. The town he created contained twelve hundred acres. Ninety-six acres were divided to create 192 half-acre lots, and the rest of the land was divided into five-acre outlots. The main portion of the town was laid out in a grid pattern made up of three avenues and five cross streets. It was located on a flat section along a slope, turning the town off traditional compass points. King Street (Main), the central avenue followed the Great Wagon Road. The other avenues, Queen Street (Muhlenburg) and Duke William Street (Church), also honored the Royal Family. Lord Fairfax and William Pitt were recognized by cross-street names. Mueller named

103. Wust, "Story of Colonial Strasburg," 14; and Couper, *History* 2:1123.
104. Fithian, *Philip Vickers Fithian*, 136.
105. "Northern Neck Grants and Surveys," H:156; and "Deed Book," Frederick County, 7:399.
106. Wayland, *History of Shenandoah*, 135.
107. Hening, *Statutes* 7:406–7; and Cartmell, *Shenandoah Valley*, 229

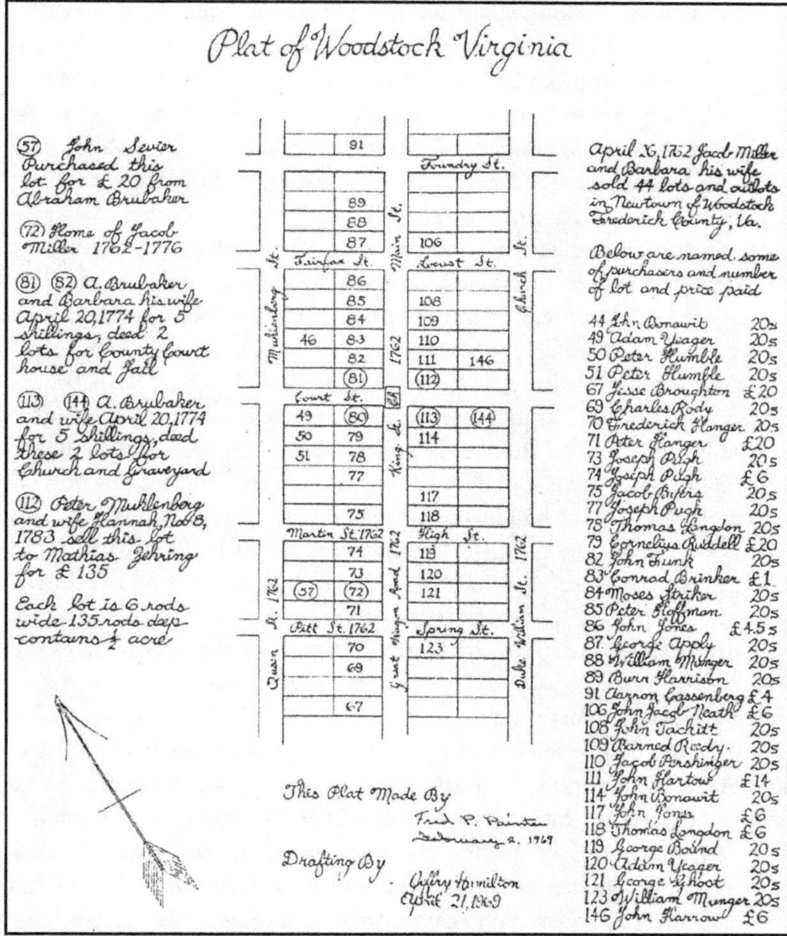

Fred Painter, "Plat of Woodstock Virginia," 1969. In "Deed Book," vol. 281: 171, Shenandoah County Courthouse, Woodstock, Virginia.

the other streets after his sons. The four blocks near the main intersection consisted of twelve lots facing the avenues, two lots deep. The next blocks, northeast and southwest of the main intersection contained only eight lots each. The focus of the town was the log church that stood in the center of the main intersection.[108]

Although the act that created Woodstock named nine men as trustees, the Assembly only granted them the authority to establish building regulations and settle land disputes.[109] Mueller remained the sole landowner as a virtual proprietor. But on April 26, 1762, Mueller and his wife Barbara sold forty-four inlots with their accompanying outlots. The empty lots among them sold for

108. Couper, *History*, 2:1121; and Wayland, *History of Shenandoah*, 131.
109. Hening, *Statutes* 7:406–7.

twenty shillings. The lots with structures on them were valued individually.[110] The success of the initial land offering was a precursor of Woodstock's development. The town quickly became a successful craft and trading center. Mueller himself opened a store in partnership with Adam Yeager.[111] Several ordinaries opened to serve the migratory traffic continuing deeper into the Valley. Early on, John Mosley opened a ropewalk, taking advantage of the regional hemp crop. Additional shops soon joined his manufactory as other craftsmen, including smiths, saddlers, and joiners made Woodstock their home.[112]

When the House of Burgesses created Dunmore (later Shenandoah) County in 1772, it recognized the importance of Woodstock by designating it as the new county seat.[113] Mueller had died six years previously, but the proprietorship had passed to his son-in-law, Abraham Brubaker. Brubaker and his wife deeded four lots to the new county to serve as sites for a courthouse, jail, new church, and cemetery.[114] The town's first resident minister, John Peter Muhlenburg, son of the founder of American Lutheranism, oversaw the construction of the church building (lots 113 and 144). The courthouse was completed in 1773 (lots 81 and 82).[115] Home to the county buildings, Woodstock was assured future success. Indeed, Brubaker laid out and sold additional town lots in 1773.[116] Two years later, when Philip Fithian passed through Woodstock, he wrote, "Here are several Taverns and stores; & perhaps fifty Families."[117] Mueller's town did not need the court to succeed, but it profited from its location nonetheless.

Although no one attempted to establish any towns between Woodstock and Staunton during the colonial period, people laid out two towns in the region in the next decade—New Market and Harrisonburg. Population may have been a factor in this slight delay. In the eighteenth century, the population of the Shenandoah Valley was concentrated in the north.[118] Nonetheless, another individual did establish a colonial town in the Great Valley as it stretched southwest from Staunton.

110. "Deed Book," Frederick County, 7:398–511 passim.

111. "Order Book," Frederick County, 10:322–26.

112. Fithian, *Philip Vickers Fithian*, 136; La Rouchefoucault Liancourt, *Travels*, 2:99; and Cartmell, *Shenandoah Valley*, 229.

113. Hening, *Statutes* 8:579; 9:420–24.

114. "Deed Book," Shenandoah County Courthouse, Woodstock, VA, B:8–12; and Couper, *History* 2:1121.

115. "Dunmore County Order Book," Shenandoah County Courthouse, Woodstock, VA, 1:261, 271, 273.

116. For example, see "Deed Book," Shenandoah County, A:259, 260, 263.

117. Fithian, *Philip Vickers Fithian*, 136.

118. According to the 1790 census, the Valley had a population (including enslaved people) of 74,767. Fifty-two percent of the people lived in the two northernmost counties: Berkeley (population 19,713) and Frederick (19,681). South from there, Shenandoah County's population stood at 10,510, Rockingham's at 7,449, Augusta's at 10,886, and Rockbridge's at 6,528. Mitchell, *Commercialism*, 99.

Fincastle

When the Virginia Assembly established Botetourt County in 1769, county officials decided to locate the court at a spring near Miller's Mill on an eighty-one-acre tract belonging to Israel Christian. Christian, a county justice, offered to give the county forty acres, reserving two half-acre lots for himself. Another magistrate by the name of William Bowyer objected, either because he thought the site unsuitable or he wanted the court on his own.[119] But the court decided to accept Christian's gift and ordered James McGavock to build a "Gaoler's House" and prison, chose Christian and Stephen Trigg to supervise construction of a "Log Cabbin Twenty four feet Long; and twenty Wide for a Court House, with a Clapboard Roof with Two small Sheds one at each end for Jury Rooms."[120] In May 1770 county surveyor William Preston began to lay off the first thirty lots containing one-half acre of land each. In the end Christian donated more land than he originally offered, a total of forty-five acres, of which the court gave him two and one-half.[121] The justices named the new town Fincastle in honor of George Murray, Lord Fincastle, the son of Governor John Murray, Lord Dunmore.[122]

Preston had a formidable challenge in laying out Fincastle because of the geography of the town site Robert Breckenridge, William Fleming, Francis Smith, Benjamin Smith, and Andrew Woods had chosen.[123] They located the town on the slope of a steep hill. Preston decided to use a simple grid pattern created by two main avenues and two cross streets. The most flat portion of the town was the area bordered by Church Street and what was eventually known as Roanoke Street. Back Street and Main Street, thirty-three feet wide, ran east-west down the steep slope of the hill. Preston designated six lots on the slope for the courthouse, perhaps envisioning a structure standing at the top of the hill oriented west to create a formal approach. However, it was eventually built on the northwest corner of Main and Roanoke streets. Lots for an Anglican church and cemetery were laid out on the northeast corner of the small town, beside the public spring. One unusual feature about Fincastle was the fact that Preston laid out the half-acre lots in squares instead of the more typical rectangles.[124]

119. Hening, *Statutes* 8:395–96; and "Order Book, Botetourt County," Botetourt County Courthouse, Fincastle, VA, 1:10.

120. "Order Book, Botetourt County," 1:44; and "Deed Book, Botetourt County," Botetourt County Courthouse, Fincastle, VA, 1:394.

121. "Order Book, Botetourt County," 1:89; and "Deed Book, Botetourt County," 1:121–22.

122. "Order Book, Botetourt County," 1:89; and Kegley, *Kegley's Virginia*, 405. Fincastle remains Botetourt County's seat. It was not part of the short-lived Fincastle County, which was carved from Botetourt in 1772 and then was itself abolished in 1776, when it was divided into three new counties: Montgomery, Washington, and Kentucky.

123. "Order Book, Botetourt County," 1:66.

124. "Deed Book, Botetourt County," 15:104. An 1821 plat of Fincastle can be found in "Deed Book, Botetourt County," 15:103.

"This Plan of the Town of Fincastle was returned to Court & Ordered to be Recd," 1778. In "Deed Book, Botetourt County," 2:347, Botetourt County Courthouse, Fincastle, Virginia.

Some houses were already standing around the mill at the foot of the hill when Fincastle was laid out. With a local population and no shortage of investors, the town lots sold quickly. The county granted licenses for three taverns in 1770; two more opened in 1771, and another in 1773.[125] The Assembly officially chartered the town in 1772 in recognition of its rapid growth.[126] Besides profiting from the business of the court, Fincastle became a collection point for the region's hemp and wheat crops, which were shipped to New London or Staunton and then onto points farther east and north. Christian, who already had mercantile connections in Staunton, was in an especially good position

125. "Order Book, Botetourt County," 1:89; Frances J. Niederer, *The Town of Fincastle, Virginia* (Charlottesville: Univ. Press of Virginia, 1965), 3, 28; and Robert Douthat Stoner, *Seed-Bed of the Republic: A Study of Pioneers in the Upper (Southern) Valley of Virginia* (Radford, VA: Commonwealth, 1962), 165.

126. Hening, *Statutes* 8:616–17.

to profit from the commercial trade. People opened several new mills, including a sawmill, on the stream at the foot of the town. As a result, the town began to profit from large-scale flour and cornmeal production. People also established tanneries and a metalworking shop by the creek. The town also began to market a new agricultural product in the region—flax.[127]

Fincastle's success during the colonial period can be measured by a list of homeowners made near the end of the century. The account records fifty-nine homes in or near the town: eleven frame houses, twenty-six hewn log houses, twenty-one cabins, and one double cabin.[128] Almost immediately, Fincastle functioned as a market center for the region and fit into the trading patterns of backcountry Virginia. Thus Botetourt's county town was guaranteed successful future development. Irish traveler and observer Isaac Weld put it succinctly when he passed through the town at the end of the century. "Fincastle," he said, "is most rapidly increasing."[129]

Martinsburg

The county town of Berkeley County (in modern West Virginia) is another example of an existing village that developed into a town after being chosen as a home for a county court. Located at the northern end of the Shenandoah Valley, Martinsburg began as a village sitting on an eight-hundred-acre tract of land in the Northern Neck granted to Adam Stephen in 1753.[130] It began to form during the French and Indian War, just as many other towns in the Valley did when settlers in the Lower Shenandoah Valley moved to the area, probably drawn by the relative security of a nearby fort.[131] By 1762 members of the settlement began to congregate, creating a village near Stephen's saw and grist mills. People constructed taverns as well as residences to benefit from the migratory trade of people moving south and from people traveling west to visit thermal and mineral springs. Stephen proposed naming the community after himself, but by that time Stephensburg had already been established to the south, so the village became known as Martinstown or Martinsville either in honor of Stephen's friend Thomas Bryan Martin, a Frederick County justice, or the Reverend Denny Martin, who was helpful in getting the county court for Martinsburg. Both men were relatives of Lord Fairfax.[132]

127. Stoner, *Seed-Bed*, 36, 47; and Niederer, *Town of Fincastle*, 3, 11.

128. Niederer, *Town of Fincastle*, 4–5.

129. Weld, *Travels* 1:214.

130. "Northern Neck Grants and Surveys," H:398. Stephen later added to his holdings. See "Northern Neck Grants and Surveys," M:128, 389.

131. Dandridge, *Historic Shepherdstown*, 36; and J. E. Norris, ed., *History of the Lower Shenandoah Counties of Frederick, Berkeley, Jefferson, and Clarke* (Chicago: A. Warner, 1890), 242.

132. Fithian, *Philip Vickers Fithian*, 11; Norris, *History*, 229, 242; Cartmell, *Shenandoah Valley*, 232; Couper, *History* 2:1094; and Lorraine Minghini and Thomas E. VanMetre, *History of Trinity Episcopal Church and Norborne Parish Martinsburg, Berkeley County, West Virginia* (Martinsburg, WV?: n.p., 1956?), 49.

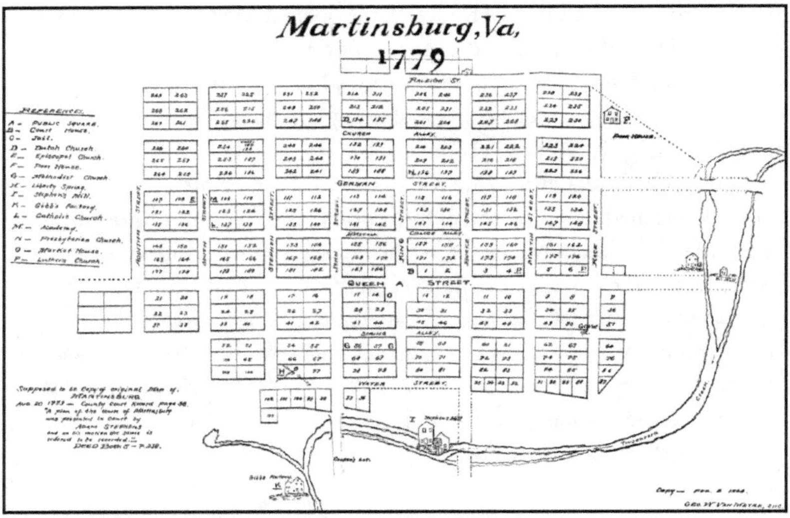

Geo. Van Metre, "Martinsburg, Va. 1779." Berkeley County Courthouse, Martinsburg, West Virginia, 1904. Courtesy of the Berkeley County Clerk's Office, Martinsburg, West Virginia.

Settlement growth in the backcountry created the need to divide Frederick County in the 1770s. Stephen was an important voice in regional politics, having risen to the rank of major general in the Virginia militia and having served as justice of the peace for the county. He was also the largest landholder in the northern part of the county and led a movement to petition the Assembly to form a new county. He was successful, and in 1772 the Assembly created Berkeley County.[133]

The new county court met at the home of Edward Beeson until Stephen, Berkeley's new sheriff, successfully lobbied to have the court moved to his property at Morgan Spring near Tuscarora Creek. In November 1772 the court provided the funds necessary to construct a prison and a courthouse. Plans for the jail were specific: it was to be a thirty-by-thirty-six-foot structure with plank walls, each floor containing three rooms. The courthouse design would be determined later. In an effort to keep the court on his property, Stephen agreed to donate an acre of land, as well as the planking and stone needed for the courthouse.[134] But there were delays, and in a move to try and speed the process, Stephen withdrew his offer to provide the lumber. He also placed the condition that construction must begin immediately if he were to provide the land and stone. Nevertheless, the delays continued while the justices debated the shape of the courthouse. Finally, in August 1773, they

133. Hening, *Statutes* 8:597–99; and Harry M. Ward, *Major General Adam Stephen and the Course of America Liberty* (Charlottesville: Univ. Press of Virginia, 1989), 102–3.

134. "Berkeley County Minute Book," Berkeley County Courthouse, Martinsburg, WV, 1:94, 104–5; and Ward, *Major General*, 103.

hired William Brown as an undertaker to build a courthouse with "the walls to be Built in a circular form instead of a square."[135] Construction was extremely slow, and the building was not completed until 1779 or 1780.[136]

Hitetown/Leetown

While finalizing the courthouse design partly caused the delay in accepting Stephen's offer, there was also another reason. Stephen had a rival, a man named Jacob Hite, the son of Yost Hite, one of the original settlers in the Shenandoah Valley. Another hamlet, which became known as Hitetown (modern Leetown, West Virginia), had developed around Jacob Hite's gristmill.[137] When the Assembly created Berkeley, Hite petitioned to have the court moved there. Stephen's offer and later ultimatum may have been an attempt to pressure the court into choosing his town over Hitetown. Suspecting fraud in the ultimate decision, Justice Hite and other members of the court petitioned the Governor's Council to reconsider the decision, but Stephen's village remained Berkeley's county town.[138]

While the court controversy was raging, a feud broke out between Stephen and Hite after Stephen, in his capacity as sheriff, confiscated fifteen of Hite's slaves and twenty-one of his horses to be auctioned off in settlement of a judgment against Hite. The incident grew as Hite, supported by Justice Horatio Gates (of Revolutionary fame) broke into the jail and reclaimed Hite's property. The fame of the feud spread across the colony as Hite presented his case to the public in *The Virginia Gazette*, making charges that Stephen, because of his position in the community, felt obligated to answer.[139] Finally, Hite, disgusted with the entire affair, sold his property to General Charles Lee and relocated his family to South Carolina. His hamlet, a simple row of lots situated at a T-shaped intersection, never really developed further.[140]

135. "Berkeley County Minute Book," 1:134–5, 182, 199. A circular courthouse would have been unusual in colonial Virginia. See Lounsbury, "Structure of Justice," 214–26; and Whiffen, "Early Courthouses," 2–10.

136. Gardiner and Gardiner, *Chronicles*, 20–23; and Norris, *History*, 232.

137. "Berkeley County Minute Book," 1:196; Thomas Blackburn, "Advertisement," *Virginia Gazette* (Rind), Oct. 8, 1772; Bryan Bruin, "Advertisement," *Virginia Gazette* (Purdie and Dixon, and Rind), Oct. 17, 1771; and Minghini and VanMetre, *History*, 49.

138. McIlwaine, Hall, and Hillman, *Executive Journals* 6:522–23; and Ward, *Major General*, 104–5.

139. They even sent their accounts to rival editors who published papers named the *Virginia Gazette*. See Jacob Hite, "Mr. Pinkney," *Virginia Gazette* (Pinkney), July 6, 1775; Adam Stephen, "To Mess. Dixon & Hunter," *Virginia Gazette* (Hunter and Dixon), Sept. 30, 1775; Hart, *Valley*, 56–57; and Ward, *Major General*, 105–6.

140. "Deed Book, Berkeley County," Berkeley County Courthouse, Martinsburg, WV: 3:463–64; Jacob Hite, "To be Sold, by public auction," *Virginia Gazette* (Pinkney), Sept. 7, 1775; Norris, *History*, 393; and Anna W. Schley and Linnie Schley, "Old Homes of the Leetown Neighborhood," *Magazine of the Jefferson County Historical Society* 7 (Dec. 1941): 7–8. For more on the Hite family, see A. D. Kenamond, "The Hite Families in Jefferson County," *Magazine of the Jefferson County Historical Society* 31 (Dec. 1965): 34–35.

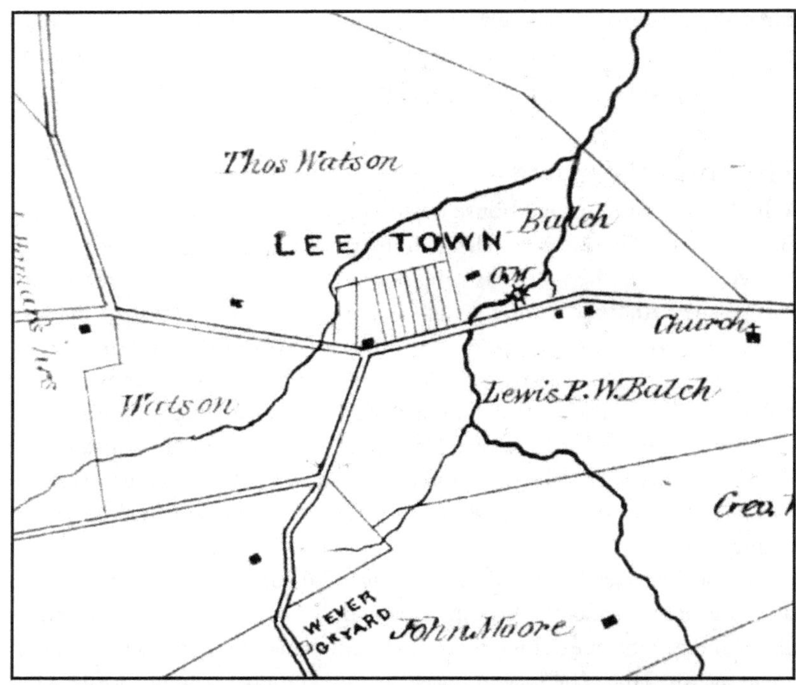

Detail of "Map of Jefferson County Va. Photographed for the Bureau of Topographical Engineers Oct. 1862." Cartographic and Architectural Branch, National Archives, College Park, Maryland.

Stephen's village was more successful. After the court controversy abated, Stephen laid out streets for the town that ultimately was named Martinsburg. Stephen was ambitious, marking off 269 half-acre lots. The central feature of the town was a Renaissance-style public square at the intersection of the two main avenues, King and Queen streets (an interesting and possibly revealing choice of names on the eve of the American Revolution). The remaining portion of the town was cut into blocks of six lots each by streets and alleys in a regular grid pattern. The streets were sixty-six feet wide, while the alleys were thirty-three. The square housed the courthouse and a market. Although the town was seated near Tuscarora Creek, the main water supply was Morgan's Spring, renamed Liberty Spring during the American Revolution (lot H). Eight small lots laid out along the creek (lots 93–103) may have been intended for industrial use.[141]

Stephen's ambitious plans for Martinsburg were not ill founded. When the streets were actually laid out, the town already contained more than twenty houses, a sawmill, a gristmill, two or three ordinaries, two stores, a blacksmith shop, a shoemaker's shop, and a distillery. It continued to grow throughout the 1770s. The banks of Tuscarora Creek developed into an industrial sector

141. "History of Berkeley County," in *Historical Hand-Atlas*, 17.

with the addition of new mills and work yards. Within a few years Martinsburg developed into a regional service center, though its trade was hampered somewhat by its proximity to Winchester.[142]

Several institutions made their home in the young town. An academy opened during the early years of the Revolution. Not surprisingly, Martinsburg had a large German population, which was even acknowledged in a street name (German Street). By 1775 a German Reformed Church constructed a sanctuary (lot 194), quickly followed by a Lutheran congregation (lot 4). But Martinsburg's ethnic diversity was reflected in the other congregations that established churches before 1779: Episcopal, Presbyterian, Methodist, and Roman Catholic (lots 108, 196, 56, and 137 respectively).[143]

In 1773 Martinsburg was in a position to develop into a successful town. However, had Hitetown been made county seat of Berkeley, it easily could have drawn away Martinsburg's commerce and population. In 1775 Philip Fithian wrote of Martinsburg, "It is yet in its Infancy—Two Years ago the Spot was high Woods—There are now perhaps thirty Houses, they have already built a Prison of stone & strong—And are now making a Courthouse of no inconsiderable size & Eligance."[144] Martinsburg had existed without the court, but only as a small village. Once it became the county town, the court assured further growth—a growth so dramatic that the Virginia General Assembly granted it a charter in 1778, just five years after Stephen had laid out his new town.[145]

From Mecklenburg to Fincastle, nine urban places stood near the Great Wagon Road as it passed through Virginia by the close of the colonial era. What is remarkable is that all of them continue to exist in the twenty-first century, revealing much about what factors were necessary to the success of towns in the colonial backcountry. Geography and the constant stream of settlers into the Great Valley provided the chief differences between the Valley towns and communities in the Piedmont and Southside. By funneling the thousands of migrants along the valley floor, the mountains to the east and west helped shape the location, development, and success of these towns.

Essentially, the Valley towns were migrant settlements along the main route into the southern backcountry, which was the source of their communication, their supplies, their trade, and most of their inhabitants. With tens of thousands of people moving into the Valley and tens of thousands more moving on into North Carolina, the towns could not help but flourish. They tended to be spaced at regular intervals, usually between six and twelve miles apart, or a day's travel by wagon.[146] They had a steady supply of new residents, a ready

142. Norris, *History*, 242–43; and Ward, *Major General*, 103.
143. Minghini and VanMetre, *History*, 50.
144. Fithian, *Philip Vickers Fithian*, 11.
145. Hening, *Statutes* 9:569–71.
146. Hofstra, *Planting*, 261–62.

market for people passing through, and excellent connections for trade with Maryland and Pennsylvania, as well as the other regions of Virginia. The migration not only benefited Valley towns: the Great Wagon Road also provided access to the Southside. It is not coincidental that New London, which had easy connections to the Valley, was the Southside town that prospered the most during the colonial period. The influx of settlers from the North also shaped the unique and divers ethnic and religious character of the Valley towns.

It was the Great Valley of Virginia with its thriving towns that saw the most successful urban development of all the regions in the Virginia backcountry during the colonial period. Two towns located at opposite ends of the Shenandoah portion of the Great Valley grew to dominate the region. In the north, Winchester, the largest backcountry town and one of the largest towns in Virginia, clearly dominated the region, serving as the hub of what became the closest thing to a true hierarchy of central places in Virginia. Staunton played a similar role in the southern part of the Valley, though its network was composed of fewer elements. Since urban systems are evolving constantly, a perfect hierarchy probably never would develop, but it is possible to think of the two networks as loosely hierarchical. Actually, the geography of the Valley helped create a system that was more linear in its arrangement than central.[147]

At the end of the eighteenth century, the northern network consisted of at least six hamlets, seven local centers with populations ranging from 250 to 650 persons, and one secondary town (Mecklenburg) with 1,100 residents. Winchester was a mercantile powerhouse, having five stores in operation by 1757 and an astounding twenty-one by 1787. It in turn was connected to the fall-zone ports of Falmouth, Fredericksburg, and Alexandria.[148] Winchester's position in the Valley was even important to larger ports to the north. Winchester was an important component of Philadelphia's cattle trade, and its connection to Baltimore was essential for the port's success, as Winchester provided direct access to the tremendous volume and variety of backcountry products. Without towns like Winchester there could not have been a Baltimore.[149]

The hierarchy of central places in the southern part of the Shenandoah Valley was in a more formative stage at the end of the colonial period than its northern counterpart, but a rudimentary system had developed. Staunton, which boasted five stores by 1764, was fed by smaller towns like Fincastle as well as a number of smaller hamlets. Staunton's hinterland extended beyond the Valley, reaching to New London in the Southside and to Warm Springs and Hot Springs in the Mountains. It was connected to fall-zone ports, particularly Richmond and Fredericksburg, and participated in the cattle trade moving through the Valley to Winchester and beyond.

147. O'Mara "Urbanization," 423; Russo, *American Towns*, 56; and Hendricks, "Town Development," 309–10.

148. Hofstra and Mitchell, "Town and Country in Backcountry Virginia," 631, 637, 639; and Mitchell, "Metropolitan," 115.

149. Earle and Hoffman, "Staple Crops," 51.

While central place theory may go a long way toward describing urban development in the Great Valley, it is not easy to discount the importance of staple theory in understanding the growth of central places there. Both Winchester and Staunton prospered before the development of a large-scale trade in secondary staples such as wheat, hemp, and cattle, and much of the processing of these products took place outside of large towns. Rarely were Valley towns collection sites for surplus agricultural products. Cattle drovers simply passed through the towns on their way north, and wheat was processed and shipped directly from mill sites.[150] However, while these observations may be true to an extent, they ignore certain realities. For example, there were important milling operations in a number of urban centers, including Fincastle, Martinsburg, Mecklenburg, Strasburg, and Staunton. Cattlemen passing through the towns supported taverns, stores, and other service industries. Industries related to the cattle trade developed in places like Winchester, leading to related industries, such as the production of butter and cheese, and byproducts like tallow and leather. Winchester's ropewalk also suggests that quantities of hemp were coming into the town's markets. Furthermore, even if the majority of trade in secondary staples such as wheat took place outside of towns, the profits from wheat and flour were greater than from tobacco, and farmers spent much of that money in Valley towns on goods and services.[151] When such elements of the towns' economies are taken into account, it seems that staple theory adds a complimentary explanation to the rise of central places in the Valley.

Along with the additional function of providing goods and services for people passing through, the Valley towns also served the same roles as backcountry towns in other regions. Four were established to serve as county towns, though three of them—Martinsburg, Staunton, and Fincastle—had existed previously as small mill communities before being laid out as towns. One other town, Woodstock, became a county seat before 1776. The other four towns, with the exception of Stephensburg's brief stint as a county seat, never served as a home to a country court during the colonial period.

During the years when there was no military conflict, Valley towns without county courts tended to fall into two categories. Stephensburg was primarily an agricultural community. Because of its proximity to Winchester, initially Stephensburg attracted few settlers and no industry or mercantile establishments. Only its brief tenure as Frederick's county seat provided Stephensburg with large numbers of investors, though despite the increase, the town's inhabitants remained primarily farmers.

Other Valley towns became centers of industry and trade, serving the needs of their surrounding community and the southward train of settlers, as well as sending the region's products to larger towns. Martinsburg, Strasburg,

150. Hofstra and Mitchell, "Town and Country in Backcountry Virginia," 621; and Mitchell, "Metropolitan," 114.

151. Mitchell and Hofstra, "Town and Country in the Colonial South," 18; and Earle and Hoffman, "Staple Crops," 28, 36.

Staunton, and Fincastle all grew up around mills. In addition to its mills, Strasburg could boast an important ceramics industry. Mecklenburg had milling operations, but it also supported a diverse number of other craftsmen. Before it became the seat of Dunmore County, Woodstock served as an important craft community as well. Each of these towns became important regional centers and had trading connections with other towns in the Valley and beyond.

The number of institutions beyond the court reflected a town's degree of development while simultaneously encouraging more settlement in the town and the surrounding area. Most of the communities had taverns and stores. However, the more successful towns also supported religious and educational institutions. Winchester, Staunton, Woodstock, Strasburg, and Martinsburg all had at least one church established before the end of the colonial period. Winchester, Staunton, Mecklenburg, Strasburg, and Martinsburg all had schools. Staunton was unique in that it was home to an orphan asylum.

Geography, population, services, and trade all affected the growth of the Valley towns, but they would not have been established at all without private initiative. Entrepreneurs played a direct role in the creation of the four court towns. James Wood set the precedent in laying out Winchester with the intention of it becoming the seat of Frederick County, although he was in the unique position of having to play a delicate game of politics with a proprietor, Lord Fairfax. Once Augusta County was formed, William Beverley took the initiative and created Staunton in an effort to attract settlers to his huge estate. Israel Christian and Adam Stephen may simply have been motivated by land speculation and the enormous profit potential of a successful town. Although Mecklenburg never became a county seat, Thomas Shepherd knew what a great benefit a court could be and reserved a space for a courthouse, just in case. Virginia's Assembly recognized the role of these individuals when it chartered many of the towns. The acts often made such references as "Whereas it hath been represented to this General Assembly, that James Wood, gentleman, did survey and lay out a parcel of land . . . for a town."[152] For the most part, each of these men had enormous tracts of land in the area being created into a new county. The achievement of acquiring the county court not only brought success and prestige for towns, but also helped raise the status and power of the men who founded them.

The town founders used different tactics to gain support from county justices to locate the court in their towns. James Wood gave Frederick County fourteen acres of land in Winchester, keeping only a few lots for himself. William Beverley kept forty-four lots in Staunton for himself but donated twenty-five acres and a courthouse (albeit shoddily built) to Augusta County. Israel Christian gave Botetourt County officials almost the entire town land of Fincastle—forty-five acres—while Adam Stephen offered Berkeley County only an acre of land and building materials for the courthouse (coincidently,

152. Hening, *Statutes* 6:268–70. For other examples, see Hening, *Statutes* 7:473–76, 8:616–17.

both counties were named in honor of Virginia's popular governor Norborne Berkeley, Baron de Botetourt). These men realized that to profit from a town located on their land, they need not maintain control of all of the town lots. Simply having the town nearby would raise the value of the surrounding property. Furthermore, Wood and Lord Fairfax successfully demonstrated that money was to be made with a town's expansion.

If gifts of land and buildings were not enough to aid in the establishment of a county seat, the town founders had other tools. William Beverley used his influence in the Assembly quite effectively, blocking opposition from the Augusta County court justices. Adam Stephen fought on the local level in his capacity of Berkeley County's sheriff to aid in his battle against rival Jacob Hite. Powerful allies also helped in the towns' development. Lord Fairfax worked with James Wood to build Winchester instead of trying to block his efforts, and Fairfax's relatives Thomas and Denny Martin assisted Adam Stephen. Other men did not restrict their involvement to one county town. Israel Christian used his mercantile connections in Staunton to help support his store in Fincastle.

Private initiative was also a factor in establishing towns that did not serve as county seats. Thomas Shepherd, Lewis Stephens, Peter Stover, and Jacob Mueller did not have to make gifts of land in order to secure a population when they founded their towns (although Mueller's son-in-law made a free gift of land to the Shenandoah County court when Woodstock became the county seat). Instead, they were proprietors in their own right. Shepherd, Stephens, Stover, and Mueller all laid out towns after a number of people had already settled on their land. They had a guaranteed market for their town lots.

It is very telling that almost half of the Valley towns arose out of the discord of the French and Indian War. Mecklenburg, Stephensburg, Strasburg, and Woodstock were all founded after groups of settlers banded together for security near a private fort, and a fort may have aided in the creation of what became Martinsburg. Much closer to the theater of battle than Piedmont or Southside citizens, Valley residents felt much more vulnerable and were quick to seek the security of greater numbers. However, a fort was not the only focus for the development of a Valley town.

Besides aiding in their creation, war also aided in the growth of Valley towns. The location of Fort Loudoun proved to be an important boon to Winchester, not only adding a measure of security but also creating economic benefits. New industries developed there to support the military, and the large numbers of troops stationed at the fort brought increased trade to other businesses. Other towns also found economic prosperity because of war, particularly Strasburg, which developed a substantial livestock and agricultural trade with the military during the French and Indian War, and Mecklenburg, with its large number of craft industries, which flourished during the Revolution by supplying the army with saddles, munitions, and other products in addition to food.

Considering the way most Valley towns developed, it should be no surprise that so many of them at least temporarily sported the names of their founders. Mecklenburg, although officially named after the queen, continued to be referred to as Shepherdstown until 1798, when the Virginia Assembly bowed to reality and officially recognized that name.[153] Stephensburg was the only town chartered under the name of its founder, though for a time Strasburg was known as Staufferstadt, and Woodstock was referred to as Muellerstadt. Hitetown became Leetown once Jacob Hite sold it to Charles Lee, and Adam Stephen would have loved to have named his town for himself if the name had not been taken already. Staunton and Fincastle, both court towns, were named after members of the ruling governor's family, and another county seat, Martinsburg, honored a relative of Lord Fairfax.

Most of the Valley towns followed the trend in other parts of the Virginia backcountry by using a gridiron street system of half-acre lots, with some variation. Winchester's grid was irregular, a reflection of several additions to the original plan. Lord Fairfax also added the five-acre outlots. Staunton had a more regular street system, but each block was small, containing only four lots. Woodstock had an alternating system of blocks with eight and twelve lots. Fincastle also had two sizes of blocks, some with four and others with six lots, although the town was unique in that the lots were square. Stephensburg was divided by two main cross streets and had linear blocks of five lots each, with accompanying outlots. Mecklenburg was based on long avenues with cross streets cutting the town into large square blocks. The design of Strasburg was very reminiscent of Mecklenburg in that it too was based on long avenues and had square blocks. Martinsburg had a Renaissance-style square that served as the location for its courthouse and market. And although Woodstock did not have a square in the traditional sense, an important building stood in the center of the town's main intersection. It was not the courthouse, but a church.

When Joshua Fry and Peter Jefferson delineated the path of the Great Wagon Road through the Great Valley of Virginia, they pointed out a corridor for migrating settlers traveling out of Pennsylvania into the backcountry. The towns that were established along the road were not created by an organized land system, nor were their locations chosen by a colonial proprietor. Instead, many of them grew out of the chaos of the French and Indian War. As the flow of immigration slowed to a trickle, the settlers along the route banded together for security, creating several villages. Other towns grew to meet the needs of local government as the population of the Valley increased. These towns made trading connections with other communities, developed industries, and became regional service centers. Although the Valley towns developed at different rates because of their individual circumstances, all of them flourished and continued to serve the flow of migrants as they moved through the Virginia backcountry.

153. Shepherd, *Statutes* 2:139.

Chapter 5

The Mountains

Settlement west beyond the Great Valley of Virginia was limited during the colonial period. It was difficult to reach arable lands in the mountains, and there was still danger of conflict with Indians—a fact that became all too evident during the French and Indian War. Still, in the northern part of the colony, where gaps made passage into the mountain valleys relatively easy, a small cadre of intrepid people began moving into the region during the second quarter of the eighteenth century. The lure of the Virginia mountains was not just openness and the possibility of land, both of which could still be had in other parts of the colony. The mountains also had other resources that drew people, not only in the northern part of the colony but also west of Staunton, where the terrain made traversing the slopes more problematic. Despite the problems of accessibility, by 1776 at least four sites in the mountains west of the Great Valley were functioning towns.

Romney

Only one mountain town developed along the lines of other Virginia towns during the colonial period. A portion of the Northern Neck stretched into the northern reaches of Virginia's mountains, and Lord Fairfax was always looking for ways to exploit his vast land holdings. Settlers moved west into the relatively accessible river valleys there by the 1730s. Among them were John and Job Pearsall, who moved with their families onto a plain along the South Branch of the Potomac River by 1738. Other people joined them, and the South Branch community on what became known as Pearsall's Flats began to grow. From the survey party he sent across his holdings in 1748, Fairfax learned that there were squatters on his land, and he began to grant land to the settlers. He also worked to encourage other people to move into the region, but Frederick County's boundaries caused him two problems. Members of the South Branch community who had any legal business were forced to cross back over the mountains and travel to the court that met at Winchester. That might discourage future settlement in the region, so Fairfax needed to push for the creation of a new county west of the Valley. On the other hand, he wanted to segregate his lands and deal with as few jurisdictions as possible. Part of the Northern Neck tract west of the mountains already spilled over into Augusta County. So in 1753 Fairfax petitioned the Assembly to create Hampshire County out of parts of both Frederick and Augusta.[1]

The act creating Hampshire County went into effect in 1754. The timing was not propitious, because that year its inhabitants found themselves in the middle of a war zone. Job Pearsall built a fort strong enough to provide protection for his immediate neighbors. George Washington, responsible for the safety of the region as an officer in the Virginia militia, visited the fort and garrisoned it with between forty and ninety men on several occasions between 1754 to 1758. Meanwhile, citizens in the rest of the county fled eastward, and in a report to Lieutenant Governor Robert Dinwiddie, Washington described Hampshire as "desolate," calling the county a place "where scarce a family lives!"[2] By 1762 tensions in the region had settled and people began returning to rebuild. Lord Fairfax was also anxious to return to his settlement project, so he sent surveyors into the region to choose a site to build a town.

The surveyors settled on Pearsall's Flats because it had a number of advantages. It was relatively level and fertile, and there were already a number of structures there, including Fort Pearsall, a church, a school, and the courthouse. Fairfax had one hundred half-acre town lots laid out into blocks of four lots each. There were also ninety-six accompanying outlots of two and a half acres. Four lots (65, 66, 75, and 76) were reserved for public use, and the courthouse stood on lot 66. The blocks were created by four sixty-foot-wide streets (Bolton, Marsham, High, and Grafton) and four sixteen-and-a-half-foot lanes (Birch, Rose, Grubb, and Gravel). Ironically, the main route into town, the road to Winchester, entered via one of the narrow lanes.[3]

1. Hening, *Statutes* 6:376–79; Selden W. Brannon, ed., *Historic Hampshire: A Symposium of Hampshire County and Its People, Past and Present* (Parsons, WV: McClain, 1976), 236; Cartmell, *Shenandoah Valley*, 230; and Federal Writers' Project, *Historic Romney, 1762–1937* (Romney, WV?: Town Council, Romney, 1937), 48.

2. George Washington, "To Robert Dinwiddie," Apr. 24, 2756, in Washington, *Papers* 3:45; Brannon, *Historic Hampshire*, 236–37; and Hu Maxwell and H. L. Swisher, *History of Hampshire County, West Virginia, from Its Earliest Settlement to the Present* (Morgantown, WV: A. Brown Boughner, 1897), 517.

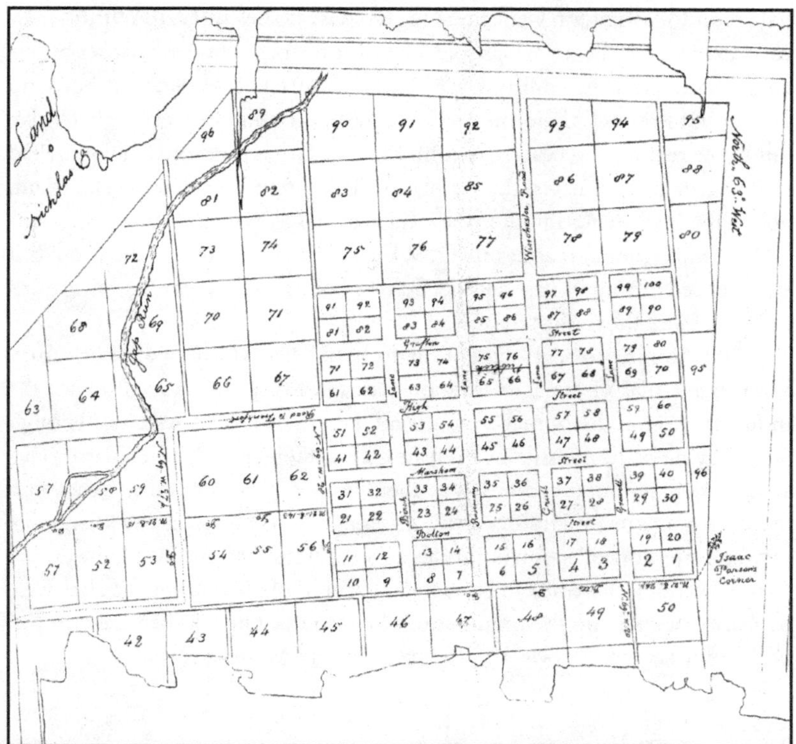

Detail of "Plan of the Town of Romney," 1790. Folded plan included in Federal Writers' Project, *Historic Romney, 1762–1937* (Romney, West Virginia [?]: Town Council, Romney, 1937).

Once his mountain town was laid out, Lord Fairfax wasted no time in asking the Assembly to grant it a charter. Hampshire's burgesses introduced the petition November 18, 1762. The resulting bill scuttled a separate petition that had been presented weeks earlier to charter another town on Fairfax land, called Tucker's Plantation. Once the burgesses saw the Fairfax document, they rejected the other petition. By December the colonial government had chartered the new town, though it neglected to include the usual list of trustees that appeared in such legislation. But the town was official. It was named Romney, possibly after the English Channel port of the same name.[4]

Lord Fairfax had no problems selling lots in Romney. There were already people living on the tract, and there were the public buildings. The same year Fairfax's surveyors laid out the town, the log school was rebuilt in stone behind the courthouse. It became a subscription school named Romney Academy. The town also became a place of commerce; nearby farmers passed through with their wheat and tobacco crops on their way to markets in the

3. (Previous page) Brannon, *Historic Hampshire*, 237–38; and Federal Writers' Project, *Historic Romney*, 9–11, 31.

4. Hening, *Statutes* 7:598–600; Brannon, *Historic Hampshire*, 237–38; and Federal Writers' Project, *Historic Romney*, 53.

Valley, and Washington went there to purchase horses in 1770. Within a few years every lot in the town was sold, and over the next ten years, scores of settlers flocked into the county. By 1774 the county had over seven thousand people, but Romney's halcyon days were past as another Indian conflict broke out in the region, and Governor John Murray, Lord Dunmore felt compelled to bring in troops. Later, the American Revolution deterred development. Following the Revolution, Romney did grow large enough to have the General Assembly name trustees in 1789, but it could not sustain the growth it experienced during its first decade. Even as late as 1833, fewer than fifty families inhabited the mountain town.[5]

While Romney's development might have been typical of a backcountry town in colonial Virginia, its location was not. Except for Pearsall's Flats the mountain region discouraged settlement, and there simply were not enough people living in the mountains to create and sustain towns. The legislature created no new mountain counties, so there was no need for county seats, and there were no great migratory roads bringing the traffic necessary to support service centers or collection points for agricultural shipments. With the exception of Romney, there had to be some unusual resource unavailable elsewhere that drew people into the mountains. The resource that sparked the creation of the other colonial towns in Virginia's mountains was hot water.

The Spa Towns

In eighteenth-century England, the emergence of a consumer society created changes in the life of the nation. With an increase and greater diffusion of wealth, the market for entertainment spread beyond the wealthy classes and members of the court to include the burgeoning middle class. As a result, entrepreneurs in most English towns began to cater to this new trade. Certain localities specialized in the leisure industry. Spas, which had existed previously as minor villages, experienced an increase in number of patrons. At first these centers—the most famous of which was Bath—catered to genuinely ill people who were seeking relief at mineral springs. In between drinking and bathing in the waters, the patrons had leisure to participate in a number of other activities, including dancing and attending concerts. Soon a new kind of "holiday" was born. Throughout the century increasing numbers of people attracted by the fashion and glamour traveled to participate in the new rituals of polite society.[6]

5. George Washington, *The Diaries of George Washington, 1748–1799*, ed. John C. Fitzpatrick, 4 vols. (Boston and New York: Houghton Mifflin, 1925), 1:406; Hening, *Statutes* 13:90–91; Maxwell and Swisher, *History of Hampshire*, 316; Brannon, *Historic Hampshire*, 239; Federal Writers' Project, *Historic Romney*, 31, 53, 55; and Kercheval, *History of the Valley*, 241.

6. P. J. Corefield, *The Impact of English Towns, 1700–1800* (Oxford: Oxford Univ. Press, 1982), 51–53, 63–64; J. H. Plumb, "The Commercialization of Leisure in Eighteenth-Century England," in Neil McKendrick, John Brewer, and J. H. Plumb, *The Birth of a Consumer Society: The Commercialization of Eighteenth-Century England* (Bloomington: Indiana Univ. Press, 1982), 282–83; and Mark Girouard, *The English Town: A History of Urban Life* (New Haven, CT: Yale Univ. Press, 1990), 77.

The attraction and mystique of the spa was not lost on the inhabitants of colonial America, where individuals tried to profit from the popularity of the English resorts. It was no coincidence, for example, that the first town established in North Carolina was named Bath. When explorers and settlers traveled into the western reaches of New England, Pennsylvania, and Virginia, they discovered mineral and thermal springs. Viewed as more than just geological curiosities, these springs quickly became centers of activity. At first they only attracted the infirm who were brave or desperate enough to endure rough trails and other hardships in search of better health. But news of the medical benefits of the springs traveled quickly. In Virginia, for example, *The Virginia Gazette* reported that "The Honourable Lewis Burwell, Esq., President of this Colony is returned from the Medicinal Springs on the Frontiers, where he has been some Time past for the Recovery of his Health, and we hear he has received much Benefit by the Waters."[7] As their numbers increased, travelers could not only "enjoy health" at the Virginia springs but could also find "good Company."[8] During the summer months, an urban economy supplied goods and services, and the sites eventually became permanent towns. By the end of the century, Virginia resorts were just as fashionable as British spas and were not only "visited by the sick alone," but by the "healthiest and most robust in search of pleasure and love."[9] Colonial spas were not as formal or extravagant as English resorts; nevertheless they played social and economic roles similar to their English counterparts. Taking the waters in Virginia soon became almost as popular as it was in the mother country.[10]

The areas around three springs in the Virginia backcountry developed into spas during the colonial period. In Augusta (modern Bath) County, two of the springs worked in tandem as resort communities in a valley on the eastern slope of the mountains. A second resort area developed in northern Frederick County (modern Morgan County, West Virginia) at the site of another thermal spring near the Potomac River.

With the arrival of European settlers in the 1730s, the lore of the spring at Frederick quickly attracted people in search of improved health. Pilgrims to the site began to erect cabins as early as 1745. Two years later, there was enough activity at the spring for Moravian missionaries L. Schnell and Vitus Handrup to observe "for a while the many sick people."[11] Further south in Augusta County the fame of the water spread as well. Explorer and surveyor Dr.

7. "Williamsburg, June 27," *Virginia Gazette* (Hunter), June 27, 1751.

8. Frances Norton Mason, ed., *John Mason & Sons, Merchants of London and Virginia* (Richmond, VA: Dietz, 1937), 189.

9. Ferdinand-Marie Bayard, *Travels of a Frenchman in Maryland and Virginia, with a Description of Philadelphia and Baltimore, in 1791; or, Travels in the Interior of the United States, to Bath, Winchester, in the Valley of the Shenandoah, etc., etc., during the Summer of 1791*, ed. and trans. Ben C. McCrary (Ann Arbor, MI: Edwards Brothers, 1950), 1.

10. Carl Bridenbaugh, "Baths and Watering Places of Colonial America," *William and Mary Quarterly*, 3rd series, vol. 3 (Apr. 1946): 179–80.

11. L. Schnell, "Moravian Diaries of Travels Through Virginia," eds. William J. Hinke and Charles E. Kemper, 12 (July 1904): 55; and *Morgan County, West Virginia, and Its People* (Berkeley Springs, WV: Morgan County Historical and Genealogical Society, 1981), 9.

Thomas Walker, who visited the area in July of 1750, wrote that "we went to the Hot Springs and found six Invalids there."[12] By 1755, a considerable population had grown up in the region surrounding the Augusta Warm Springs, and visitors, including people traveling to the spring from other colonies, frequented the area, though reaching it was not an easy task.

Descriptions of life at the springs during this period are scarce. In 1765 North Carolina Attorney General Robert Jones Jr. wrote the influential lawyer Edmund Fanning that although he "received very considerable Benefit from bathing" at the Augusta springs, the "Great Difficulty of getting Provisions, the Solitude of the Place," and "the want of agreeable Company" brought a quick end to his visit. He also wondered if the trip was worth the effort because travel to and from the facilities "through Drought, Heat, & Bad Roads; my Health (and that of my Horses) was much impaired" before he reached home.[13] It is likely that the areas resembled the scene at a Pennsylvania spring Philip Fithian described some years later:

> It looks indeed like an *Infirmary* or Hospital. Many of them are by no Means in Health. They must, in strong Belief, at least, be indisposed, or they would not submit to the Inconveniences, for any Length of Time, which the Situation of the Place makes necessary. It is quite in the woods. Not a single House, nor any cleared Land, between it & the Town. They must carry all of their provisions, & supply themselves. They live in low Cabbins built with Slabbs, & Boughs, and dress their Dinners at one great common Fire.[14]

Because of the springs' remote locations along the frontier, Indians remained a part of life, especially in times of strife. The Frederick spring lay about thirty-five miles, or one day's journey, from Winchester, the nearest town. Staunton was the closest town to the Augusta springs, some fifty miles, or two days, away.[15] At the start of the French and Indian War, the Presbyterian minister Hugh McAden preached at different locations in the region in July 1755 and described the alarm of the inhabitants at the news of General

12. Thomas Walker, "Extracts from the Journal of Dr. Thomas Walker," ed. J. T. McAllister, *Virginia Magazine of History and Biography* 19 (Apr. 1911): 172. The spring in Frederick County was also known as Warm Springs, Hot Springs, and by a number of variations, which has caused some confusion among historians. Bridenbaugh, for example, mistakenly puts Walker in Frederick County. See Bridenbaugh, "Baths," 160. Similarly, Dorothy Gilcrest confuses references made by Johann David Schoepf. See Dorothy Gilcrest, "The Virginia Springs: A Mirror of Ante-Bellum Society," M.A. thesis, Univ. of Virginia, 1943, 22–23; and Schoepf, *Travels*, 1:310–11.

13. "Letter from the Attorney General [Robert Jones Junr.] to Edward Fanning, Ocanechy, July 25th 1765," in Saunders, *Colonial Records* 7:100.

14. Fithian, *Philip Vickers Fithian*, 114.

15. The rate of travel in the middle of the eighteenth century depended on a number of variables: the purpose of the trip, the mode of transportation (horseback or chaise), weather, and the quality of roads. While in the Tidewater, a traveler could expect to travel fifty miles in a day, in the backcountry the roads were not as good, and the approaches to the Virginia springs were notoriously bad. Fithian described them as "mountainous and stoney." (Fithian, *Philip Vickers Fithian*, 162) During his travels to the region in 1759 and 1760, Andrew Burnaby averaged around thirty-five miles a day. See Burnaby, *Travels*, passim.

Braddock's defeat, declaring that "the whole inhabitants were put into an universal confusion."[16] That same year George Washington toured the area and established Fort Dinwiddie, only five miles from the Augusta springs on the Jackson River, to protect the local populace.[17] The people frequenting the Frederick spring benefited from the proximity of Winchester's Fort Loudoun. Despite these defenses, however, the number of visitors to the springs declined. Andrew Burnaby, for example, almost traveled to see the Augusta springs in 1759, having been assured they "were extremely well worth visiting: but as the Cherokees had been scalping in those parts only a few days before," he "judged it prudent" not to go.[18] Even after the war, the springs were still very much a part of the frontier. In 1775 Indian negotiator and Augusta County magistrate John Connolly wrote a friend in Richmond that he escorted three Indians to the springs to impress them by giving them the "opportunity of seeing as many Gentlemen of Virginia at that place & this season generally bring together."[19]

The lure of the waters' curative powers overcame apprehension of physical danger, and people continued to travel to the springs. Explorers, scientists, and dilettanti traveled to the areas. Thomas Walker, George Washington, Thomas Jefferson, Bishop James Madison, and others recorded their analyses of the waters' character. Washington described the Frederick water as devoid of medical taste, with a consistent temperature of seventy-four degrees.[20] Flavor was no more of a deterrent than danger, though. Jefferson and others found the Augusta water contained sulfur and other minerals, which according to Philip Fithian, made it smell and taste "strongly like the Washings of a foul Gun." Its temperature, "warmer than New Milk," was about 96 degrees, while the smaller spring ran at 112; both hot enough to cook eggs.[21]

People used the Augusta and Frederick springs as cures for various ailments. Most travelers bathed in the waters seeking relief from rheumatoid arthritis, while others drank the waters to cure rheumatic and other less specific "ague & fever."[22] People also believed the springs could cure gonorrhea

16. As quoted in William Henry Foote, *Sketches of North Carolina, Historical and Biographical, Illustrative of the Principles of a Portion of Her Early Settlers* (New York: Robert Carter, 1846), 163.

17. Washington initially sent Peter Hogg to the area, instructing him to proceed without delay "to Jackson River or the Head-Quarters of Captain Lewis's Company," where "above all; you are to be particularly careful in using your best Endeavors to Guard and Protect the Inhabitants and Settlers in those Parts." Washington "To Captain Peter Hogg[,] September 6, 1755," in *Papers* 2:18–19. Washington arrived a few weeks later and directed the fort's completion. Washington, "Memorandum, 24 Sept. 1755," *Papers*, 2:59; and Washington, "To Captain Peter Hogg[,] Sept. 24, 1755," *Papers* 2:60–61.

18. Burnaby, *Travels*, 46.

19. John Connolly, "John Connolly to George Routes," *Virginia Magazine of History and Biography* 14 (July 1906): 78.

20. Frederick T. Newbraugh, *Warm Springs Echoes about Berkeley Springs and Morgan*, 3 vols. (Hagerstown, MD: Automated Systems, 1967), 1:6.

21. Fithian, *Philip Vickers Fithian*, 162; Jefferson, *Jefferson's Notes*, 34; and Thomas R. Joynes, "Memoranda Made by Thomas R. Joynes on a Journey to the States of Ohio and Kentucky, 1810," *William and Mary College Quarterly Historical Magazine*, 1st series, vol. 10 (Jan. 1902): 149.

22. Mason, *John Mason*, 263; Walker, "Extracts," 166; Jefferson, *Jefferson's Notes*, 34–35; and Schoepf, *Travels* 1:310.

and syphilis. Andrew Burnaby reported that a "soldier in the Virginia regiment, whose case was almost desperate, by drinking and bathing in these waters, was, after a few days, entirely cured," though he was disappointed to learn that Colonel Washington could not verify the story.[23] Later in the century, people flocked to the springs for the "Establishment" of their general health and to avoid "the unwholesome air of the cities, during the excessive heat of dog-days."[24]

Warm Springs and Hot Springs

With the reputation of their medicinal qualities growing, the thermal springs were ripe for development. Ownership of both the Warm Springs and the Little Warm Springs, or Hot Springs, fell to descendants of John Lewis, an early settler who came to the region in the 1740s. Hot Springs was included in a three-hundred-acre tract patented by Lewis's son, Augusta County surveyor Andrew Lewis, for himself, his brother Thomas, and Thomas Bullitt.[25] The three men intended to profit from visitors to the spring by building an inn and "properly stock[ing] it with wines, etc."[26] They constructed the tavern in 1766 and improved the springs, though the facilities were somewhat primitive. Spa promoter John Rouelle described the spa at the end of the century, saying that "the springs are upon a hillock, and come out among mud and grasses of different kinds; some holes have been cut . . . to make a kind of bath."[27] The partnership did not last long, and Bullitt became the sole proprietor of the operation in 1769.

Warm Springs lay just five miles north of Hot Springs. In 1751 a 140-acre tract of land that included the thermal spring was surveyed for John Lewis (son of Andrew or Thomas) and his son John.[28] The facilities were more luxurious at Warm Springs, and in 1761 the Lewises created a pool "inclosed with an octangular wall; about ten yards across and in the center about 5 feet 5 Inches deep, shallower at the sides."[29] The bath was not covered, but the Lewises added a wall to "keep the bathers out of sight."[30]

23. Burnaby, *Travels*, 46. See also Newbraugh, *Warms Springs Echoes* 1:7.

24. Mason, *John Mason*, 263; and Bayard, *Travels*, 1.

25. "Land Office Patents," 35:484; and "Surveyors Record, Augusta County," Augusta County Courthouse, Staunton, VA, 2:29.

26. J. T. McAllister, *Historical Sketches of Virginia Hot Springs, Warm Sulphur Springs, and Bath County, Virginia* (Salem, VA: Salem Printing and Publishing, 1908), 5; Oden F. Morton, *Annals of Bath County, Virginia* (Staunton, VA: McClure, 1917), 47; and Stan Cohen, *Historic Springs of the Virginias: A Pictorial History* (Charleston, WV: Pictorial Histories, 1981), 56.

27. John Rouelle, *A Complete Treatise on the Mineral Waters of Virginia: Containing a Description of their Situation, their Natural History, their Analysis, Contents, and their Use in Medicine* (Philadelphia: Charles Cist, 1792), 55.

28. "Will Book, Augusta County," Augusta County Courthouse, Staunton, VA, 3:221–22. See also "Will Book, Bath County," Bath County Courthouse, Warm Springs, VA, 1:298–99; and "Deed Book," Augusta County Courthouse, Staunton, VA, 18:291–92.

29. Briggs, "Journal," 13; and Cohen, *Historic Springs*, 113.

30. Rouelle, *Complete Treatise*, 45.

After the French and Indian War, the increasing popularity of the Augusta springs encouraged wealthy residents of eastern Virginia to push for the construction of roads to help develop the area as a health resort. In 1768 *The Virginia Gazette* ran an advertisement for a group of Fredericksburg businessmen detailing a scheme for a lottery "[f]or raising the sum of nine hundred pounds, to make a road over the mountain to the warm and hot springs in Augusta county."[31] Two years later, residents of Augusta, Botetourt, Hanover, and Albemarle counties sent a petition to the House of Burgesses revealing that the springs were frequented by people from all levels of society. The petition asked the Assembly for funds not only to build a road to the springs but also "for building Houses for the Reception and Security of the poor Sick who resort to the Springs."[32] The Assembly passed a law in 1772 calling for a toll road to be constructed from Jennings Gap to Warm Springs and the construction of the houses for the poor.[33] The new road was finished the same year and vastly improved travel from Staunton.

Philip Fithian's experience traveling to the springs was much different from Robert Jones's twelve years earlier. Fithian found his route into town "nearly intolerable; frozen some on the Surface but not hard enough to bear my Horse; exceedingly hilly, Spurrs running from the Mountains, and all stony" in January of 1776. He took the coach road to Staunton when he left a few days later and was delighted to find that on the new road "You may gallop a Horse, & not hurt him nor yourself, from Foot to Foot of a very high Mountain—pray believe me, it is true, I can prove it."[34]

Because they were resort communities, the populations of Hot Springs and Warm Springs were highly seasonal, reaching their peak during the summer months. With increasing accessibility to the resorts, wealthy Tidewater Virginians competed to buy up land and construction rights. In addition to the homes of the permanent residents of Warm Springs, "about a dozen log cabins" housed summer visitors, which Fithian estimated in 1776 to number "between two & three hundred."[35] Nor did the growing popularity of the resorts rely on word of mouth alone. Thomas Bullitt advertised in *The Virginia Gazette* by 1770.[36]

The summer population brought an increase in the number and variety of economic and social activities, transforming the spring settlements into urban centers reminiscent of Public Times in Williamsburg or court days at

31. "A Scheme of a Lottery," *Virginia Gazette* (Rind), July 21, 1768; Mitchell, "Upper Shenandoah," 409–10; and Gilcrest, "Virginia Springs," 27.

32. Kennedy and McIlwaine, *Journals of the House* 12:126.

33. Hening, *Statutes* 8:546–50.

34. Fithian, *Philip Vickers Fithian*, 161, 163.

35. Joynes, "Memoranda," 149; Fithian, *Philip Vickers Fithian*, 162–63; Jefferson, *Jefferson's Notes*, 35; and Mitchell, "Upper Shenandoah," 440. Other period references to the springs include Mason, *John Mason*, 263, 275, 276; and La Rouchefoucault Liancourt, *Travels* 2:91.

36. "Advertisement," *Virginia Gazette* (Purdie and Dixon), June 7, 1770.

isolated county courthouses.[37] The economy of the region was based primarily on this summer traffic. Merchants with ties in Staunton opened stores in Warm Springs, providing town residents with manufactured goods, ammunition, and whiskey, but these businesses, too, operated on a seasonal basis. To supplement their incomes in the off season, many of Hot Springs' and Warm Springs' permanent residents pursued other activities. Thomas Bullitt, in addition to operating the Hot Springs tavern, developed a market in horses, specializing in racing stock. Other people operated gristmills on the streams running into the Jackson River; however, most residents were farmers, who took advantage of the valley's rich farmland by growing hemp and raising livestock, including cattle, sheep, and hogs.[38]

Although the settlements at the Augusta springs functioned together to attract resort business to the valley, they grew at different rates. Hot Springs remained the smaller village, but people continued to settle around the spring throughout the colonial period. Residents petitioned to charter the town as early as 1778, the year it was platted, although it was not chartered until 1793.[39] Similarly, people settled in Warm Springs until it prospered beyond the constraints of its seasonal industry. During the American Revolution, when the Virginia government had to leave Richmond, Warm Springs was large enough to be chosen as a possible meeting place, and when the General Assembly created Bath County in 1790, Warm Springs became its county town.[40] In the 1780s the Staunton mercantile firm of White, Kirk, and Company set up permanent operations, joined in 1788 by Staunton merchant William Bowyer. In the 1790s other firms including Mustoe and Chambers began operations in Bath County. Partner Anthony Mustoe eventually moved to Warm Springs and was an important force in marketing textiles produced in Staunton.[41]

Bath/Berkeley Springs

Frederick Warm Springs was included in Lord Fairfax's Northern Neck tract. In 1748 he sent a survey party (including sixteen-year-old George Washington, who kept a journal of the trip) to explore the region. During their journey, the group specifically traveled to "see y. Fam'd Warm Springs."[42] Fairfax set the area aside "for the welfare of suffering humanity."[43] This was at the same time

37. Mitchell, "Upper Shenandoah," 440. For Public Times, see James Soltow, *The Economic Role of Williamsburg* (Williamsburg, VA: Colonial Williamsburg Foundation, 1965), 6–19. For court days see Isaac, *Transformation*, 78–93; Charles S. Sydnor, *Gentleman Freeholders: Political Practices in Washington's Virginia* (Chapel Hill: Published for the Institute of Early American History and Culture at Williamsburg, VA, by Univ. of North Carolina Press, 1952), 78–93; Roeber, *Faithful Magistrates*, 73–80; and Shepard, "'Being Court Day,'" 459–70.

38. Mitchell, "Upper Shenandoah," 440; Morton, *Annals*, 66–67; and McAllister, *Historical Sketches*, 7.

39. Morton, *Annals*, 46. Actually, the town was chartered as Hot Bath. See Shepherd, *Statutes* 1:266.

40. Hening, *Statutes* 13:165–67; and Morton, *Annals*, 48.

41. Mitchell, "Upper Shenandoah," 442; and Mitchell, *Commercialism*, 219–20.

42. Washington, *Diaries* 1:6.

43. As quoted in Bridenbaugh, *Myths*, 180. See also Gilcrest, "Virginia Springs," 4.

Fairfax was developing his Hampshire County lands, and he may have intended to lay out a town at the spring. Certainly Fairfax's move was not an empty gesture, for the spring continued to attract ever greater numbers of patrons. Indeed, more people traveled to the Frederick spring than the springs in Augusta County because of its closer proximity to population centers and its greater accessability.[44] While Lord Fairfax erected a house at the spring for himself, most visitors threw up rough huts, staked tents, or sought whatever shelter was available. Despite the rough conditions, people carried out their activities at the spring with some decorum. Gradually, a protocol developed at the spring around bathing whereby men and women bathed alternately, called to the "hollow scooped in the sand" by the blast of a horn.[45]

Washington's interest in the spring continued after his first visit, and in 1760 he approached Fairfax about purchasing the property.[46] Washington visited the spring many times throughout his life, leaving a record of its development. When he traveled to the area in 1761, for example, Washington "found of both sexes about 2[5]0 People . . . full of all many of diseases & Complaints."[47] He discovered that food and provisions were readily available, but lodging was still available only to those people who were willing to construct it: "had we not succeeded in getting a Tent & marquee from Winchester we should have been in a most miserable situation here."[48] By 1767 conditions at the spring had improved enough for him to start bringing Martha, and the couple returned two years later with his stepdaughter, Patsy Custis, hoping to relieve her epilepsy. They stayed two months, occupying the house of Washington's friend James Mercer, though they had to call workers to make some repairs to the building. By this time there was a plentiful supply of labor at the spring, for Washington also ordered an arbor to be constructed for Patsy and arranged for the delivery of meat, poultry, eggs, butter, and vegetables. He also hired the services of a baker and a blacksmith. Services of this sort were certainly necessary, for if Washington was typical, visits to the springs lasted a fortnight, three weeks, or even longer. There was also plenty to do to pass the time beyond taking the waters. The Washingtons attended church and dined or went to tea with the Fairfaxes. Later, Washington's visits became so frequent that he had his own cottage built at the spring, which he used during his presidency.[49]

44. Jefferson, *Jefferson's Notes*, 35.

45. J. J. Moorman, *The Virginia Springs, and Springs of the South and West* (Philadelphia: J. B. Lippincott, 1859), 308–9; Schoepf, *Travels* 1:310–11; and Cartmell, *Shenandoah Valley*, 23.

46. Washington, *Diaries* 1:161.

47. Washington, "To Charles Green," Aug. 26[–30], 1761, *Papers* 7:68.

48. Ibid., 7:69.

49. Ibid., 7:69; Washington, *Diaries* 1:336, 340; Bridenbaugh, "Baths," 160–61; Newbraugh, *Warm Springs Echoes* 1:8; and Cohen, *Historic Springs*, 133. Although evidence is scarce, visits to Virginia's springs may have been even longer. Residents in Williamsburg wrote to London merchant John Norton about his son's visit to Warm Springs in 1772. Norton left the first week in August and did not return until the end of September. See Mason, *John Mason*, 263, 275.

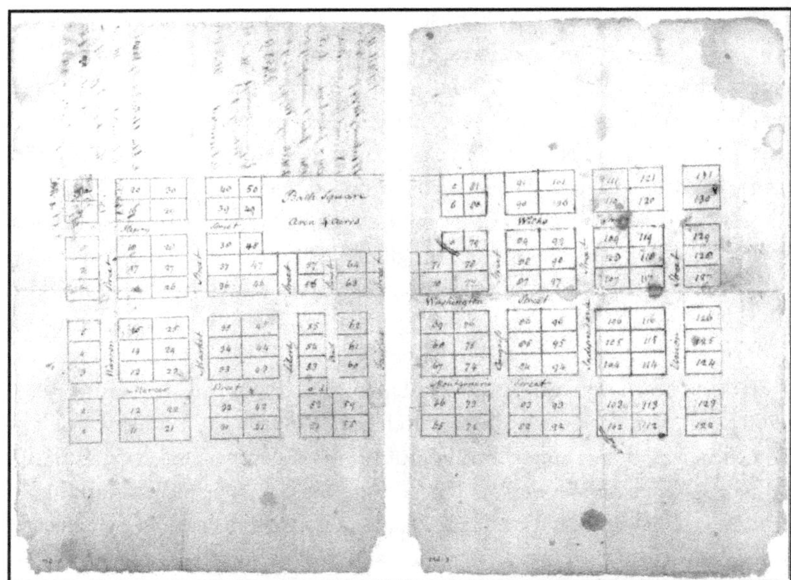

"Plan of the Town of Bath [Berkeley Springs, West Virginia], Showing Streets, Lots, etc., with Endorsements, N. D.," c. 1777. Fairfax Family Proprietary Papers, 1688–1810, Accession 24062, Box 2, folder I-101, Personal Papers Collection, Library of Virginia, Richmond. Courtesy of the Library of Virginia.

Travel to and from the spring improved with the creation of new roads. Washington wrote a friend in 1761, "[O]ur Journey (as you may imagine) was not of the most agreeable sort through such Weather & such Roads as we had to encounter; these last for 20 or 25 Miles from hence are almost impassible for Carriages; not so much from the Mountainous Country (but this in fact is very rugged) as from Trees that have fallen across the Road, and rendered the ways intolerable."[50] Once the Assembly cut Berkeley County off Frederick in 1772 and made Martinsburg the county seat, conditions improved. That year the county authorized two new roads to be cut to the spa.[51]

At the close of the colonial period, the Virginia legislature finally attempted to accommodate the hordes of people flocking to the Frederick spring and bring order to the odd collection of buildings that they had constructed there. In 1776 the Assembly chartered fifty acres of land as the town of Bath (modern Berkeley Springs, West Virginia). Lots sold at public auction after being advertised in *The Virginia Gazette* for three months. The act prevented the sale of lots that contained any houses built by Lord Fairfax, but houses built by other people were to be removed or destroyed within six months. The spring itself was once again reserved "to and for the publick use and benefit."[52]

50. Washington, "To Charles Green," Aug. 26[–30], 1761, *Papers* 7:68.
51. Newbraugh, *Warm Springs Echoes* 1:9.
52. Hening, *Statutes* 9:247–49. See also "Advertisement," *Virginia Gazette* (Purdie), June 27, 1777.

When the town was laid out the next year, it consisted of a grid arrangement of streets cutting the town into blocks of mostly six half-acre lots each. Bath Square, comprising four acres, was set off around the spring in a modified Renaissance style. It was entered from the north by Wilks Street, from the south by Henry Street, and from the east by Bath Street in typical Renaissance fashion. However, two other streets, Liberty and Fairfax, also entered the square on its eastern side. While the Fairfax name was an obvious nod to the land's proprietor, Wilks Street, named for British Whig politician John Wilkes, and Henry Street, named after Virginia Governor Patrick Henry, reveal the fervor of local support for the American Revolution. Other patriotic street names included Liberty, Congress, Independence, Union, and Washington streets. As the town lay in a gorge, space was limited, and houses built on the west end of town were constructed right up against the side of a cliff. To prevent their houses from being destroyed by rockslides during the spring thaw, people frequently built palisades to protect them.[53]

Even before the General Assembly created the town of Bath, Frederick's spring was a flourishing resort where members of all classes gathered. Philip Fithian traveled to the spring in 1775, a year before the Assembly granted it a charter. In September he found the place filled with four hundred people, about half of whom were "visibly disposed," and "Many in sore Distress."[54] The town also abounded with people who came for other reasons than to take the waters. Fithian described the nightlife: "In one Part of the little bush Village a splendid Ball—At some Distance, & within hearing, a Methodist Preacher was haranguing the People. Frequent Writings on the Plates, &c—In our dining Room Companies at Cards. Five & forty, Whist, Alfours, Callico-Betty &c. I walked out among the Bushes here also was—Amusements in all Shapes, & in high Degrees, are constantly taking Place among so promiscuous Company." Late at night he found that throughout the town, the air was filled with "soft & continual Serenades of different Houses where the Ladies Lodge," as the search for marriage partners ensued, occasionally creating havoc, as in the case of the Scot who broke into the "Lodging Room of a buxom Kate . . . compell'd, by the irresistible Call of Renewed Nature," the result of the "Vigor-giving Waters."[55]

Later in the century, Bath remained a flourishing resort town. People in search of relief for their ailments continued to frequent the community, though German doctor Johann David Schoepf noted during his visit that "very few of them came for their health or the water; they seek society and distraction, and make little journeys on horse-back of 2-300 miles, for frequently acquaintances living very far apart have appointments fixed for Bath-town."[56] After

53. Bayard, *Travels*, 39.
54. Fithian, *Philip Vickers Fithian*, 125; and Bridenbaugh, "Baths," 161.
55. Fithian, *Philip Vickers Fithian*, 126.
56. Schoepf, *Travels* 2:311.

Lord Fairfax died, his house became a ballroom and assembly hall for social gatherings. Later, an entrepreneur built a log theater. Taking tea, card playing, and gambling were still popular, and Schoepf found, "The public amusements are horse-racing, play, and dancing; at the balls one or at most two blacks supply the company with woful horn-pipes and jigs."[57]

Like the resorts in Augusta County, Bath's economy continued to be highly seasonal. Residents made what money they could "living in winter on what they can earn during the 'genteel season.'"[58] Unlike the people of Warm Springs and Hot Springs who tried to diversify their economies and provide a measure of self-sufficiency, the residents of Bath preferred "to bring in everything from abroad," making living in the settlement a very expensive prospect.[59] During the summer months, market days were lively, complete with groups of "drunken champions" who roamed the streets looking for fights.[60] But once the season passed, even the merchants left town.[61] According to Methodist Bishop Francis Asbury, Bath was truly a "place of wickedness" after the best English fashion.[62]

Four towns stood in the Virginia mountains at the end of the colonial period.[63] Romney followed a typical pattern of development, evolving to meet the needs of the Pearsall's Flats community, where a fort, church, school, and courthouse had emerged already. With its unique geographical setting on a large mountain plain literally blocked off from competition, Romney cornered the market on urban places in that part of the colony. But the other towns followed a pattern different from any other backcountry towns.

Originally attracted by their curative powers, Virginians began traveling to the Augusta and Frederick thermal springs early in the eighteenth century. The number of pilgrims crossing the mountains steadily increased, so that by midcentury "bush villages" developed during the summer months. Planters and merchants from the Tidewater began to invest in land near the springs. Local settlers established taverns, grew crops, built mills to supply the transient population with food, worked to improve the facilities, and petitioned the Assembly for further improvements such as roads and houses for the poor. Merchants from Staunton and Winchester operated branches of their stores

57. Ibid., 2:310–11; Bayard, *Travels*, 39, 47; and Francis Asbury, *The Journal and Letters of Francis Asbury*, ed. Elmer T. Clark, J. Manning Potts, and Jacob S. Payton, 3 vols. (Nashville, TN: Abingdon, 1958), 1:490.

58. Schoepf, *Travels* 2:311.

59. Ibid.; and Asbury, *Journal and Letters* 1:492.

60. Bayard, *Travels*, 42.

61. Schoepf, *Travels* 2:311.

62. Asbury, *Journal and Letters* 1:518.

63. Although Hot Springs was not formally platted until 1778, it is included because it had full-time residents in addition to its summer traffic during the colonial period and because of its association with nearby Warm Springs. Certainly Frederick Warm Springs can be classified as a town long before it had a new formal street plan imposed upon it in 1776.

at the springs throughout the summer. The impromptu entertainments of a few pilgrims soon developed into a full-scale industry as individuals and groups sponsored balls, assemblies, and theater productions held in appropriate facilities. Resembling the brief life that emerged at isolated county courthouses throughout the colony, the summer seasons of the mountain spas led to thriving urban places—as long as there was warm weather.

Economically, the functionalist approach best explains the story of these towns, as people constructed the inns, bathing facilities, and seasonal stores to meet the summer traffic before the sites reverted to their isolated existence in winter. But by the third quarter of the eighteenth century, Warm Springs, Hot Springs, and Bath were full-scale resort communities, and by the close of the century, each of them had overcome its seasonal status, attracted permanent residents, and was a chartered town. Crucial to their creation was the promise of improved health and social diversion, and the facilities that grew to provide these functions gradually led to the creation of traditional towns. But even before they developed into recognizable towns with year-round residents, the areas around the thermal springs of the Virginia mountains were places that provided urban services. Functionalist adherents argue that the activities on court or market days mark a geographic location as an urban place for the few weeks of activity a year, even if it lacked many facilities or full-time residents.[64] Even with only a few permanent citizens, the spas were full-scale towns for at least three or four months out of the year.

The other important story of the Virginia mountain towns was the power and influence of Thomas, Lord Fairfax. Possibly even more than his activities in shaping towns in the Valley, Fairfax's involvement in the creation of Romney and Bath reveal the deference Virginians on all levels of society paid to the colony's resident nobleman. By the time Fairfax had set up permanent residence in Virginia, the Valley already had a large number of people. So while he had interests in Valley towns, particularly Winchester, Fairfax was always forced to deal with existing communities and other leaders. Romney was his only chance to create a town of his own design, and ironically he built a fairly typical Virginia backcountry town with a gridiron plan, sixty-foot-wide roads, and four-lot blocks. But Fairfax may have had a much easier time than other founders in creating his town. His position led the General Assembly to bow to his request to fashion a county for him and drop a rival town's petition the moment his hit the burgesses' desks.

With Frederick Warm Springs, Fairfax was not quite so heavy handed. Indeed, he regularly allowed visitors on his property, even allowing them to pitch tents and build houses. Perhaps the special nature of the spring persuaded him to be more magnanimous than he had been with the squatters or even legal residents in other parts of the Northern Neck. When he laid out the town of

64. For example, see Ernst and Merrens, "'Camden's turrets,'" 549–74.

Bath, he was generous enough to donate to the town the four acres of land surrounding the spring. Fairfax held enough influence in the General Assembly, however, to insist that all of the structures in the new town except for his own be moved or pulled down. The respect for Lord Fairfax continued despite the fact that he was a loyalist. During the heady early days of the American Revolution when Bath's streets were named, Fairfax Street stood side by side with Liberty, Congress, Independence, and Union streets.

Of all of the regions in the Virginia backcountry, the story of the mountain towns is the most unusual because the four towns owed their success almost exclusively to the growth of service industries. As a county town, Romney's primary purpose was as home to the court, providing legal services for the only colonial county in the mountains. It soon grew to support an academy and provide crafts and market services for the Pearsall's Flats community. As resorts, the three spa towns were unique during the colonial period, but they were just the beginning. Entrepreneurs developed other thermal and mineral springs in Virginia following the Revolution. Books, pamphlets, and other material heralding the benefits of specific waters circulated widely, and during the antebellum years, Virginia spas drew members of all levels of society. Like the English resorts before them, the springs of Virginia became less the refuge of the sick in search of relief and more places of fashion where people of all ranks could mingle in search of social diversion—truly places of both health and good society.

Chapter 6

To Cohabit in Towns

By the end of the colonial period, Virginians literally were going to town in the backcountry. They had made at least twenty-five attempts to establish backcountry towns, bringing about significant changes to the landscape, economy, and culture of the backcountry as people began to congregate and settle together in urban settings. In 1776 nineteen of these towns were functioning urban places, though after the Revolution four of them (Chatham, Westham, New London, and Peytonsburg) lost much of their population and trade, rapidly declining to function as agricultural hamlets or crossroads stores. The four earliest towns (Brent Town, Germanna, King William's Town, and Eden) had failed outright, and Hitetown was puttering along as a small hamlet without much chance of future development. The others continued to grow and flourish and became the vanguard of an important urban explosion during the last quarter of the eighteenth century. People had established the twenty-five towns for a variety of purposes, under differing circumstances, and with varying degrees of success. Nevertheless, by the close of the colonial period, towns and town life were firmly rooted in the southern backcountry. The formula Francis Makemie had laid out in 1705 had been correct. Towns were the means to increasing the value of land, attracting a variety of people, improving trade, and fostering religion and education in the Virginia backcountry.[1]

1. Makemie, "Plain & Friendly," 261–65.

That being said, Virginians had a somewhat ambivalent attitude toward towns. The idea of the town as the origin of civilization was an important theme that was integral to their cultural identity, and yet it had to compete with an innate desire to own land and be independent.[2] The availability of affordable land made it possible for people to carve out a life of self-reliance for themselves, though even if they insisted on living in rural areas, the ties to urban places proved unavoidable. Indeed, one of the factors that may have obscured this important southern urban movement was that backcountry towns, even those not officially chartered by the colonial government, were an essential part of rural society and agriculture, hastening backcountry settlement. Farmers could not and did not wish to function without urban places, and towns needed agricultural communities in order to survive. Together they were part of a larger economic system.[3] Though they were small and relatively few in number, towns provided a wide range of services, helping shape the economic, social, and political lives of people living far beyond their bounds. Rural populations needed towns as collection points for their agricultural products and the locations for retail distribution. Towns also served as centers for the dissemination of government, news, and culture. Towns were the means by which Virginians were settling the backcountry.[4]

The ambivalence over the rural/urban nature of backcountry Virginia may be one explanation for the majority of southern towns' remaining generally small when compared to towns in the middle and New England colonies.[5] At the end of the colonial period, Leesburg had a population of about five hundred people, Staunton and Mecklenburg about one thousand, and Winchester had surpassed fifteen hundred. But these were exceptions. The majority of the backcountry towns were much smaller, with residential populations of only one hundred or so residents, but that did not negate the importance of their role in backcountry life. The existence of a town made it possible to establish weekly markets servicing a surrounding area of three or four miles, hold annual fairs that drew people from a dozen or more miles away, and provide a place for an assemblage of stores, taverns, houses of worship, schools, and courthouses, all of which brought opportunities for trading, socializing, spreading news and information, and receiving justice.[6] A place did not have to provide all of these functions to be a viable town, and in Virginia, many of these activities took place in isolated locations that could not possibly be con-

2. Fries, *Urban Idea*, 31.

3. Rutman with Rutman, *Small Worlds*, 233, 250–51; Mitchell, "Settlement," 35; and Ernst and Merrens, "'Camden's turrets,'" 573.

4. Farmer, *In The Absence*, 2.

5. In discussing the population of Pennsylvania towns in 1800, for example, James T. Lemon categorizes county seats with populations of between three hundred and five hundred people as "Weak, stagnant." And he identifies six backcountry towns with populations of more five hundred people in southeastern Pennsylvania alone. See Lemon, *Best Poor Man's*, 118–23.

6. Mitchell and Hofstra, "Town and Country in the Colonial South," 7.

sidered urban. What was necessary was centrality, or the ability to provide goods and services beyond the needs of the local residents, and a commitment to the idea of towns. People had to be willing to purchase lots, build homes, open businesses, and participate in town life.[7] If these other factors were in place, the size of a town's population was not particularly important. In backcountry Virginia, a place with a hundred residents was a town and an important regional center.[8]

During the seventeenth century, the Virginia government failed several times in its attempts to create towns through legislation. It should be no surprise then that legislative activity did not greatly influence the success of eighteenth-century towns. Acts creating or chartering towns most often reflected physical reality. The Assembly simply recognized backcountry towns that already existed. In other instances, it acted on petitions made by individuals, groups, or county governments. Because there was legislative zeal to create towns in some instances and a seeming reluctance to grant charters in others, charters were a poor measure of a community's success.[9] Of the twenty-five backcountry towns, the Assembly chartered nine when they were little more than place names, while another nine—including Waterford, which flourished throughout the second half of the century—were never chartered, or were not recognized until after the colonial period.[10] The seven remaining towns were recognized legally within five years on average of their establishment.[11] The one major exception was Staunton, which, after its initial act of incorporation was rescinded, had to wait fourteen years for official recognition.

While a charter provides little insight into such factors as population growth and economic importance, it does give hints about the motives behind the establishment of a town.[12] Defense is mentioned in the acts recognizing seven towns, six of which were chartered during the French and Indian War.[13] Concerns over inland trade are mentioned in five acts, while three charters recognize that an individual or group made a gift of land to establish a county seat.[14] Charters name courthouses as the central feature of eight towns, and a

7. Mitchell, "Metropolitan," 108–9.

8. Farmer, *In the Absence*, 21; and O'Mara "Urbanization," 427–28.

9. Armstrong, "Urban Vision," 14.

10. The nine towns chartered the year they were laid out include Bath, Charlottesville, Chatham, Leesburg, Peytonsburg, Romney, Stephensburg, Strasburg, and Woodstock. Towns not chartered during the colonial period were Brent Town, Eden, Germanna, Hitetown, Hot Springs, King William's Town, Martinsburg, Warm Springs, and Waterford. Hot Springs, Martinsburg, Warm Springs, and Waterford were all chartered after 1776.

11. The towns, with the number of years between their founding date and receiving a charter, include Dalstonburg, 2; Fincastle, 2; Mecklenburg, 4; New London, 4; Staunton, 14; Westham, 1; and Winchester, 8.

12. Wellenreuther, "Urbanization," 662–64.

13. Dalstonburg, New London, Peytonsburg, Staunton, Strasburg, and Woodstock were all chartered during the French and Indian War. Fincastle was chartered in 1770.

14. Trade is mentioned specifically in the acts chartering Charlottesville, Chatham, Mecklenburg, Westham, and Woodstock. Gifts are mentioned in the acts for Fincastle, New London, and Staunton.

magazine is named in one.[15] However, legislative charters make it clear that, in the eyes of the legislature at least, the single most significant factor in recognizing a town was that someone had taken the personal initiative to found it. Over and over again, it is clear that personal initiative was a key factor in town development. Fifteen of the sixteen colonial charters state as a reason for granting a charter that an entrepreneur had laid out streets and lots.[16] Charlottesville's charter is distinct in not mentioning an entrepreneur because the county government purchased the land and laid out the town.

The individuals who founded backcountry towns were not driven by an invisible hand; clearly they had personal motives, though the circumstances behind each attempt to build a town varied widely. Economic gain was often a powerful motivating force, though occasionally more altruistic motives came into play. (When landowners in the Valley found refugees on their doorsteps during the Seven Years War, for example, profit was not among their immediate concerns.) A tract of land was worth more broken into smaller blocks and sold off, but such a scheme succeeded only if people had a reason to invest in a given location. Entrepreneurs were not the only people interested in making money through the sale of lots or the associated economic opportunities that a town attracted. Other individuals or mercantile firms often purchased lots as speculative ventures, hoping the value of the land would increase with time or improvement. At the end of the eighteenth century, Ferdinand-Marie Bayard found that a number of individuals had gotten very wealthy in land speculation: "I do not doubt that chance has favored the speculators; however, there is a calculation of probability which implies shrewdness."[17] Speculating in land, whether in a town or in the countryside, was risky, and speculators often wished simply to hold their land to see if it increased in value. For towns, this was a mixed blessing. It meant that lots would be sold, raising land values, but it also meant that a number of the owners did not participate in the life of the town, to its detriment.[18] In an attempt to alleviate some of the negative effects of speculation, most town charters required owners to build on their lots within two years or the land would revert to the previous owner. However, such stipulations went largely ignored and unenforced.

Another important factor that frequently influenced the progress of a town was the status of the people involved. Deference was a powerful force in colonial Virginia, and being well connected was quite advantageous. People like the William Byrds, Lord Fairfax, and William Beverley got special consideration when they petitioned the legislature, to the point of having rival towns

15. Courthouses are mentioned for Charlottesville, Chatham, Fincastle, Leesburg, Martinsburg, Peytonsburg, Romney, and Winchester, and Dalstonburg was built around the magazine.

16. These include Chatham, Dalstonburg, Fincastle, Leesburg, Martinsburg, Mecklenburg, New London, Peytonsburg, Romney, Staunton (in both of its charters), Stephensburg, Strasburg, Westham, Winchester, and Woodstock.

17. Bayard, *Travels*, 90.

18. Mitchell, "Metropolitan," 109, 116.

quashed without much difficulty. Many of the individuals who created towns, while not quite as well connected as they, were still important members of the local society, and they curried favor from people they felt could help them. Position and connections, as Jacob Hite learned in his struggles with Adam Stephen, meant everything (see chapter 4).

When individuals were working to establish their towns, they knew that capturing the county court was a particularly effective way to build interest in a town. Speculation and courthouses frequently went hand in hand.[19] Mills, forts, taverns, even a magazine might work to help build a thriving town. But nothing worked quite like a court, and county seats made up the majority of backcountry Virginia towns. Ten of the twenty-five towns were founded to be county towns, four more existing towns became county seats as new counties were created, and one served as a county seat temporarily. Gaining a court certainly did not guarantee a town's success, nor was having a court necessary for a town to develop. Mecklenburg, for example, grew to be one of the largest and most prosperous towns in Virginia—far larger than the majority of the county towns—though it was never home to a court except for a brief period during the Civil War. However, the administrative functions the court provided helped many towns develop more diverse economies or at least kept them alive until after the colonial period, when they could eventually prosper. There was danger in relying solely on a court. The practice of relocating the court to the center of the county each time a new county was created sounded the death knell for several towns and inhibited town development.[20]

Apart from serving as administrative centers, trade was the most important factor in the success of backcountry towns. Founders recognized that markets had definable territories and worked to locate their towns along important roads to help expedite trade.[21] Farmers understood both the necessity and the convenience of being tied to a town and even positioned their homes along roads—symbolically locking themselves into the economic order—and participating in annual fairs in Winchester, Staunton, New London, Strasburg, and Mecklenburg.[22] What is more, rural farmers and townspeople alike knew that they were part of a much larger economic system, part of the Atlantic world. In 1774 Nicholas Cresswell tried to break into the booming wheat trade in the backcountry. He wrote that "Great quantities of this article is brought down from the back Country in waggons . . . as good Wheat as ever I saw in England" and that flour was sent to the coastal ports and on "to the West Indies, and sometimes Lisbon and up the Streights."[23] Several stores based in coastal or fall-zone cities, or in Scotland, invested in backcountry towns,

19. Wellenreuther, "Urbanization," 664.

20. Mitchell, *Commercialism*, 13–14; and Farmer, *In the Absence*, 63.

21. O'Mara, "Urbanization," 349.

22. Warren R. Hofstra, "Ethnicity and Community Formation on the Shenandoah Valley Frontier," in Puglisi, *Accommodation*, 61; and Wellenreuther, "Urbanization," 667.

23. Cresswell, *Journal*, 47.

and set up branch operations or created connections with backcountry merchants. Much of the trade that went on in the backcountry occurred in the Great Valley as tens of thousands of people migrated to Virginia or passed through on their way to North Carolina. This traffic helped create several towns in the Valley that not only became homes for the migrants but also served as way stations or service centers providing them with supplies.[24]

The great backcountry migration also influenced developing towns' ethnicity and religion, both of which contributed importantly to shaping the character of towns. Many groups of Germans settled in towns in the northern part of the Great Valley, and Ulster Scots moved farther south. They were joined by people of other national origins and religious persuasions to create a very diverse population.[25] Religion also played an important part in the settlement of Piedmont and Southside towns, particularly in the first four towns, whose founders attempted to bring religious refugees to Virginia and the Quaker town of Waterford.

Backcountry migration and trade were also influenced by both the French and Indian War and the American Revolution. During the first conflict, people gathered together to seek protection and thus created a number of towns. Several towns benefited during both wars from business generated by the military. Two of the early towns, Brent Town and Germanna, had forts to serve as protection from Indians. During the French and Indian War, forts formed the foundation for three towns (Mecklenburg, Stephensburg, and Woodstock), and a fort brought new life and prosperity to a fourth (Winchester). Two towns were home to powder magazines (Dalstonburg and New London), one became the home of a weapons foundry (Westham), and two served as a site for prisoners of war (Charlottesville and New London). War stimulated craft industries and the growth and processing of new agricultural products such as hemp.[26] And at least once, in the case of Westham, war led to the destruction of a backcountry Virginia town.

The presence of public institutions other than courts in backcountry communities was important to their development. Eleven towns had neither churches nor schools during the colonial period that can be identified easily. For the most part, these were towns that failed (Brent Town, Chatham, Eden, and Peytonsburg), developed very slowly (Dalstonburg, Hitetown, and Westham), or had seasonal populations until late in the period (Warm Springs, Hot Springs, and Bath). Generally, the more successful towns had a couple of public institutions. People established schools, for example, in Mecklenburg, New London, Romney, Strasburg, Winchester, and Woodstock. Communities supporting at least one congregation included Charlottesville, Germanna, King

24. Earle and Hoffman, "Staple Crops," 55–56; and Wellenreuther, "Urbanization," 666.

25. Warren R. Hofstra, "Land Policy and Settlement in the Northern Shenandoah Valley," in Robert D. Mitchell, ed., *Appalachian Frontiers: Settlement, Society, and Development in the Preindustrial Era* (Lexington: Univ. Press of Kentucky, 1991), 118.

26. Hofstra, "Land Policy," 117.

William's Town, Martinsburg, Mecklenburg, New London, Romney, Staunton, Strasburg, Winchester, and Woodstock. However, as La Rouchefoucauld-Liancourt noted when he traveled to Stephensburg late in the eighteenth century, the fact that a town had a church did not mean that people regularly attended: "we seldom meet with any in Virginia where divine service is performed; from time to time we see indeed old buildings called meeting-places, but no sermons are delivered there, no prayers read, and they do not of course deserve the name of church."[27] Nevertheless, the presence of both churches and schools does much to reveal the vitality of a community in addition the importance such institutions held for town citizens. Such institutions helped differentiate a town from a cluster of residences.[28]

Another feature was a town's actual form. Colonial street plans survive for twenty of the twenty-five backcountry towns, and certain patterns become readily apparent. One pattern that dominated backcountry towns was the grid, or more accurately, orthogonal arrangement, where streets were laid out parallel to each other and came together at right angles. This scheme was used in seventeen of the known designs and probably was used in other towns for which plans no longer exist. There were many advantages in a rectilinear street system, particularly for a frontier community. Surveying the land was easy, requiring only simple tools. Lots, which were almost exclusively one-half acre in size, could be divided evenly. The system made for a regular and efficient use of space, and the lots could be easily identified and sold. Straight roads made for efficient flow of traffic and made designation of space for specific areas of use (domestic, government, and manufacture) possible. It was an orderly and logical arrangement, and the basic street system could be expanded and adjusted as the town grew. An orthogonal plan was ideal for a society that was more concerned with landownership and speculation than an aesthetic or communal vision.[29] The orthogonal plan also appealed to eighteenth-century Virginians' penchant for rationalism, balance, and order. Often proprietors used a plat of the town as a sales device at lot offerings, and an orthogonal scheme impressed initial investors, increasing lot sales.[30]

Two main features appeared in backcountry town designs that made certain towns different from the norm: outlots and squares. Outlots were a holdover of European town design in which people would live together in villages but have separate acreage for different uses. Outlots were used in six of the

27. La Rouchefoucault Liancourt, *Travels*, 2:101.

28. Ernst and Merrens, "'Camden's turrets,'" 560.

29. Fries, *Urban Idea*, 26–28; Pillsbury, "Urban Street," 437; Kornwolf with Kornwolf, *Architecture* 1:612–13; and Dan Pezzoni, "Town Form," M.A. thesis, Virginia Polytechnic Institute and State Univ., 1987, 2, 11. Although the rectilinear system dates back to the ancient period and was used in seventeenth-century Virginia, Pillsbury states that its widespread use in Pennsylvania antedated "its general national acceptance" (436), suggesting that migrants coming into the backcountry down the Great Wagon Road might have brought its use, or at least acceptance of it, with them. Kornwolf states, however, that the grid plan was already dominant in Virginia during the seventeenth century.

30. Kornwolf with Kornwolf, *Architecture* 1:613; and Pezzoni, "Town Form," 5, 11–13.

plans. These lots usually contained five or so acres, but in one case, Brent Town, outlots had one hundred acres. Interestingly, the use of outlots appears to occur in towns built or planned very early on the frontier, such as Brent Town and King William's Town, or towns in the Valley and mountains that were built on the eve of or during the French and Indian War (Winchester, Stephensburg, Woodstock, and Romney), lending credence to the notion that security and the need for self-sufficiency were motivating factors for their use—one of their original purposes in Europe.[31] Their practical effect on an orthogonal design was the creation of different grids in the same streetscape. So-called minigrids could also be created when later additions were made to an existing town. These later additions might be differentiated by the width of their streets as standard widths increased.[32]

The other primary feature disrupting the rectilinear norm was the square, which appeared in five of the plans and was suggested in a sixth. Its use was innovative. William Byrd I used the first square in the backcountry in King William's Town, designating it as the proper location for important structures, though not in the center as was typical, but in each corner. It would be interesting to speculate how he intended the streets to operate in such an arrangement. His son used similar squares in each of his villages in the design for Eden. Later, the towns of Martinsburg and Bath incorporated a square into their designs. Charlottesville's design also included a square, though ironically it stood on the edge of town instead of in the center. The plan of a sixth town, Woodstock, created a square by leaving the church in the middle of the town's main intersection, though without providing additional space for it. This trick was also used in the design of two North Carolina backcountry towns, Salisbury (1755) and Charlotte (1768), though in both of those instances, the main intersection served as the location for a courthouse rather than a church.[33]

Only three towns grew up in the Virginia backcountry without any formal system of roads. Of these, Dalstonburg may have had a rectilinear road system originally and Waterford had orthogonal additions made to it later. The simplest design belonged to the hamlet of Hitetown. A linear design typically reflects a lack of concern for town development, but had Hitetown won the battle for the Berkeley County court, Jacob Hite might have laid out a more elaborate scheme. Certainly there had been no concern for street design at the future sites of places like Staunton, Martinsburg, Fincastle, and Bath before their street plans were laid out. The irregular plan of Waterford, on the other hand, was shaped by the geography of the area—tall hills and a stream. Waterford's plan may also reflect cultural origins rather than a general lack of concern for design. Irregular street plans were prevalent in southeastern Penn-

31. Hofstra, *Planting*, 193–94, 261. German urban design may also have influenced the use of outlots in the Shenandoah Valley because of the origins of many of the inhabitants.

32. Paul Groth, "Streetgrids as Frameworks for Urban Society," *Harvard Architectural Review* 2 (Spring 1981): 74–75.

33. Hendricks, "Town Development," 85–96, 111–18.

sylvania and in Wales, points of origin for the majority of Waterford's residents.[34] A fourth town, Germanna, had a simple linear arrangement, but it differed from Hitetown in that its single road was laid out perfectly straight instead of following a preexisting route. It could easily have been expanded into a rectilinear plan, had Germanna prospered.

The urban colonial movement in the Virginia backcountry took place in two discrete phases. The first period lasted from 1687 to 1738, and although there was only a six-year gap between the demise of the William Byrd II's Eden project and the founding of Winchester in 1744, the differences between the two movements they represent are striking. Brent Town, Germanna, King William's Town, and Eden all failed, though had they survived and developed, they might have significantly changed the way the region developed.[35] As it is, their stories show that before the formation of the later successful towns, there was an impetus—a human thrust that demonstrated a natural and important movement—to form towns. These four early places clearly anticipated the much more deliberate and successful movement to come.

In many ways the history of the first four backcountry towns was merely a continuation of the same kinds of bad decisions and unrealistic expectations that had plagued Virginia's settlement beginning in 1607. George Brent, Alexander Spotswood, and the first two William Byrds approached their colonies with a general naivety driven by a desire for wealth bordering on unbridled avarice. They all tried to create instant communities in a wild frontier. The sites were too far into the frontier for the comfort and safety of the colonists, despite the feeble efforts of the founders and the colonial government to provide some protection through increased patrols or the construction of block houses. Furthermore, the settlements were simply too far away from the populated parts of the colony to establish good economic ties and regular trade and thus provide a way for town residents to survive. Finding residents to inhabit their towns was difficult for the four early founders. Like the leaders of Jamestown and the other early Virginia communities, these men wanted to bring in large groups of people, have them build towns, and then sit back and watch the profits roll in. But that was just not going to happen. It had not worked with the early Virginia settlements, and it did not work in the backcountry a century later.

At the turn of the eighteenth century, the obvious place to look for a large disaffected group of people desperate enough to move en masse into the wilderness was continental Europe, where decades of religious war and economic turmoil created many groups of refugees. The problem was that town founders competed with each other for the same groups of Huguenots, Lutherans, and in one instance Catholics, forcing a false scarcity of colonists.

34. Pillsbury, "Urban Street," 432, 434; and Harrison, *Landmarks*, 267–68.
35. For speculation about the potential impact of Eden, for example, see Farmer, *In the Absence*, 39.

As a result, if they were able to get their hands on a group of people, the founders embarked on extremely paternalistic and authoritarian policies to try and keep them. Certainly groups of European refugees wanted to immigrate to the American colonies, but few of them had any desire to settle in the wilderness. And, as had been the case in Jamestown, the leaders were attracting the wrong sort of settler. What they needed were farmers and housewrights who could clear the land and subsist until civilization caught up with them. Instead, they were vying for people who often practiced specialized trades that needed larger urban markets. Had the first founders established their towns and been patient enough to allow people who were genuinely interested in moving there to settle in them, the communities could have survived. But gambling on acquiring a ready-made population for a town meant that if they did not get that particular group, the project died in its tracks. It was little wonder that the founders often had to coerce their colonists into settling on their lands, which in turn caused new problems.

During the early years of backcountry settlement, the treatment of residents at the hands of town founders was a recurring issue. Alexander Spotswood was motivated primarily by profit and wanted his Germans to work his mines. As a result, he provided insufficient monetary assistance to his colonists for the first two years, and they struggled. The time they spent building shelter left them little time to clear fields and grow crops, and there was a constant shortage of food. Similarly, when William Byrd I helped with the creation of King William's Town, he provided too little money and other assistance for the colonists, and they remained on the brink of starvation. And Byrd was very quick to look for ways to enrich himself, selling the Huguenots supplies and assuming control of a coal deposit settlers had discovered. But there was one major difference between the residents of these early, chronically underfunded backcountry towns and Virginia's earliest settlers. They could and did leave as soon as their financial obligations were over; ultimately the deaths of these towns illustrate how settlers felt about the founders. Heavy-handed rule, inadequate financial support, and proprietorial self-aggrandizement pushed away the very colonists whom founders had struggled to attract in the first place.

The second phase of backcountry urban development lasted from 1744 to the end of the colonial period and is distinguishable from the earlier one by a number of factors. First, during this period, there was a greater level of direct involvement on the part of town founders in the towns themselves. The first founders (with the exception of Alexander Spotswood, who moved to Germanna after he left office) were not invested physically in their communities. The founders of the second phase, by contrast, typically lived in the towns they started, working side by side with the rest of the community. But that is only one of a host of factors that shaped the second and more successful period of backcountry town development. The number of towns and the sheer size of the territory that they covered led to regional variations.

Another chief factor differentiating the first and second phases was how the towns functioned economically. A town did not function as an isolated unit but was linked to the countryside, other areas, and other towns in several ways. On one level, the town was linked to its surrounding community in a mutually beneficial system of exchange. The needs of a region could be met by a traveling merchant or solitary Scots store, allowing local farmers to trade their products for manufactured or imported foods in an early stage of development. As the area's population increased, the needs of a community surpassed the capabilities of a single merchant. More settlers meant that a larger volume of agricultural products was produced for sale. To profit from their labors and compete with farmers in other regions, farmers needed to tie into a commercial trading system. On the other hand, larger numbers of farmers placed demands on merchants to provide a greater volume and a wider range of products. Similarly, a growing population created the additional demand needed for artisans to begin producing items for local consumption. This reciprocal system of connections between a town and the surrounding rural community served farmers as well as merchants, craftsmen, and, in several instances, governmental or court officials.[36] Towns were linked to one another, again in a reciprocal system of exchange.

While economic models are useful in describing how the towns and regions in the backcountry functioned, they do not provide an explanation of how they came about. What does explain urban development in the Virginia backcountry are the deliberate intentions of intelligent people who worked to bring these towns, and ultimately these economic systems, into being. In each instance an individual or small group decided to found a town. Their motivation varied widely: many sought profit, others wanted to establish government, a few found themselves surrounded by neighbors asking for help in a period of crisis, and some were part of ethnic or religious groups wanting a new start. They decided a particular piece of land would be a good site. That decision could have been influenced by a number of factors: an important road passed nearby, there was a river ford, it had a good water source, it was in the geographic center of a county, or there was some building—a church, store, mill, courthouse, fort, etc.—already present. Once they hit upon a site, a few people chose to simply let the site develop naturally, but the majority of them drew up plans and laid out systems to divide and distribute the land. They sought to build institutions to provide social services—government, religion, education—for the population. They bought and exchanged goods, established stores, created systems of credit, processed and manufactured goods, and built ties to other towns, both nearby and far away, as a way to obtain goods and services they could not provide for themselves. All the while,

36. Farmer, *In the Absence*, 555; Mitchell and Hofstra, "Town and Country in the Colonial South," 5; and Camblin, *Town in Ulster*, viii.

these individuals and their actions attracted people interested in their designs: individuals who hoped to move into areas to settle where land might be cheaper or more readily available; speculators who thought that the value of a town lot might increase quickly; investors from other towns who felt they might expand their mercantile operations into new markets; travelers who merely passed through, availing themselves of whatever services the town had to offer; and people who were not necessarily interested in living in a town but were attracted to the advantages of having a town nearby. Towns brought people, economic activity, society, and family to the Virginia backcountry. They stimulated faster expansion of settlement frontiers.

In many respects, Winchester serves as the prototypical backcountry town, combining all of the major influences that shaped the later colonial towns. The first permanent town in the Virginia backcountry, Winchester was founded by James Wood, a member of the local gentry. Although an important man in his own right, Wood nevertheless had to defer to the real power broker in the region, Lord Fairfax, making careful arrangements to gain his approval for the project. Fairfax complied, at first tacitly, then actively, making his own additions to the town and actively pursuing legislative recognition for the town.

Wood used his knowledge from serving in the county government to site the town in a prime location for the Frederick County courthouse to serve the majority of the residents rather than attempting to build at the geographical center. Initially he laid out fifteen acres, retaining only two for himself, and donating the rest to the county. This magnanimous gesture was later repaid when the town succeeded, because he later added 106 more acres to the town. Not to be outdone, Lord Fairfax first added 490 acres of his own to be divided into outlots and later added 173 town lots. The outlots and the later additions with their wider streets were arranged in an orthogonal pattern, though the outlots and additions created variations in the town's form. A number of people purchased lots, including men who later founded towns of their own. Many people purchased lots for speculation.

Much of the early success of Winchester came from its prime location along the Great Wagon Road, which brought new settlers into the region and supplied people moving farther south, helping to establish Winchester as a key point along a linear arrangement of service centers. The migration brought a variety of ethnic and religious groups into Winchester, creating a diverse population. A number of Germans and Ulster Scots moved into Winchester. By the end of the colonial period there were Anglican, Lutheran, and Reformed congregations worshiping in the town, and there was at least one school operating.

In 1752, eight years after it was established, Winchester had a population of about three hundred people, and Lord Fairfax and Wood petitioned the General Assembly to officially recognize Winchester by granting it a charter. Winchester thus gained status and the right to hold fairs twice a year. Within another five years it was home to five storekeepers, seven taverns or ordinaries, and a variety of craftsmen.[37]

Much of Winchester's growth during the 1750s was stimulated by the French and Indian War. Its population doubled within three years when people came flooding into the town from the west for safety, requiring new town lots to be laid out. Winchester became home to Fort Loudoun and a garrison of soldiers because, as Colonel George Washington pointed out in 1756, although Winchester was "trifling in itself," it was "a place of utmost importance to the country in general" because of "its centrical situation." It stood at a major crossroads, and Washington noted that Winchester "commands the communication from east to west, as well as from north to south, for at this place do almost all the roads center, and secures the great roads of one half of our frontiers to the markets of the neighbouring colonies, as well as to those on Rappahannock and Potomack &c."[38] With the arrival of troops, the economy flourished. Winchester became a collection and distribution point for a number of locally produced crops, its craft population grew, and it began to be woven into the wholesale merchant trade, acquiring links with mercantile firms in several fall-zone and port towns in Virginia, as well as Baltimore and Philadelphia.[39]

By 1759 Winchester had developed into a promising town. After surviving a few years of slow growth, in the 1750s the community reaped the benefits of trade, migration, and a military presence. However, in 1759 an epidemic of smallpox broke out. In July, to help contain the spread of the disease, the county court decided to relocate to the town of Stephensburg "during the time the Small Pox rageth in the Town of Winchester."[40] Stephensburg instantly became a rival home for the Frederick County court. In spite of fifteen years of progress during which Winchester had developed a fairly diverse economy, its town leaders quickly became alarmed. In October they petitioned the court to return, noting that cases of smallpox had developed in Stephensburg. The justices agreed and ordered the court to return.[41] But despite that order, the battle continued, and the court remained in Stephensburg. Finally in March of 1760, the Winchester faction produced a writ of adjournment in court, and the justices once again agreed to return.[42]

This backcountry version of the Babylonian Captivity reflects the importance the leaders of Winchester and Stephensburg placed on retaining the Frederick County court. By 1759 Winchester was a successful town, no longer

37. Mitchell, "Metropolitan," 114.

38. Washington, "To John Robinson," Apr. 24, 1756, *Papers* 3:50; Washington, "To Governor Dinwiddie," Apr. 27, 1756, *Papers* 3:60; and Mitchell, "'Over the Hills,'" 77.

39. Hofstra, *Planting*, 8; and Robert D. Mitchell, "'Over the Hills,'" 77.

40. "Order Book," Frederick and Winchester Judicial Center, Winchester, VA, 8:280.

41. Ibid., 8:330.

42. Ibid., 9:11.

dependent on the court for its existence. On the other hand, the people of Stephensburg were determined to retain the court because it brought new life to their community. Yet Winchester's leaders fought for the court's return, perhaps with some justification. For although the court was no longer the central feature of the town's economy, it did bring money, people, trade, and status to the town. And in the end, they were correct. Winchester continued to grow and prosper while Stephensburg grew at a much slower pace. Winchester dominated not only Stephensburg but all of the towns in the Lower Shenandoah Valley.

The economic growth that continued in Winchester following the conclusion of the French and Indian War was due in part to new crops that were being raised in the Valley, including wheat and hemp. Cattlemen passed through the town driving their herds north to Pennsylvania. These changes profited Winchester in a number of ways, as it became home to some processing, sold goods to the farmers and drovers, and continued to develop as a mercantile powerhouse. The number of merchants and stores kept increasing, as did the variety and quality of the products they sold. The increasingly complex economic development came about through elaborate systems of credit, which merchants provided to landowners using town lots in a number of Valley towns and nearby farmland as collateral. This credit system benefited both the shopkeepers and their customers.[43]

The Virginia General Assembly recognized Winchester's tremendous growth and economic prosperity in 1779 when it incorporated the town, something it had done for only three other towns—Williamsburg (the state capital) and Alexandria and Norfolk, both large port cities. The act gave Winchester the right to elect its own government, levy taxes, and pass its own laws.[44] The legislation truly marked the success of a place that had begun as a backcountry town.

Winchester's story and the narratives of all of the colonial backcountry towns form a crucial part of the history of the southern backcountry, with implications expanding beyond the borders of Virginia. Backcountry town development had not occurred spontaneously. Residents wanted towns and worked diligently to create them and help them survive. They saw towns as a natural and essential part of their culture and humanity, and they knew what elements were necessary for towns to succeed. The twenty-five attempts to found them signaled a deliberate drive on the part of individuals who worked to settle the backcountry. By the end of the colonial period, Virginians clearly had overcome what in 1724 Hugh Jones had called their lack of inclination "to cohabit in towns."[45]

43. Hofstra and Mitchell, "Town and Country in Backcountry Virginia," 631–34, 636–41.
44. Mitchell, "Metropolitan," 115.
45. Jones, *Present State,* 73.

In 1775, five decades after Jones made his remark, Philip Fithian traveled through the newly established backcountry town of Martinsburg. He was impressed with the progress that had been made in building the town just two years after it had been laid out. He was equally enamored of the vision its citizens held for the future. Inspired, he recorded in his diary what proved to be a very prophetic statement: "Probably, if American liberty can be established, for which we are now contending even in Blood, this, with many other infant Villages, in a Series of Years, will be populous & wealthy Towns, grand in Appearance, & busy with Commerce. . . . But the Glory of America, her Wealth, & Inhabitants, and inchanting Habitations, are remote yet, & to be obtained by Time, & Industry."[46] Serving as trading and administrative centers, agricultural villages, religious settlements, as well as resorts and service centers, towns were already a central part of life in the Virginia backcountry, and the future of urban growth looked promising. All that was required to fulfill this promise were a few key elements: planning, dedication, hard work, and a little luck.

46. Fithian, *Philip Vickers Fithian*, 11.

Bibliography

Primary Sources

Anbury, Thomas. *Travels through the Interior Parts of America*. Boston: Houghton Mifflin, 1923.

Arnold, Benedict. "Arnold's Expedition to Richmond, Virginia, 1781." *William and Mary Quarterly*, 2nd series, vol. 12 (July 1932): 187–90.

Asbury, Francis. *The Journal and Letters of Francis Asbury*. Edited by Elmer T. Clark, J. Manning Potts, and Jacob S. Payton. 3 vols. Nashville: Abingdon, 1958.

"Augusta Parish Registry" [photostat]. Alderman Library Special Collections, Univ. of Virginia, Charlottesville.

Bayard, Ferdinand-Marie. *Travels of a Frenchman in Maryland and Virginia with a Description of Philadelphia and Baltimore in 1791; or, Travels in the Interior of the United States, to Bath, Winchester, in the Valley of the Shenandoah, etc., etc., during the Summer of 1791*. Edited and translated by Ben C. McCrary. Ann Arbor, MI: Edwards Brothers, 1950.

Beverley, Robert. *The History and Present State of Virginia*. Chapel Hill: Univ. of North Carolina Press, 1947.

Briggs, John Howell. "Journal of a Trip to the Sweet Springs, Commencing July 23d and Ending September 29th 1804." In *First Resorts: A Visit to Virginia's Springs*, 11–32. Richmond: Virginia Historical Society, 1987.

Brock, R. A., ed. *Documents, Chiefly Unpublished, Relating to the Huguenot Emigration to Virginia*. Richmond: Virginia Historical Society, 1886.

Burnaby, Andrew. *Travels through the Middle Settlement in North America, in the Years 1759 and 1760; with Observations Upon the State of the Colonies*. 3rd ed. London: T. Payne, 1798.

Byrd, William, I, William Byrd II, and William Byrd III. *The Correspondence of the Three William Byrds of Westover, Virginia, 1684–1776*. 2 vols. Edited by Marion Tinling. Charlottesville: Published for the Virginia Historical Society by Univ. Press of Virginia, 1977.

Byrd, William, II. *The London Diary (1717–1721) and Other Writings*. Edited by Louis B. Wright and Marion Tinling. New York: Oxford Univ. Press, 1958.

———. *The Prose Works of William Byrd of Westover: Narratives of a Colonial Virginian*. Edited by Louis B. Wright. Cambridge, MA: Belknap Press of Harvard Univ. Press, 1961.

———. *The Secret Diary of William Byrd of Westover, 1709–1772.* Edited by Louis B. Wright and Marion Tinling. Richmond, VA: Dietz, 1941.

———. *William Byrd's Histories of the Dividing Line Betwixt Virginia and North Carolina.* Edited by William K. Boyd. Raleigh, NC: Edwards and Broughton, 1929.

———. *William Byrd's Natural History of Virginia, or the Newly Discovered Eden.* Edited by Richard Croom Beatty and William J. Mulloy. Richmond, VA: Dietz, 1940.

Caldwell, John Edwards. *A Tour Through Part of Virginia, in the Summer of 1808.* New York: R. C. Southwick, 1809.

Chalkey, Lyman, ed. *Chronicles of the Scotch-Irish Settlement in Virginia Extracted from the Original Court Records of Augusta County 1745–1800.* 3 vols. Baltimore: Genealogical Publishing, 1965.

Chastellux, François Jean, Marquis de. *Travels in North-America in the Years 1780, 1781, and 1782.* 2 vols. London: G. G. J. and J. Robinson, 1787.

Clayton, John. "A Letter from Mr. John Clayton Rector of Crofton at Wakefield in Yorkshire to the Royal Society, May 12, 1688." In Peter Force, ed., *Tracts and Other Papers, Relating Principally to the Origin, Settlement, and Progress of the Colonies in North America, From the Discovery of the Country to the Year 1776*, vol. 3, tract 13. Washington, DC: Peter Force and Wm. Q. Force, 1844.

"Complaint by Germans against Governor Spotswood." *Virginia Magazine of History and Biography* 6 (1898–99): 385–86.

Connolly, John. "John Connolly to George Routes." *Virginia Magazine of History and Biography* 14 (July 1906): 78–79.

Cresswell, Nicholas. *The Journal of Nicholas Cresswell, 1774–1777.* New York: Dial, 1924.

Culpeper, Thomas, Lord. "Speech of Governor Lord Culpeper." *Virginia Magazine of History and Biography* 14 (Apr. 1967): 362–66.

Dauphiné, Durand de. *A Huguenot Exile in Virginia, or Voyages of a Frenchman Exiled for His Religion, with a Description of Virginia and Maryland.* Edited by Gilbert Chinard. 1687. New York: Press of the Pioneers, 1934.

Dinwiddie, Robert. *The Official Records of Robert Dinwiddie, Lieutenant-Governor of the Colony of Virginia, 1751–1758.* Edited by R. A. Brock. 2 vols. Richmond: Virginia Historical Society, 1884.

Feltman, William. *The Journal of William Feltman of the First Pennsylvania Regiment, 1781–82.* Philadelphia: Historical Society of Pennsylvania, 1853.

Fife, R. H., trans. and ed. "The Vestry Book of King William Parish, VA., 1707–1750." With an introduction by R. L. Maury. *Virginia Magazine of History and Biography* 11 (1903–4): 289–304.

Fithian, Philip Vickers. *Philip Vickers Fithian: Journal, 1775–1776, Written on the Virginia-Pennsylvania Frontier and in the Army Around New York.* Edited by Robert Greenhalgh Albion and Leonidas Dodson. Princeton, NJ: Princeton Univ. Press, 1934.

Fitzhugh, William. "Letters of William Fitzhugh." *Virginia Magazine of History and Biography* 1 (1893–94): 17–55, 105–26, 253–77, 391–410; 2 (1894–95): 15–36, 121–42, 259–75, 370–79; 3 (1895–96): 1–15, 161–68, 253–61, 268–73.

Fontaine, John. *Memoirs of a Huguenot Family.* Edited by Ann Maury. New York: Putnam's, 1907.

Force, Peter, ed. *Tracts and Other Papers, Relating Principally to the Origin, Settlement, and Progress of the Colonies in North America, From the Discovery of the Country to the Year 1776.* 4 vols. Washington, DC: Peter Force and Wm. Q. Force, 1836–46.

Gottschalk, Matthias Gottlieb. "Moravian Diaries of Travels through Virginia." Edited by William J. Hinke and Charles E. Kemper. *Virginia Magazine of History and Biography* 11 (1903–4): 225–42.

Graffenried, Christoph von. *Christoph von Graffenried's Account of the Founding of New Bern.* Edited by Todd H. Vincent. Raleigh: North Carolina Historical Commission, 1920.

[Grube, Bernhard Adam?]. "Diary of a Journey of Moravians from Bethlehem, Pennsylvania, to Bethabara in Wachovia, North Carolina, 1753." Translated by Adelaide L. Fries. In Newton D. Mereness, ed., *Travels in the American Colonies*, 327–56. New York: Macmillan, 1916.

Hartwell, Henry, James Blair, and Edward Chilton. *The Present State of Virginia and the College.* Edited by Hunter Dickinson Farish. 1727. Williamsburg, VA: Colonial Williamsburg, 1940.

Hening, William Waller, ed. *The Statutes at Large; Being a Collection of all the Laws of Virginia, From the First Session of the Legislature in the Year 1619.* 13 vols. Charlottesville: Univ. Press of Virginia, 1969.

"Instructions to William Berkeley, 1642." *Virginia Magazine of History and Biography* 2 (1895): 281–88.

Jefferson, Thomas. *Jefferson's Notes on the State of Virginia.* Baltimore, MD: W. Pechin, 1800.

———. *The Papers of Thomas Jefferson.* Edited by Julian P. Boyd et al. 29 vols. Princeton, NJ: Princeton Univ. Press, 1950–2002.

Jones, Hugh. *The Present State of Virginia: From Whence is Inferred a Short View of Maryland and North Carolina.* Edited by Richard L. Morton. Chapel Hill: Published for the Virginia Historical Society by the Univ. of North Carolina Press, 1956.

"Journals of the Council of Virginia in Executive Sessions, 1737–1763." *Virginia Magazine of History and Biography* 15 (1907–8): 373–89.

Joynes, Thomas R. "Memoranda Made by Thomas R. Joynes on a Journey to the States of Ohio and Kentucky, 1810." *William and Mary College Quarterly Historical Magazine*, 1st series, vol. 10 (Jan. 1902): 145–58.

Kangas, M. N. and D. E. Payne, eds. *Frederick County, Virginia: Wills & Administrations 1795–1816.* Baltimore: Genealogical Publishing, 1983.

Kemper, Charles E., ed. "Documents Relating to Early Projected Swiss Colonies in the Valley of Virginia 1706–1709." *Virginia Magazine of History and Biography* 29 (1921): 1–17.

———, ed. "The Early Westward Movement of Virginia, 1722–1734. As Shown by the Proceedings of the Colonial Council." *Virginia Magazine of History and Biography* 13 (1905): 113–38.

Kennedy, John Pendleton and H. R. McIlwaine, eds. *Journals of the House of Burgesses of Virginia.* 13 vols. Richmond: Colonial Press, E. Woddey, 1905–15.

"Land Office Patents." Library of Virginia, Richmond.
Langston, Anthony. "On Towns and Corporations; And on the Manufacture of Iron." *William and Mary Quarterly Historical Magazine*, 2nd series, vol. 1 (Jan. 1921): 100–106.
La Rouchefoucault Liancourt. *Travels through the United States of North America, the Country of the Iroquois, and Upper Canada, in the Years 1795, 1796, and 1797; With an Authentic Account of Lower Canada.* Translated by H. Neuman. 2 vols. London: R. Phillips, 1799.
Lederer, John. *The Discoveries of John Lederer.* Edited by William P. Cumming. Charlottesville: Univ. Press of Virginia, 1958.
Makemie, Francis. "A Plain & Friendly Perswasive to the Inhabitants of Virginia and Maryland For Promoting Towns & Cohabitation. By a Well-Wisher to Both Governments." *Virginia Magazine of History and Biography* 4 (Jan. 1897): 255–71.
Mason, Frances Norton, ed. *John Mason & Sons, Merchants of London and Virginia.* Richmond, VA: Dietz, 1937.
Maury, James. "Letter of Rev. James Maury to Philip Ludwell on the Defense of the Frontiers of Virginia, 1756." *Virginia Magazine of History and Biography* 19 (1911): 292–304.
McIliwaine, H. R., ed. *Legislative Journals of the Council of Colonial Virginia.* 3 vols. Richmond, VA: Colonial Press, Everett Waddey, 1918–19.
———, Wilmer Lee Hall, and Benjamin Jennings Hillman, eds. *Executive Journals of the Council of Colonial Virginia.* 6 vols. Richmond: Virginia State Library, 1925–67.
Mereness, Newton D., ed. *Travels in the American Colonies.* New York: Macmillan, 1916.
Michel, François Louis. "Report of the Journey of François Louis Michel from Berne, Switzerland, to Virginia, October 2, 1701–December 1, 1702." Translated and edited by William J. Hinke. *Virginia Magazine of History and Biography* 24 (1916): 1–43, 113–41, 275–303.
Neu-gefundenes Eden. Oder: Aussführlicher Bericht von Sud- und Nord-Carolina, Pensilphania, Mary-Land, & Virginia: Entworffen durch zwey in dise Provintzen gemachten Reisen, Reiss-Journal, und ville Brieffen, dardurch der gegenwärtige Zustand diser Länderen warhafftig entdecket, und dem Nebenmenschen zu Gutem an Tag gelegt wird. Samt beygefügtem Anhang, oder freye Unterweisung zu dem verlohrnen, nun aber wieder gefundenen Lapide Philosophorum, dardurch man bald zur Vergnüügung, und wahrer Reichthum gelangen kan. Bern, Switzerland: In Truck verfertiget durch Befelch der Helvetischen Societät, 1737.
"Northern Neck Grants and Surveys." Library of Virginia, Richmond.
"Public Meeting in Loudoun in 1774." *William and Mary Quarterly*, 1st series, vol. 12 (Apr. 1904): 232–33.
R. G. "Virginia's Cure, or An Advisive Narrative Concerning Virginia: Discovering the True Ground of that Churches Unhappiness, and the Only True Remedy." In Peter Force, ed., *Tracts and Other Papers, Relating Principally to the Origin, Settlement, and Progress of the Colonies in North America, From the Discovery*

of the Country to the Year 1776, vol. 3, tract 15. Washington, DC: Peter Force and Wm. Q. Force, 1844.

Reichel, John Frederick. "Travel Diary of Bishop Reichel, Mrs. Reichel, and Their Company from Lititz, Pa. To Salem, N.C., 1780." In Newton D. Mereness, ed., *Travels in the American Colonies*, 586–99. New York: Macmillan, 1916.

Rose, Robert. *The Diary of Robert Rose: A View of Virginia by a Colonial Parson, 1746–1751*. Edited by Robert Emmett Fall. Verona, VA: McClung, 1977.

Rouelle, John. *A Complete Treatise on the Mineral Waters of Virginia: Containing a Description of their Situation, their Natural History, their Analysis, Contents, and their Use in Medicine*. Philadelphia: Charles Cist, 1792.

Sainsbury, W. Noel, et al., eds. *Calendar of State Papers, Colonial Series.* 40 vols. London: Public Record Office, 1860–1938.

Sallé, Abraham. "Abraham Salle to George I." *Virginia Historical Magazine* 34 (1926): 159–60.

Saunders, William L., ed. *The Colonial Records of North Carolina*. 16 vols. Winston, NC: M. I. & J. C. Stewart, Printers to the State, 1895–96; Goldsboro, NC: Nash Brothers, Book and Job Printers, 1896–1906.

Schnell, L. "Moravian Diaries of Travels Through Virginia." Edited by William J. Hinke and Charles E. Kemper. *Virginia Magazine of History and Biography* 12 (July 1904): 55–82.

Schoepf, Johann David. *Travels in the Confederation*. Translated and edited by Alfred J. Morrison. 2 vols. New York: Bergman, 1968.

Shepherd, Samuel, ed. *The Statutes at Large of Virginia, From October Session 1792, to December Session 1806, Inclusive, in Three Volumes, (New Series) Being a Continuation of Hening*. 3 vols. New York: AMS, 1970.

Simcoe, John Graves. *Journal of the Operations of the Queen's Rangers*. New York: New York Times and Arno Press, 1968.

Smith, William Loughton. *Journal of William Loughton Smith*. Edited by Albert Matthews. Cambridge, MA: The Univ. Press, 1917.

Smyth, J. F. D. *A Tour in the United States of America*. 2 vols. London: G. Robinson and J. Sewell, 1784.

Spotswood, Alexander. *The Official Letters of Alexander Spotswood*. Edited by R. A. Brock. 2 vols. Richmond: Virginia Historical Society, 1882–85.

Toulmin, Harry. *The Western Country in 1793*. Edited by Marion Tingling and Godfrey Davies. San Marino, CA: Henry E. Huntington Library and Art Gallery, 1948.

The Virginia Gazette, Williamsburg, 1736–80.

Vitruvius Pollio, Marcus. *The Ten Books on Architecture*. New York: Dover, 1960.

Walker, Thomas. "Extracts from the Journal of Dr. Thomas Walker." Edited by J. T. McAllister. *Virginia Magazine of History and Biography* 19 (Apr. 1911): 166–72.

Washington, George. *The Diaries of George Washington, 1748–1799*. Edited by John C. Fitzpatrick. 4 vols. Boston and New York: Houghton Mifflin, 1925.

———. *The Papers of George Washington, Colonial Series*. Edited by W. W. Abbot et al. 10 vols. Charlottesville: Univ. Press of Virginia, 1983–95.

Weld, Isaac. *Travels Through the States of North America, and the Provinces of Upper and Lower Canada During the Years 1795, 1796, and 1797*. 2 vols. London: John Stockdale, 1807.

Winfree, Waverley K., and Randolph Church, eds. *The Laws of Virginia: Being a Supplement to Hening's The Statutes at Large.* Richmond: Virginia State Library, 1971.

Wood, James. "A List of Ticketts in the Winchester Lottery. Signed and Sold by James Wood, 1760." Handley Library, Winchester, VA.

County Records

Albemarle County, VA

"Albemarle County Surveyors Book, 1756–1790." Albemarle County Courthouse, Charlottesville, VA.

Augusta County, VA

"Court of Chancery." Augusta County Courthouse, Staunton, VA.

"Deed Book." Augusta County Courthouse, Staunton, VA.

"Order Book, Augusta County." Augusta County Courthouse, Staunton, VA.

"Surveyors Record, Augusta County." Augusta County Courthouse, Staunton, VA.

Bath County, VA

"Will Book, Bath County." Bath County Courthouse, Warm Springs, VA.

Bedford County, VA

"Bedford County Order Book." Bedford County Courthouse, Bedford, VA.

"Deed Book." Bedford County Courthouse, Bedford, VA.

Berkeley County, WV

"Berkeley County Minute Book." Berkeley County Courthouse, Martinsburg, WV.

"Deed Book, Berkeley County." Berkeley County Courthouse, Martinsburg, WV.

"Will Book, Berkeley County." Berkeley County Courthouse, Martinsburg, WV.

Botetourt County, VA

"Deed Book, Botetourt County." Botetourt County Courthouse, Fincastle, VA.

"Order Book, Botetourt County." Botetourt County Courthouse, Fincastle, VA.

Charlotte County, VA

"Deed Book, Charlotte County." Charlotte County Clerk's Office, Charlotte Court House, VA.

"Order Book, Charlotte County." Charlotte County Clerk's Office, Charlotte Court House, VA.

Frederick County, VA

"Common Law Order Book." Frederick and Winchester Judicial Center, Winchester, VA.

"Deed Book." Frederick and Winchester Judicial Center, Winchester, VA.

"Surveys." Frederick and Winchester Judicial Center, Winchester, VA.

"Order Book." Frederick and Winchester Judicial Center, Winchester, VA.

"Will Book." Frederick and Winchester Judicial Center, Winchester, VA.

Halifax County, VA

"Book of Pleas." Halifax County Courthouse, Halifax, VA.

"Deed Book, Halifax County." Halifax County Courthouse, Halifax, VA.

Jefferson County, WV

"Deed Book." Jefferson County Courthouse, Charles Town, WV.

Loudoun County, VA

"Loudoun Will Book." Loudoun County Courthouse, Leesburg, VA.

Lunenburg County, VA

"Deed Book." Lunenburg County Courthouse, Lunenburg, VA.

"Order Book." Lunenburg County Courthouse, Lunenburg, VA.

"Will Book." Lunenburg County Courthouse, Lunenburg, VA.

Pittsylvania County, VA

"Deed Book." Pittsylvania County Courthouse, Chatham, VA.

"Pittsylvania County Court Records." Pittsylvania County Courthouse, Chatham, VA.

Shenandoah County, VA

"Deed Book." Shenandoah County Courthouse, Woodstock, VA.

"Dunmore County Order Book, 1772–1774." Shenandoah County Courthouse, Woodstock, VA.

"Minute Book, Shenandoah County." Shenandoah County Courthouse, Woodstock, VA.

"Will Book, Shenandoah County." Shenandoah County Courthouse, Woodstock, VA.

Maps

Bellin, Earle, Sr. *Carte de la Virginie, Avec Parte du Maryland et de la Pensilvanie. Suivant ce que les Anglois en ont publie de plus recent. Earle Sr. Bellin ingenieur de la Marine; Covered 1755*. 1755.

Bellin, J. N. *Carte de la Virgini Mari–Land &a. Tiree des meileurs Cartes Angloises*. 1764.

Fry, Joshua, and Peter Jefferson. *A Map of the most Inhabited part of Virginia containing the Whole Province of Maryland with Part of Pensilvania, New Jersey and North Carolina. Drawn by Joshua Fry and Peter Jefferson in 1751*. London: Thos. Jeffreys, 1755.

———. *A Map of the most Inhabited part of Virginia containing the Whole Province of Maryland with Part of Pensilvania, New Jersey and North Carolina. Drawn by Joshua Fry and Peter Jefferson in 1775*. London: Laurie & Whittle, 1794.

Henry, John. *A New and Accurate Map of Virginia Wherein most of the Counties are laid down from Actual Surveys. With a Concise Account of the Number of inhabitants, the Trade, Soil and Produce of that province. By John Henry*. London: Thos. Jeffreys, 1770.

Hite, Alexander. "A Plat for the Town of Strasburg or Stover Made by Alexander Hite." 1783. Strasburg Town Hall, Strasburg, VA.

Hough, John. "Plan of Leesburg." 1759. Loudoun Museum, Leesburg, VA.

"Map of Jefferson County Va. Photographed for the Bureau of Topographical Engineers Oct. 1862." 1862. Cartographic and Architectural Branch, National Archives, College Park, MD.

"Map of a Section of Territory Adjacent to Marysville or Charlotte Court House." C. 1840. Archives and Records Division, Map Collection, Library of Virginia, Richmond.

"This Original platt of the Town of Winchester, and of the Commons, which was deposited in Lord Fairfax's Office, was returned into Court by Robert Macky and on his motion is admitted to record." 1794. In "Deed Book," 24B:91. Frederick and Winchester Judicial Center, Winchester, VA.

Painter, Fred. "Plat of Woodstock Virginia." 1969. In "Deed Book," 281:171. Shenandoah County Courthouse, Woodstock, VA.

"Plan of New London Town." In "Deed Book," A:434. Bedford County Courthouse, Bedford, VA.

"Plan of the Out Lots and a Sketch of the situation of the Lots in the Town and to them." In "Stephens City, Virginia Records." Handley Regional Library, Winchester, VA.

"Plan of the Town of Bath [Berkeley Springs, West Virginia], Showing Streets, Lots, etc., with Endorsements, N. D." C. 1777. Fairfax Family Proprietary Papers, 1688–1810, Accession 24062. Box 2, folder I-101. Personal Papers Collection. Library of Virginia, Richmond.

A Plan of the Town of Charlottesville. Charlottesville, VA?: n.p., 1818?.

"A Plan of the Town of Charlottesville in the County of Albemarle." C. 1765. In "Albemarle County Surveyors Book, 1756–1790," Vol. 1, pt. 2:77. Albemarle County Courthouse, Charlottesville, VA.

"A Plan of the Town of Staunton Augusta County." 1749–50. In "Deed Book," 2:410. Augusta County Courthouse, Staunton, VA.

"A Plan of the Ways Leading to the Albemarle Courthouse." Papers of the Randolph Family of Edgehill, 1726–1826. MSS 5533. Special Collections, University of Virginia Library, Charlottesville.

"This is a Plan of the Town of Beverley." 1756. Ambler Family Papers, 1638–1809. MMC-2527. Library of Congress, Washington, DC..

"This Plan of the Town of Fincastle was returned to Court & Ordered to be Recd." 1778. In "Deed Book, Botetourt County," 2:347. Botetourt County Courthouse, Fincastle, VA.

"The Town of Patonsburg Layed off According to Act of Assembly by Sherd. Walton." 1761. In "Deed Book, Halifax County," 3:149. Halifax County Courthouse, Halifax, VA.

Van Metre, Geo. "Martinsburg, Va. 1779." 1904. Berkeley County Courthouse, Martinsburg, WV.

Varle, Chas. "Plan of Winchester." Inset in *Map of Frederick, Berkeley, & Jefferson Counties in the State of Virginia.* Philadelphia: Benjamin Jones, 1809.

Wood, James, Jr. "The Rod lines include the Town of Winchester containing 84 Lotts already Tested by act of Assembly." 1758. In "Surveys," 66. Frederick and Winchester Judicial Center, Winchester, VA.

Secondary Materials

Aailsworth, Timothy S., et al. *Charlotte County: Rich Indeed.* Richmond: Whittet & Shepperson, 1979.

Adams, Percy G. "The Real Author of William Byrd's Natural History of Virginia." *American Literature* 28 (1956): 211–20.

Alderfer, E. G. *The Ephrata Commune: An Early American Counterculture.* Pittsburgh: Univ. of Pittsburgh Press, 1985.

Aler, Vernon F. *Aler's History of Martinsburg and Berkeley County, West Virginia.* Hagerstown, MD: Mail Publishing, 1888.

Alexander, James. *Early Charlottesville Recollections.* Edited by Mary Rawlings. Charlottesville, VA: Albemarle County Historical Society, 1942.

Armstrong, Thomas Field. "Urban Vision in Virginia: A Comparative Study of Ante-Bellum Fredericksburg, Lynchburg, and Staunton." M.A. thesis, Univ. of Virginia, 1974.

An Atlas of Frederick County, Virginia, From Actual Surveys by J. M. Lathrop and A. W. Baton. Philadelphia: D. J. Lake, 1885.

Aull, Edward. *Early History of Staunton and Beverley Manor in Augusta County, Virginia.* Staunton, VA: McClure, 1963.

Beeman, Richard R. *The Evolution of the Southern Backcountry: A Case Study of Lunenburg County, Virginia, 1746–1832.* Philadelphia: Univ. of Pennsylvania Press, 1984.

Bell, Landon C. *The Old Free State: A Contribution to the History of Lunenburg County and Southside Virginia.* Baltimore: Genealogical Publishing, 1974.

Bentley, George E. "Old Quaker Town." In *Waterford Perspectives*, 13–14. Waterford, VA: Waterford Foundation, 1983.

Billings, Warren M., John E. Selby, and Thad W. Tate. *Colonial Virginia: A History.* White Plains, NY: KTO, 1986.

Boeschenstein, Warren. *Historic American Towns along the Atlantic Coast.* Baltimore: Johns Hopkins Univ. Press, 1999.

Brannon, Selden W., ed. *Historic Hampshire: A Symposium of Hampshire County and Its People, Past and Present.* Parsons, WV: McClain, 1976.

Bridenbaugh, Carl. "Baths and Watering Places of Colonial America." *William and Mary Quarterly*, 3rd series, vol. 3 (Apr. 1946): 151–81.

———. *Cities in Revolt: Urban Life in Colonial America, 1743–1776.* New York: Knopf, 1955.

———. *Cities in the Wilderness: The First Century of Urban Life in America, 1625–1742.* Oxford: Oxford Univ. Press, 1938.

———. *Myths and Realities: Societies in the Colonial South.* Baton Rouge: Louisiana State Univ. Press, 1955.

Brownell, Blaine A., and David R. Goldfield, eds. *The City in Southern History: The Growth of Urban Civilization in the South.* Port Washington, NY: Kennikut, 1977.

Bugg, James L., Jr. "The French Huguenot Frontier Settlement of Manakin Town." *Virginia Magazine of History and Biography* 61 (Oct. 1953): 359–94.

Bushong, Millard Kessler. *A History of Jefferson County, West Virginia.* Charles Town, WV: Jefferson, 1941.

Cadden, Virginia Hinkins. *The Story of Strasburg.* Strasburg, VA: n.p., 1961.

Camblin, Gilbert. *The Town in Ulster.* Belfast, Northern Ireland: Wm. Mullan & Son, 1951.

Cappon, Lester J., and Stella F. Duff. *Virginia Gazette Index, 1736–1780.* 2 vols. Williamsburg, VA: Institute of Early American History and Culture, 1950.

Carr, Lois Green, ed. *The Chesapeake and Beyond: A Celebration*. Crownsville: Maryland Historical and Cultural Publications, 1992.

———. "The Metropolis of Maryland: A Comment on Town Development along the Tobacco Coast." *Maryland Historical Magazine* 69 (Summer 1974): 123–45.

Cartmell, T. K. *Shenandoah Valley Pioneers and Their Decedents: A History of Frederick County, Virginia*. Winchester, VA: Eddy, 1909.

Chappell, Edward A. "Acculturation in the Shenandoah Valley: Rhenish Houses of the Massanutten Settlement." *Proceedings of the American Philosophical Society* 124 (1980): 55–89. Reprinted in Dell Upton and Michael Vlach, eds., *Common Places: Readings in American Vernacular Architecture*, 252–74. Athens: Univ. of Georgia Press, 1986.

Charlottesville, 1762–1962. Charlottesville, VA: Charlottesville 200th Anniversary Commission, 1962.

Chernichowski, Beth-Anne. "Legislated Towns in Virginia, 1680–1705; Growth and Function: 1680–1780." M.A. thesis, College of William and Mary in Virginia, 1974.

Chilton, W. B., ed. "The Brent Family." *Virginia Magazine of History and Biography* 17 (1909): 308–11; 18 (1910): 96–102.

Christaller, Walter. *Central Places in Southern Germany*. Translated by C. W. Baskin. Englewood Cliffs, NJ: Prentice-Hall, 1966.

Clark, Thomas D., ed. *Travels in the Old South: A Bibliography*. 2 vols. Norman: Univ. of Oklahoma Press, 1956.

Clement, Maud Carter. *The History of Pittsylvania County, Virginia*. Lynchburg, VA: J. P. Bell, 1929.

Cohen, Stan. *Historic Springs of the Virginias: A Pictorial History*. Charleston, WV: Pictorial Histories, 1981.

Corefield, P. J. *The Impact of English Towns, 1700–1800*. Oxford: Oxford Univ. Press, 1982.

Couper, William. *History of the Shenandoah Valley*. 3 vols. New York: Lewis Historical, 1952.

Crass, David Colin, et al., eds. *The Southern Colonial Backcountry: Interdisciplinary Perspectives on Frontier Communities*. Knoxville: Univ. of Tennessee Press, 1998.

Craven, Avery Odell. *Soil Exhaustion as a Factor in the Agricultural History of Virginia and Maryland, 1606–1860*. Gloucester, MA: P. Smith, 1965.

Cumming, William P. *The Southeast in Early Maps*. Princeton, NJ: Princeton University Press, 1958.

Dandridge, Danske. *Historic Shepherdstown*. Charlottesville, VA: Michie, 1910.

Darter, Oscar H. *Colonial Fredericksburg and Neighborhood in Perspective*. New York: Twayne, 1957.

Doddridge, Joseph. *Notes on the Settlement and Indian Wars of Western Pennsylvania from 1763 to 1783, inclusive, together with a Review of the State of society and Manners of the First Settlers of the Western Country*. Pittsburgh: John S. Ritenour and Wm. T. Lindsey, 1912.

Dodson, Leonidas. *Alexander Spotswood: Governor of Colonial Virginia, 1710–1722*. Philadelphia: Univ. of Pennsylvania Press, 1932.

Doran, Michael F. *Atlas of County Boundary Changes in Virginia, 1634–1895*. Athens, GA: Iberian, 1987.

Duncan, Richard R. *Theses and Dissertations on Virginia History: A Bibliography*. Richmond: Virginia State Library, 1986.

Earle, Carville, and Ronald Hoffman. "Staple Crops and Urban Development in the Eighteenth-Century South." *Perspectives in American History* 10 (1972): 7–80.

———. "The Urban South: The First Two Centuries." In Blaine A. Brownell and David R. Goldfield, eds., *The City in Southern History: The Growth of Urban Civilization in the South*, 23–51. Port Washington, NY: Kennikut, 1977.

Ebert, Rebecca A., and Teresa Lazazzera. *Frederick County, Virginia: From Frontier to the Future*. Norfolk, VA: Donning, 1988.

Edmunds, Pocahontas Wight. *History of Halifax*. 2 vols. N.p.: n.p., 1978?.

Elliot, James. *The City in Maps: Urban Mapping to 1900*. London: British Library, 1987.

Ernst, Joseph A., and H. Roy Merrens. "'Camden's turrets pierce the skies!': The Urban Process in the Southern Colonies during the Eighteenth Century." *William and Mary Quarterly*, 3rd series, vol. 30 (Oct. 1973): 549–74.

Evans, James D. "Resolutions of Loudoun County." *William and Mary Quarterly*, 1st series, vol. 12 (Apr. 1904): 231–33.

Farmer, Charles J. *In the Absence of Towns: Settlement and County Trade in Southside Virginia, 1730–1800*. Lanham, MD: Rowman & Littlefield, 1993.

Federal Writers' Project. *Historic Romney, 1762–1937*. Romney, WV?: Town Council, Romney, 1937.

Feiss, Carl. "Early American Public Squares." In Paul Zucker, *Town and Square: From the Agora to the Village Green*, 237–55. New York: Columbia Univ. Press, 1959.

Ferrari, Mary Catherine. "Artisans of the South: A Comparative Study of Norfolk, Charleston, and Alexandria, 1763–1800." Ph.D. diss., College of William and Mary in Virginia, 1992.

Fischer, David Hackett, and James C. Kelly. *Bound Away: Virginia and the Westward Movement*. Charlottesville: Univ. Press of Virginia, 2000.

Fitzgerald, Madalene Vaden. *Pittsylvania: Homes and People of the Past*. Chatham, VA: Madalene Vaden Fitzgerald, 1974.

Foote, William Henry. *Sketches of North Carolina, Historical and Biographical, Illustrative of the Principles of a Portion of Her Early Settlers*. New York: Robert Carter, 1846.

Fries, Sylvia Doughty. *The Urban Idea in Colonial America*. Philadelphia: Temple Univ. Press, 1977.

Gardiner, Mabel Henshaw, and Ann Henshaw Gardiner. *Chronicles of Old Berkeley*. Durham, NC: Seeman, 1938.

Gilcrest, Dorothy. "The Virginia Springs: A Mirror of Ante-Bellum Society." M.A. thesis, Univ. of Virginia, 1943.

Gilreath, Amelia C. *Shenandoah County, Virginia, Abstracts of Wills, 1772–1850*. Nokesville, VA: n.p., 1980.

Girouard, Mark. *The English Town: A History of Urban Life*. New Haven, CT: Yale Univ. Press, 1990.

Goldfield, David R. "Pearls on the Coast and Lights in the Forest: The Colonial South." In Raymond A. Mohl, ed., *The Making of Urban America*, 12–23. Wilmington, DE: Scholarly Resources, 1984.

Greene, Katherine Glass. *Winchester, Virginia, and Its Beginnings, 1743–1814.* Strasburg, VA: Shenandoah, 1926.

Groome, H. C. *Fauquier during the Proprietorship.* Richmond, VA: Old Dominion, 1927.

Groth, Paul. "Streetgrids as Frameworks for Urban Society." *Harvard Architectural Review* 2 (Spring 1981): 68–75.

Hackley, W. B. "The Original Survey of German Town." *Germanna Record* 6 (Apr. 1962): 5–10.

Hale, John P. *Trans-Allegheny Pioneers.* Charleston, WV: Kanawha Valley, 1931.

Hale, John S. *A Historical Atlas of Virginia.* Verona, VA: McClure, 1978.

Harrison, Fairfax. *Landmarks of Old Prince William: A Study of Origins in Northern Virginia.* Richmond, VA: Old Dominion, 1924.

Hart, Freeman H. *The Valley of Virginia in the American Revolution, 1763–1789.* Chapel Hill: Univ. of North Carolina Press, 1942.

Hartzell, Gladys. *On This Rock: The Story of St. Peter's Church Shepherdstown, 1765–1965.* Shepherdstown, WV: Shepherdstown Register, 1970.

Head, James W. *History and Comprehensive Description of Loudoun County Virginia.* Washington, DC: Park View, 1908.

Heite, Edward F. "An English View of Virginia." *Virginia Cavalcade* 17 (Spring 1968): 169–75.

———. "Markets and Ports." *Virginia Cavalcade* 16 (1966): 29–41.

Hendricks, Christopher Edwin. "Town Development in the Colonial Backcountry—Virginia and North Carolina." Ph.D. diss., College of William and Mary in Virginia, 1991.

Herman, Bernard, Thomas Ryan, and David Schuyler. "Townhouse: From Borough to City, Lancaster's Changing Streetscape." In *Architecture and Landscape of the Pennsylvania Germans, 1720–1920*, Guidebook for the Vernacular Architecture Forum Annual Conference, "Architecture and Landscape of the Pennsylvania Germans," Harrisburg, Pennsylvania, May 12–14, 2004: 78–88.

Historical Hand-Atlas Illustrated. Chicago: H. H. Hardesty, 1883.

Hofstra, Warren R. "Ethnicity and Community Formation on the Shenandoah Valley Frontier." In Michael J. Puglisi, ed., *Diversity and Accommodation: Essays on the Cultural Composition of the Virginia Frontier*, 59–81. Knoxville: Univ. of Tennessee Press, 1997.

———, ed. *George Washington and the Virginia Backcountry.* Madison, WI: Madison House, 1998.

———. "Land, Ethnicity, and Community at the Opequon Settlement, Virginia, 1730–1800." *Virginia Magazine of History and Biography* 98 (1990): 423–48.

———. "Land Policy and Settlement in the Northern Shenandoah Valley." In Robert D. Mitchell, ed., *Appalachian Frontiers: Settlement, Society, and Development in the Preindustrial Era*, 105–26. Lexington: Univ. Press of Kentucky, 1991.

———. "'A Parcel of Barbarian's and an Uncooth Set of People': Settlers and Settlements in the Shenandoah Valley." In Warren R. Hofstra, ed., *George Washington and the Virginia Backcountry*, 87–114. Madison, WI: Madison House, 1998.

———. *The Planting of a New Virginia: Settlement and Landscape in the Shenandoah Valley*. Baltimore: Johns Hopkins Univ. Press, 2004.

———, and Robert D. Mitchell. "Town and Country in Backcountry Virginia: Winchester and the Shenandoah Valley, 1730–1800." *Journal of Southern History* 59 (Nov. 1993): 619–46.

Hohenburg, Paul M., and Lynn Hollen Lees. *The Making of Urban Europe, 1000–1950*. Cambridge, MA: Harvard Univ. Press, 1985.

Holtzclaw, B. C. "Germantown Revived." *Germanna Record* 2 (1962): 11–83.

———. "The Second German Colony of 1717, Other Germanna Pioneers, the So-Called Third Colony of 1719, and Later Comers to the Hebron Church Community." *Germanna Record* 6 (1965): 3–95.

Howe, Henry. *Historical Collections of Virginia; Containing a Collection of the Most Interesting Facts, Traditions, Biographical Sketches, Anecdotes, &c. Relating to Its History and Antiquities, Together with Geographical and Statistical Descriptions*. Charleston, SC: Babcock, 1845.

Hughes, Sarah S. *Surveyors and Statesmen: Land Measuring in Colonial Virginia*. Richmond: Virginia Surveyors Foundation, Virginia Association of Surveyors, 1979.

Hurt, Frances Hallam. *Eighteenth-Century Landmarks of Pittsylvania County, Virginia*. Lynchburg, VA: Blue Ridge Lithographic, 1967.

Hutton, James V., Jr. "Local History Articles." Handley Library, Winchester, VA, 1971.

Isaac, Rhys. *The Transformation of Virginia, 1740–1790*. Chapel Hill: Published for Institute of Early American History and Culture at Williamsburg, VA, by Univ. of North Carolina Press, 1982.

Jackson, Kenneth T., and Stanley Schultz, eds. *Cities in American History*. New York: Knopf, 1972.

Janney, Asa Moore. "The Quaker Settlement at Waterford." In *Waterford Perspectives*, 11–12. Waterford, VA: Waterford Foundation, 1983.

———, and Werner Janney. *Ye Meetg Hous Smal: A Short Account of Friends in Loudoun County, Virginia, 1732–1980*. Lincoln, VA: n.p., 1980.

Jones, Emrys. *Towns and Cities*. New York: Oxford Univ. Press, 1966.

Kegley, F. B. *Kegley's Virginia Frontier: The Beginning of the Southwest, The Roanoke of Colonial Days, 1740–1783*. Roanoke: Southwest Virginia Historical Society, 1938.

Keister, E. E. *Strasburg, Virginia, and the Keister Family*. Strasburg, VA: Shenandoah, 1972.

Keith, Arthur Leslie. "The German Colony of 1717." *William and Mary Quarterly*, 1st series, vol. 26 (1917–18): 234–39.

Kenamond, A. D. "Early Shepherdstown and Its Churches." *Magazine of the Jefferson County Historical Society* 11 (Dec. 1945): 34–41.

———. "The Hite Families in Jefferson County." *Magazine of the Jefferson County Historical Society* 31 (Dec. 1965): 28–45.

———. *Prominent Men of Shepherdstown during Its First 200 Years*. Charles Town, WV: Jefferson County Historical Society, 1963.

———. "The Sheetz Gunsmiths," *Magazine of the Jefferson County Historical Society* 24 (Dec. 1958): 18–19.

———. "Shepherdstown's Schools, 1762–1782," *Magazine of the Jefferson County Historical Society* 5 (Dec. 1939): 28–37.

Kercheval, Samuel. *A History of the Valley of Virginia*. Winchester, VA: Samuel H. Davis, 1833.

Kidney, Walter C. *Winchester: Limestone, Sycamores, and Architecture*. Winchester, VA: Preservation of Historic Winchester, 1977.

Koons, Kenneth E., and Warren R. Hofstra, eds. *After the Backcountry: Rural Life in the Great Valley of Virginia, 1800–1900*. Knoxville: Univ. of Tennessee Press, 2000.

Kornwolf, James D., with Georgiana W. Kornwolf. *Architecture and Town Planning in Colonial North America*. 3 vols. Baltimore: Johns Hopkins Univ. Press, 2002.

Larsen, Lawrence H. *The Urban South: A History*. Lexington: Univ. Press of Kentucky, 1990.

Lemon, James T. *The Best Poor Man's Country: A Geographical Study of Early Southeastern Pennsylvania*. Baltimore: Johns Hopkins Univ. Press, 1972.

———. "Urbanization and the Development of Eighteenth-Century Southeastern Pennsylvania and Adjacent Delaware." *William and Mary Quarterly*, 3rd series, vol. 24 (Oct. 1967): 501–42.

Lewis, Kenneth E. "Economic Development in the South Carolina Backcountry: A View from Camden." In David Colin Crass et al., eds., *The Southern Colonial Backcountry: Interdisciplinary Perspectives on Frontier Communities*, 87–107. Knoxville: Univ. of Tennessee Press, 1998.

Lingeman, Richard. *Small Town America: A Narrative History, 1620–The Present*. New York: Putnam's, 1980.

Lounsbury, Carl. "The Structure of Justice: The Courthouses of Colonial Virginia." In Thomas Carter and Bernard L. Herman, eds., *Perspectives in Vernacular Architecture, III*, 214–26. Columbia: Univ. of Missouri Press, 1989.

Manarin, Louis, and Clifford Dowdey. *The History of Henrico County*. Charlottesville: Univ. Press of Virginia, 1984.

Mansfield, James Roger. *A History of Early Spotsylvania*. Orange, VA: Green, 1977.

Marraro, Howard R. "Count Luigi Casiglioni: An Early Italian Traveler to Virginia (1785–1786)." *Virginia Magazine of History and Biography* 58 (Oct. 1950): 473–91.

Marsh, Helen Hurst. "Early Loudoun Water Mills." *Bulletin of the Loudoun County Historical Society* 1 (1958): 21–26.

Martin, Ann Smart. "Buying into the World of Goods: Eighteenth-Century Consumerism and the Retail Trade from London to the Virginia Frontier." Ph.D. diss., College of William and Mary in Virginia, 1993.

———. "Commercial Space as Consumption Arena: Retail Stores in Early Virginia." In Sally McMurry and Annmarie Adams, eds., *People, Power, Places*, Perspectives in Vernacular Architecture, VIII, 201–18. Knoxville: Univ. of Tennessee Press, 2000.

Martin, Joseph. *A New and Comprehensive Gazetteer of Virginia and the District of Columbia.* Charlottesville, VA: Moseley & Tompkins, 1836.

Mason, George Carrington. "The Colonial Churches of Spotsylvania and Caroline Counties, Virginia." *Virginia Magazine of History and Biography* 58 (1950): 442–72.

Maury, Richard L. Introduction to R. H. Fife, trans. and ed., "The Vestry Book of King William Parish, VA., 1707–1750," *Virginia Magazine of History and Biography* 11 (1903–4): 289–93.

Maxwell, Hu, and H. L. Swisher. *History of Hampshire County, West Virginia, from Its Earliest Settlement to the Present.* Morgantown, WV: A. Brown Boughner, 1897.

McAllister, J. T. *Historical Sketches of Virginia Hot Springs, Warm Sulphur Springs, and Bath County, Virginia.* Salem, VA: Salem Printing and Publishing, 1908.

McCleary, Ann E. "Ethnic Influences on the Vernacular Architecture of the Shenandoah Valley." In Michael J. Puglisi, ed., *Diversity and Accommodation: Essays on the Cultural Composition of the Virginia Frontier*, 252–74. Knoxville: Univ. of Tennessee Press, 1997.

McCleskey, Turk. "Rich Land, Poor Prospects: Real Estate and the Formation of a Social Elite in Augusta County, Virginia, 1738–1770." *Virginia Magazine of History and Biography* 98 (July 1990): 449–86.

McIlwaine, H. R. "The Huguenot Settlement at Manakin Towne." *Huguenot* 6 (1933): 66–77.

McKelvey, Blake. *The City in American History*. New York: Barnes and Noble, 1969.

McKendrick, Neil, John Brewer, and J. H. Plumb. *The Birth of a Consumer Society: The Commercialization of Eighteenth-Century England.* Bloomington: Indiana Univ. Press, 1982.

Merrens, Harry Roy. *Colonial North Carolina in the Eighteenth Century: A Study of Historical Geography*. Chapel Hill: Univ. of North Carolina Press, 1964.

Middleton, Arthur Pierce. *Tobacco Coast: A Maritime History of the Chesapeake Bay in the Colonial Era.* Newport News, VA: Mariner's Museum, 1953.

Minghini, Lorraine, and Thomas E. VanMetre. *History of Trinity Episcopal Church and Norborne Parish, Martinsburg, Berkeley County, West Virginia.* Martinsburg, WV?: n.p., 1956?.

Mitchell, Robert D., ed. *Appalachian Frontiers: Settlement, Society, and Development in the Preindustrial Era.* Lexington: Univ. Press of Kentucky, 1991.

———. *Commercialism and Frontier: Perspectives on the Early Shenandoah Valley.* Charlottesville: Univ. Press of Virginia, 1977.

———. "'From the Ground Up': Space, Place, and Diversity in Frontier Studies." In Michael J. Puglisi, ed., *Diversity and Accommodation: Essays on the Cultural Composition of the Virginia Frontier*, 23–58. Knoxville: Univ. of Tennessee Press, 1997.

———. "Metropolitan Chesapeake: Reflections on Town Formation in Colonial Virginia and Maryland." In Lois Green Carr, ed., *The Chesapeake and Beyond: A Celebration*, 105–25. Crownsville: Maryland Historical and Cultural Publications, 1992.

———. "'Over the Hills and Far Away': George Washington and the Changing Virginia Backcountry." In Warren R. Hofstra, ed., *George Washington and the Virginia Backcountry*, 63–86. Madison, WI: Madison House, 1998.

———. "The Settlement Fabric of the Shenandoah Valley, 1790–1860: Pattern, Process, and Structure." In Kenneth E. Koons and Warren R. Hofstra, eds., *After the Backcountry: Rural Life in the Great Valley of Virginia, 1800–1900.* Knoxville: Univ. of Tennessee Press, 2000.

———. "The Shenandoah Valley Frontier." *Annals of the Association of American Geographers* 61 (Sept. 1972): 461–86.

———. "The Southern Backcountry: A Geographical House Divided." In David Colin Crass et al., eds., *The Southern Colonial Backcountry: Interdisciplinary Perspectives on Frontier Communities*, 1–35. Knoxville: Univ. of Tennessee Press, 1998.

———. "The Upper Shenandoah Valley during the Eighteenth Century: A Study in Historical Geography." Ph.D. diss., Univ. of Wisconsin, 1969.

———, and Warren R. Hofstra. "Town and Country in the Colonial South: Winchester and Frederick County, Virginia, 1738–1783." Paper presented to the Eastern Historical Geography Association, Oct. 24, 1986.

Mohl, Raymond A., ed. *The Making of Urban America.* Wilmington, DE: Scholarly Resources, 1984.

Monkkonen, Eric H. *America Becomes Urban: The Development of U.S. Cities and Towns, 1780–1980.* Berkeley: Univ. of California Press, 1988.

Moorman, J. J. *The Virginia Springs, and Springs of the South and West.* Philadelphia: J. B. Lippincott, 1859.

———. *The Virginia Springs with their Analysis; and Some Remarks on Their Character, Together with a Directory for the Use of the White Sulphur Water, and an Account of the Diseases to which it is Applicable: To Which is added a Review of a Portion of Wm. Burke's Book on the Mineral Springs of Western Virginia, Etc. and an Account of the Different Routes to the Springs.* Philadelphia: Lindsay & Blakiston, 1847.

Morgan County, West Virginia, and Its People. Berkeley Springs, WV: Morgan County Historical and Genealogical Society, 1981.

Morton, Frederic. *The Story of Winchester in Virginia.* Strasburg, VA: Shenandoah, 1925.

Morton, Oden F. *Annals of Bath County, Virginia.* Staunton, VA: McClure, 1917.

Mumford, Lewis. *The City in History: Its Origins, Its Transformations, and Its Prospects.* London: Secker & Warburg, 1961.

Murtagh, William J. *Moravian Architecture and Town Planning: Bethlehem, Pennsylvania, and Other Eighteenth-Century American Settlements.* Chapel Hill: Univ. of North Carolina Press, 1967.

Musser, Clifford S. *Two Hundred Years' History of Shepherdstown, 1730–1931.* Shepherdstown, WV: The Independent, 1931.

Nash, Francis. "The Borough Towns of North Carolina." *North Carolina Booklet* 4 (Oct. 1906): 83–102.

Newbraugh, Frederick T. *Warm Springs Echoes about Berkeley Springs and Morgan.* 3 vols. Hagerstown, MD: Automated Systems, 1967.

Nicholls, Michael L. "Origins of the Virginia Southside, 1703–1753: A Social and Economic Study." Ph.D. diss., College of William and Mary in Virginia, 1972.

Niederer, Frances J. *The Town of Fincastle, Virginia.* Charlottesville: Univ. Press of Virginia, 1965.

Norris, J. E., ed. *History of the Lower Shenandoah Counties of Frederick, Berkeley, Jefferson, and Clarke.* Chicago: A. Warner, 1890.

O'Mara, James. "Urbanization in Tidewater Virginia during the Eighteenth Century: A Study in Historical Geography." Ph.D. diss., York Univ., 1979.

Painter, Fred. *Yesterday in Woodstock.* Woodstock, VA: Woodstock Museum of Shenandoah County, 1981.

Philyaw, L. Scott. *Virginia's Western Vision: Political and Cultural Expansion on an Early American Frontier.* Knoxville: Univ. of Tennessee Press, 2004.

Peyton, J. Lewis. *History of Augusta County, Virginia.* Bridgewater, VA: C. J. Carrier, 1953.

Pezzoni, Dan. "Town Form." M.A. thesis, Virginia Polytechnic Institute and State Univ., 1987.

Pierson, Willard, Jr. "John Hook: 'A Merchant of Colonial Virginia.'" Honors thesis, Duke Univ., 1962.

Pillsbury, Richard. "The Urban Street Pattern as a Culture Indicator: Pennsylvania, 1682–1815." *Annals of the Association of American Geographers* 60 (1970): 428–46.

Plumb, J. H. "The Commercialization of Leisure in Eighteenth-Century England." In Neil McKendrick, John Brewer, and J. H. Plumb, *The Birth of a Consumer Society: The Commercialization of Eighteenth-Century England,* 265–85. Bloomington: Indiana Univ. Press, 1982.

Poland, Charles P., Jr. *From Frontier to Suburbia.* Marceline, MO: Walsworth, 1976.

Preisser, Thomas H. "Eighteenth-Century Alexandria, Virginia, before the Revolution, 1749–1776." Ph.D. diss., College of William and Mary in Virginia, 1977.

Puglisi, Michael J., ed. *Diversity and Accommodation: Essays on the Cultural Composition of the Virginia Frontier.* Knoxville: Univ. of Tennessee Press, 1997.

Quarles, Garland A. *The Churches of Winchester, Virginia: A Brief History of Those Established Prior to 1825.* Winchester, VA: n.p., 1960.

Rainbolt, James C. "The Absence of Towns in Seventeenth-Century Virginia." In Kenneth T. Jackson and Stanley Schultz, eds., *Cities in American History,* 50–65. New York: Knopf, 1972.

Ramsey, Robert W. *Carolina Cradle: Settlement of the Northwest North Carolina Frontier, 1747–1762.* Chapel Hill: Univ. of North Carolina Press, 1964.

Read, Daisy I. *New London: Today and Yesterday.* Lynchburg, VA: J. P. Bell, 1950.

Remer, Richard George. "The Great Wagon Road." M.A. thesis, College of William and Mary in Virginia, 1974.

Reps, John W. *The Making of Urban America: City Planning in the United States.* Princeton, NJ: Princeton Univ. Press, 1965.

———. *Tidewater Towns: City Planning in Colonial Virginia and Maryland.* Williamsburg, VA: Colonial Williamsburg Foundation, 1972.

———. *Town Planning in Frontier America.* Princeton, NJ: Princeton Univ. Press, 1969.

Riley, Edward M. "The Town Acts of Colonial Virginia." *Journal of Southern History* 16 (Aug. 1950): 306–23.

Roberts, William Garner, Jr. "Determinants of Physical Characteristics of the Eighteenth-Century North Carolina Town." M.A. thesis, Univ. of North Carolina, 1963.

Robinson, Morgan Poitiaux. "Virginia Counties: Those Resulting from Virginia Legislation." *Bulletin of the Virginia State Library* 9 (Jan., Apr., July, 1916).

Robinson, Philip R. *The Plantation of Ulster.* New York: St. Martin's, 1984.

Roeber, A. G. *Faithful Magistrates and Republican Lawyers: Creators of Virginia Legal Culture, 1680–1810.* Chapel Hill: Univ. of North Carolina Press, 1981.

Rouse, Alice Read. *Clement and Madame Read of Bushy Forest, Lunenburg County, Virginia, Their Eight Children, Their Descendants and Allied Families.* Cincinnati: Johnson & Hardin, 1930.

Royster, Charles. *The Fabulous History of the Dismal Swamp Company: A Story of George Washington's Times.* New York: Borzoi Books, 1999.

Russo, David J. *American Towns: An Interpretive History.* Chicago: Dee, 2001.

Rutman, Darrett B., with Anita H. Rutman. *Small Worlds, Large Questions: Explorations in Early American Social History, 1600–1800.* Charlottesville: Univ. Press of Virginia, 1994.

Sanchez-Saavedra, E. M. *A Description of the Country: Virginia's Cartographers and Their Maps, 1607–1881.* 2 vols. Richmond: Virginia State Library, 1975.

Scheel, Eugene M. "An Archaeological Plan for the Waterford Historic District. Loudoun County, Virginia." Vertical File, Thomas Balch Library, Leesburg, VA, 1979.

———. "Leesburg Originally a Grant from Lord Fairfax." *Leesburg Times-Mirror,* Feb. 23, 1978.

Schley, Anna W., and Linnie Schley. "Old Homes of the Leetown Neighborhood." *Magazine of the Jefferson County Historical Society* 7 (Dec. 1941): 4–18.

Schultz, Stanley K. "The Growth of Urban America in War and Peace, 1740–1810." In William M. Fowler Jr. and Wallace Coyle, eds., *The American Revolution: Changing Perspectives,* 127–48. Boston: Northeastern Univ. Press, 1979.

Scribner, Richard L. "Manakinetowne in Virginia." *Virginia Cavalcade* 3 (Winter 1953): 37–41.

Sellars, Leila. *Charleston Business on the Eve of the American Revolution.* Chapel Hill: Univ. of North Carolina Press, 1934.

Shepard, E. Lee. "'This Being Court Day': Courthouses and Community Life in Rural Virginia." *Virginia Magazine of History and Biography* 103 (Oct. 1995): 459–70.

Siener, William H. "Economic Development in Revolutionary Virginia: Fredericksburg, 1750–1810." Ph.D. diss., College of William and Mary in Virginia, 1982.

Skinner, Anne. "The Attempt to Build a Town at Westham." Maude Howlett Papers, Virginia Historical Society, Richmond, VA. 1945.

Smith, Mary Phlegar. "Borough Representation in North Carolina." *North Carolina Historical Review* 7 (Apr. 1930): 177–89.

———. "Municipal Development in North Carolina, 1665–1930: A History of Urbanization." Ph.D. diss., Univ. of North Carolina, 1930.

Soltow, James. *The Economic Role of Williamsburg.* Williamsburg, VA: Colonial Williamsburg Foundation, 1965.

Steadman, Melvin Lee, Jr. *A Walking Tour of Leesburg.* Leesburg, VA: Potomac, 1967.

———. *Leesburg's Old Stone Church, 1766.* Manassas, VA: Virginia-Craft Print, 1964.

Stephenson, Richard W., and Marianne M. McKee, eds. *Virginia in Maps: Four Centuries of Settlement Growth and Development*. Richmond: Library of Virginia, 2000.

Stilgo, John. *Common Landscape of America, 1580–1845*. New Haven, CT: Yale Univ. Press, 1982.

Stoner, Robert Douthat. *Seed-Bed of the Republic: A Study of Pioneers in the Upper (Southern) Valley of Virginia*. Radford, VA: Commonwealth, 1962.

Summers, Lewis Preston. *Annals of Southwest Virginia, 1796–1800*. Kingsport, TN: Kingsport Press, 1929.

Swem, Earl Greg, ed. *Virginia Historical Index*. 2 vols. Gloucester, MA: P. Smith, 1965.

Sydnor, Charles S. *Gentleman Freeholders: Political Practices in Washington's Virginia*. Chapel Hill: Published for the Institute of Early American History and Culture at Williamsburg, VA, by Univ. of North Carolina Press, 1952.

Talapar, Morris. *The Sociology of Colonial Virginia*. New York: Philosophical Library, 1960.

Thompson, Michael D. *Calendar and Index to Recorded Survey Plats in Jefferson County, West Virginia (Virginia) Courthouse, 1801–1901*. Charles Town, WV: Jefferson County Historical Society, 1984.

Tillson, Albert H., Jr. *Gentry and Commonfolk: Political Culture on a Virginia Frontier, 1740–1789*. Lexington: Univ. Press of Kentucky, 1991.

———. "Political Culture and Social Conflict in the Upper Valley of Virginia, 1740–1789." Ph.D. diss., Univ. of Texas at Austin, 1986.

Tobias, Leslie. "Manakin Town: The Development and Demise of a French Protestant Refugee Colony in Colonial Virginia, 1700–1750." M.A. thesis, College of William and Mary in Virginia, 1982.

Tolbert, Lisa C. *Constructing Townscapes: Space and Society in Antebellum Tennessee*. Chapel Hill: Univ. of North Carolina Press, 1999.

Turner, Allaynae Claire. "The Development of the Shenandoah Valley between 1710–1770: A Comparative Study of the Shenandoah Frontier and the Tidewater Area of Virginia." M.A. thesis, Univ. of Minnesota, 1951.

Tyler, Lyon Gardiner, ed. *Encyclopedia of Virginia Biography*. 5 vols. New York: Lewis Historical, 1915.

Ullman, Edward. "A Theory of Location for Cities." *American Journal of Sociology* 46 (May 1941): 854–61.

Upton, Dell, and Michael Vlach, eds. *Common Places: Readings in American Vernacular Architecture*. Athens: Univ. of Georgia Press, 1986.

Vance, James E. *The Merchant's World: The Geography of Wholesaling*. Englewood Cliffs, NJ: Prentice-Hall, 1970.

Vann, Elizabeth Chapman Denny, and Margaret Collins Denny Dixon. *Virginia's First German Colony*. Richmond, VA: n.p., 1961.

Virginia Writers' Project. *Jefferson's Albemarle: A Guide to Albemarle County, Virginia*. N.p.: Virginia Conservation Commission, 1941.

———. *Prince William: The Story of Its People and Its Places*. 4th ed. Manassas, VA: Bethlehem Good Housekeeping Club, 1961.

Waddell, Joseph A. *Annals of Augusta County, Virginia, from 1726 to 1871*. Staunton, VA: C. Russell Caldwell, 1902.

Ward, Harry M. *Major General Adam Stephen and the Course of America Liberty.* Charlottesville: Univ. Press of Virginia, 1989.

Waterford Perspectives. Waterford, VA: Waterford Foundation, 1983.

Watson, Walter A. *Notes on Southside Virginia.* Edited by Constance T. Watson. Baltimore: Genealogical Publishing, 1977.

Wayland, John W. *Germanna: Outpost of Adventure, 1714–1956.* Staunton, VA: Memorial Foundation of the German Colonies in Virginia, 1956.

———. "The Germans of the Valley." *Virginia Magazine of History and Biography* 10 (July 1902): 33–48.

———. *A History of Shenandoah County, Virginia.* Strasburg, VA: Shenandoah, 1927.

Wellenreuther, Herman. "Urbanization in the Colonial South: A Critique." *William and Mary Quarterly*, 3rd series, vol. 31 (Oct. 1974): 653–71.

Wertenbaker, Thomas Jefferson. *Norfolk: Historic Southern Port.* Durham, NC: Duke Univ. Press, 1931.

Whiffen, Marcus. "The Early Courthouses of Virginia." *Journal of the Society of Architectural Historians* 18 (Mar. 1959): 2–10.

Williams, Harrison. *Legends of Loudoun.* Richmond, VA: Garrett and Massie, 1938.

Williams, Lloyd Haynes. "The Tragic Shipwreck of the Protestant Switzers." *William and Mary Quarterly*, 3rd series, vol. 9 (1952): 539–42.

Wolf, Stephanie Grauman. *Urban Village: Populations, Community, and Family Structure in Germantown, Pennsylvania, 1683–1800.* Princeton, NJ: Princeton Univ. Press, 1976.

Woods, Edgar. *Albemarle County in Virginia.* Charlottesville, VA: Michie, 1901.

Wust, Klaus. "The Story of Colonial Strasburg." In E. E. Keister, *Strasburg, Virginia, and the Keister Family*, 8–17. Strasburg, VA: Shenandoah, 1972.

———. *The Virginia Germans.* Charlottesville: Univ. Press of Virginia, 1969.

Young, Arthur D., comp. *Cities and Towns in American History: A Bibliography of Doctoral Dissertations.* New York: Greenwood, 1989.

Zelinsky, Wilbur. "The Pennsylvania Town: An Overdue Geographical Account." *Geographical Review* 67 (Apr. 1977): 127–47.

Zucker, Paul. *Town and Square: From the Agora to the Village Green.* New York: Columbia Univ. Press, 1959.

Index

www.ingramcontent.com/pod-product-compliance
Lightning Source LLC
Chambersburg PA
CBHW021904020426
42334CB00013B/471